SOUL OF THE LION

BY WILLARD M. WALLACE

*Appeal to Arms: A Military History of
the American Revolution.* 1951

*Traitorous Hero: The Life and Fortunes of
Benedict Arnold.* 1954

Friend William. 1958

Sir Walter Raleigh. 1959

SOUL
OF THE
LION

A BIOGRAPHY OF GENERAL
JOSHUA L. CHAMBERLAIN

by

WILLARD M. WALLACE

 Stan Clark Military Books
Gettysburg, Pennsylvania

Reprinted in 1995 by:
STAN CLARK MILITARY BOOKS
915 Fairview Avenue
Gettysburg, Pennsylvania 17325
(717) 337-1728

Cover photographs courtesy National Archives

ISBN: 1-879664-00-3 (cloth)
ISBN: 1-879664-01-1 (paper)

PRINTED AND BOUND IN THE UNITED STATES OF AMERICA

TO
Wilbert Snow
AND
Bruce Catton

"Colonel Chamberlain, your gallantry was magnificent, and your coolness and skill saved us."

—Colonel James Rice (commanding 3rd Brigade, 1st Division, Fifth Corps) *re* Little Round Top, Gettysburg, July 2, 1863

"Colonel J. L. Chamberlain was wounded . . . gallantly leading his brigade. . . . I promoted him on the spot."

—U. S. Grant, speaking of Chamberlain at Rives' Salient, Petersburg, June 18, 1864

"General, you have the soul of the lion and the heart of the woman."

—General Horatio G. Sickel to Chamberlain at the Quaker Road, Virginia, March 29, 1865

"The document does you great honor. It is able, bold, clear, comprehensive and statesmanlike."

—James G. Blaine to Chamberlain on the General's first inaugural address as Governor of Maine, January, 1867

"I say this is a good age, and we need not quarrel with it. We must understand it if we can. At least we must do our work in it. We must have the spirit of reverence and faith, we must balance the mind and heart with God's higher revelation, but we must also take hold of this which we call science, and which makes knowledge power."

—Chamberlain, in his inaugural address as President of Bowdoin College, July, 1872

"You understand what you want, do you? I am here to preserve the peace and honor of this State, until the rightful government is seated [and] it is for me to see that the laws of this State are put into effect, without fraud, without force, but with calm thought and sincere purpose. I am here for that, and I shall do it. If anybody wants to kill me for it, here I am."

—Chamberlain to the mob threatening to kill him at Augusta during the crisis of January, 1880

". . . true greatness is not in nor of the single self; it is of that larger personality, that shared and sharing life with others, in which, each giving of his best for their betterment, we are greater than ourselves; and self-surrender for the sake of that great belonging, is the true nobility."

—Chamberlain, speaking of Abraham Lincoln at Philadelphia, February 12, 1909

Contents

Illustrations

(AFTER PAGE 160)

Bangor Theological Seminary
Bowdoin College, 1860
Marye's Heights, Fredericksburg
The Stonewall, Marye's Heights
Little Round Top defense works, Gettysburg
Little Round Top
Rives' Salient, Petersburg
Fort Mahone, Petersburg
Joshua L. Chamberlain as a brigadier general
Surrender of Lee's troops at Appomattox
Joshua L. Chamberlain in the 1890's
Harold Wyllys Chamberlain
Grace Chamberlain Allen
The Chamberlain House, Brunswick
Joshua L. Chamberlain at the age of 83

Maps

SOUL OF THE LION

≋ ≋ ≋ **I** ≋ ≋ ≋

SCHOLAR TO SOLDIER

THE slim, erect officer in the Union blue, looking taller than he was, peered down the rocky slopes of Little Round Top. Clouds of smoke and dust obscured his view, but what he saw forced his face into lines of decision. His vivid blue eyes narrowed, and the lips, almost covered by a sweeping brown mustache, drew into a thin line as he calculated the effects of a move which he could scarcely hope to carry off but which he must make to save his command from defeat or capture and prevent the entire left flank of the Union line at Gettysburg from being rolled up. Once the Confederates seized Little Round Top, the battle was lost for the Union and Lee's invasion of the North would be a real political threat, encouraging the peace party elements in the North and perhaps influencing the European powers to reconsider the question of recognizing the Confederacy.

Colonel Joshua Lawrence Chamberlain of the embattled 20th Maine Infantry, former Bowdoin College professor and Bangor Theological seminarian, literally had his back to the wall, at least to the rocky hillside of Little Round Top. Before him, pushing in grim silence up the hill in what was certain to be the final charge that would crash through the thin blue ranks of the 20th and take the hard-pressed defenders of the west side of the hill in the rear, were large elements of regiments from Alabama. Chamberlain's own regiment was riddled with casualties, outnumbered nearly three to one, and over-extended to the left to keep from being flanked. Worse still, it had run out of ammunition. To try to stave off the onrushing Southerners with musket butts and stones would be hopeless and tragic. At the moment of decision a young officer asked Chamberlain if he might go forward and bring off one or two wounded men before the enemy closed in.

"Yes, sir, in a moment!" the Colonel replied. He stepped to the colors, and the men looked toward him.

"Bayonet!"

The men set up a shout. Instantly there came the snicker of two hundred bayonets drawn from leather sheaths and the grating clash of steel as their loops slid over the rifle barrels. Whipping out his sabre, Chamberlain strode forward, and the entire regiment plunged down the hill in a great wheeling movement to the right.

Puzzled, the enemy checked his attack, then fell back before the shouting, thrusting blue line. An officer fired his pistol point-blank at Chamberlain's face but missed; the next instant, the Colonel's sabre at his throat, he surrendered. He was but one of hundreds of men in grey to be captured as the 20th Maine, achieving a complete psychological surprise, scythed its way between the Round Tops. It thus took the pressure off the defenders on the west slope and contributed mightily to the repulse of one of the hardest fighting units in the Confederate Army, the great division of John Bell Hood belonging to Longstreet's corps. Well earned indeed was the Congressional Medal of Honor that was subsequently awarded to the Bowdoin College professor. Nor were truer words ever written than those of the Confederate commander whose troops Chamberlain had thrown back when he said that Chamberlain's skill and the valor of his men had saved Little Round Top and the Army of the Potomac from defeat.

But Gettysburg was only one extraordinary incident in the extraordinary military and civilian life of Joshua Lawrence Chamberlain.

Chamberlain—called "Lawrence" by his parents—was born on September 8, 1828 in Brewer, Maine, of a family that had originally acquired its name when Richard de Tankerville, grandson of a Norman knight, became chamberlain to King Stephen of England in the twelfth century. Lawrence's father, also named Joshua, was a Brewer farmer who took a leading citizen's part in civil and military affairs, holding at one time the office of county commissioner and serving as lieutenant-colonel commanding the militia regiment sent eastward by Governor John Fairchild at the time of Maine's famous "Aroostook War" with New Brunswick. Lawrence's father was one of a numerous brood, two of whom, John Quincy Adams Chamberlain and Elbridge Gerry Chamberlain, moved to the then West, the latter becoming a lawyer in Indiana and a representative in Congress. Lawrence's grandfather, the first Joshua, whose own father, Ebenezer, had been a New Hampshire soldier in the Revolution and in the French and Indian War, came to Orrington on the lower Penobscot River from Massachusetts about 1799. His prosperous ship-building business was ruined in the War of 1812 when the British seized Castine and, sailing up the river, burned two of his vessels and his shipyard. He then became a colonel and commanded the garrison at Eastport. In 1817, he moved to Brewer, bought a large farm and divided his time, with the help of his sons, between farming and shipbuilding. From Ebenezer to Colonel Chamberlain to Lawrence's father there was a tradition of military service and it was particularly strong in the last.

Lawrence's mother was Sarah Dupee Brastow, daughter of Billings and Lydia Dupee Brastow of Holden, Maine. Lydia Dupee had been the fourth daughter of Charles Depuis whose name on the army lists of the Revolution was changed to Dupee. Charles was the son of an earlier Charles who had fought in the colonial wars. He, in turn, had been the second son of Jean Dupuis, a Huguenot of La Rochelle, France, who had fled to Boston, Massachusetts in 1685 when King Louis XIV revoked the Edict of Nantes which had afforded religious toleration for nearly a century.

Joshua (born in 1800) and Sarah Dupee Brastow (born in 1803) seemed to be examples of the "opposites attract" school. He was a silent man, rather severe in countenance and occasionally in attitude, but fundamentally indulgent toward his family and tolerant on the bitter political and social issues of the day. He manifested little of the aggressiveness or business perspicacity that had made his own father a conspicuous financial success before the War of 1812. Like his father, however, he named his sons after great men he admired. One of his boyhood heroes was Captain James Lawrence, the American naval captain of the frigate *Chesapeake* who fought a losing battle with H.M.S. *Shannon* in 1813 and, on being mortally wounded, cried out, "Don't give up the ship!" Hence, the name "Joshua Lawrence Chamberlain." One of Lawrence Chamberlain's brothers bore the name of "John Calhoun" after the Southern statesman whom Joshua admired for his position on the rights of the states. Joshua earlier had made a trip to the West to see his brother in Indiana and returned through the South. As a result of his travels in the South, he developed an affection for the region and its way of life that he never lost. Though he liked military activities, loyally supported the Union in the Civil War and had three sons who served, he deplored the conflict as unnecessary.

Lawrence's mother was quite different indeed from her husband. Where he was silent and stern in appearance, she was all laughter and liveliness. Where he was indulgent, she was firm. Filled with energy and industry, she kept all about her—herself included—busy with activity, her husband and the hired man at their chores, the hired girl at her kitchen tasks, her children at their studies. While she loved all of her five children—Lawrence, Horace, Sarah, John, and Thomas, in order of appearance—her eyes glowed especially brightly when she spoke of her oldest son. She early resolved that eventually he should devote himself to the Lord's work. That her husband was equally determined on a military career for Lawrence seemed not to disturb her greatly. She was adept at winning her way on the larger issues by yielding small concessions and maintaining a constant good humor. Her husband and children adored her for all that they came to recognize her technique of persuasion. Yet in their affection for this lively little woman with the three saucy curls on each side of her head they never lost their respect for her. Underneath her gaiety there was something formidable. She was, after all, a descendant of French Calvinists.

Lawrence had a full life as a boy. There was work to be done on the hundred-acre farm: barn chores, wood to cut, fields to clear and plow, planting, weeding, harvesting—an endless round, for a farm is a kind of tyrant. As a boy Lawrence learned that few things are so difficult that they cannot be mastered. Once when he told his father that he and his brothers could not clear away a large stone from a field, the older Chamberlain merely looked at him and barked, "Move it!" And the stone was moved. There was also work in the shipyard with saw and adze; and when his father experienced a temporary financial hardship, Lawrence worked for pay in a neighboring brickyard and in a ropewalk, making anything of hemp from fish lines to ships' cables.

But life was not all work. When he was a boy, Bangor was becoming the greatest lumber port in the world and one of the largest builders of ships. A land boom was starting, and the muddy streets were crowded with lumberjacks, shipbuilders, speculators, and sailors from all over the globe. To a Brewer boy just across the Penobscot, colorful, boisterous Bangor was like a city out of the *Arabian Nights.* But Lawrence did not have to cross the river for excitement. He learned to sail the family sloop *Lapwing* on the two-week vacation down the bay after haying time was over. He liked to plant his hat on the main truck of every vessel launched in Brewer. He became a strong swimmer and a skillful player of the old game of "round ball." Sometimes he slipped off to the Indian camp a mile or so away in the woods and listened to the dark and fascinating stories of ancient raids by the savage Mohawks, of mysterious Katahdin where the storm god lived, of the Saguenay far to the north where death awaited its seeker. He learned to shoot, though he preferred to observe wild life rather than destroy it. To his delight, his father taught him and his brothers how to use effectively a heavy broadsword. But of even greater pleasure to him was the music he heard in church and school. He learned to sing, and loved choral music, but of all instruments the bass viol appealed to him most, probably because a local singing master whom he liked used one. Lawrence reportedly made an imitation viol out of a cornstalk which he notched for strings and stops of the scale and, with another stalk for a bow, learned many of the principles of the instrument before he acquired the genuine article.

And, of course, there were his studies and a career to choose. With his eye on the army, Joshua sent Lawrence to Major Whiting's military academy down in Ellsworth. Lawrence did very well at the academy, military drill, Latin and the required modern language, French, having no terrors for him. Stringent family circumstances, however, led him to try his hand at "keeping school," as teaching was often called at the time, and he early acquired a high opinion of its value and a love for the work itself. Still, teaching was not an unmixed joy, for he had to thrash the usual school bully, a boy as large as himself, before he could establish his mastery over the room. Thereafter he had no trouble. Presently, moreover, he brought out his bass viol, a real one on which he had become an accomplished player, and established a winter evening singing school which proved very popular.

He was now nearing the end of his teens with no decision reached about a career. Actually his mother had been in little doubt for years: he should become a minister, and she put forth her desire in cogent and appealing terms. His father hoped he would consider West Point and a military career. Sally Chamberlain won—at least up to a point. In the mid-1840's, Lawrence had become a member of the Congregational Church in Brewer, and religion in its social as well as its spiritual significance began to possess him. He now agreed to become a minister of the gospel—but not the conventional type. He would be a missionary to some country where he could "keep school" and teach the social as well as the spiritual message of Christianity.

To carry out his purpose, he had to acquire a college education, and the college in Maine which produced many aspirants to the Congregational ministry at that time was Bowdoin College in Brunswick. Unfortunately for Lawrence's peace of mind, a knowledge of Greek was required for entrance. Latin and French he had in hand, but of Greek he knew nothing except that by reputation it was a very difficult language. He now threw himself into learning it with the concentration for which he later became celebrated. Previously he had built a room for himself in the garret of his father's home, and in this room he spent the better part of each day and evening for six months. It is said that he actually memorized Kühner's entire grammar in the unabridged Greek, interrupting his studying to split wood or to fence with his father with broadswords. To his joy he was finally admitted to Bowdoin in 1848 "conditioned" in Greek but with "advanced standing" otherwise.

Lawrence achieved a splendid record at Bowdoin. In the dreaded Greek he attained first rank and in French first honors. In higher mathematics and in astronomy, subjects which had also intimidated him initially, he was honored by being permitted to submit original problems for the Junior and Senior examinations. He was a first assistant in chemistry and an assistant librarian. He gave the German Junior Part at the scholarly Exhibition in the spring of 1851. The premium for Declamation in August, 1851—thirty dollars—was divided between Lawrence and a classmate, John H. Goodenow, who later became a lawyer, president of the Maine Senate, and United States Consul-General at Constantinople. In March, 1852, Lawrence was one of seven appointed to present English orations at the Spring Exhibition, while he was one of three who delivered English orations at his own Commencement in August, 1852. Likewise at the end of his Senior year he received the second prize of five dollars for English composition. His election to Phi Beta Kappa set the seal on a fine beginning as a scholar.

Studies did not occupy all of Lawrence's time, although a good deal of hard, sustained work must have gone on at his quarters in 21 Maine Hall. He became a member of one of the two literary societies, the Peucinian Society, and composed poems for it. He joined the Alpha Delta Phi Fraternity. Continuing his interest in religion, he taught Sunday school two miles outside Brunswick during his Freshman and Sophomore years and was leader of the choir in the Congregational Church—the First Parish Church, just off the campus—during his Junior and Senior years. The Reverend George E. Adams, D.D., was pastor of the church from 1829 to 1870. A learned, warmhearted, but crusty person, he enjoyed a reputation for giving scholarly sermons. After all, this was the church which many of the Bowdoin faculty attended and to which students came for Baccalaureate services and Commencement exercises. No doubt Lawrence, as an aspirant minister, should have followed the Reverend Adams' discourses more closely, but he found his eyes straying increasingly to the organ bench where sat a trim, lively girl who was the minister's daughter, Fanny. As a dignified Senior, he began to squire Fanny to prayer meetings and various college festivities. Soon he was deeply in love with her.

But while Lawrence was reaping scholastic honors and becoming interested in Fanny Adams, was he also aware of an extraordinary person on the faculty and that person's even more extraordinary wife? For Calvin Stowe was professor of natural and revealed religion from 1850 to 1852, and while he spent a good part of those two years away lecturing at Andover Theological Seminary, Bowdoin with only 120 students and about a dozen faculty members was scarcely so large that Lawrence could have missed at least hearing of Stowe's erudition and gift of mimicry.

Certainly he must have known Stowe's energetic little wife with her brood of seven children who lived on Federal Street and, during her husband's absence, used to work in Stowe's office at Appleton Hall on some book she was said to be writing. Very likely Lawrence was singing in the choir at the communion service on March 2, 1851 when, after listening to scripture readings by Dr. Adams, Harriet Beecher Stowe, sitting in Pew 23 in the Broad Aisle, had her vision of the death of Uncle Tom to whom Christ seemed to be speaking through her. Lawrence could not have known, however, that, stirred up as the country was over the Fugitive Slave Act passed by Congress in late 1850, it would become even more violently agitated by what Mrs. Stowe was writing and by the sermons, lectures, and mock slave auctions presented by her New York preacher-brother, Henry Ward Beecher. Nor could he have known that from this little college town with its overarching elms and stately houses on Federal and Maine Streets, its new industries starting up along the river, its family shipyards down on Casco Bay from which the men who built the ships sailed them to London, Bombay, and Canton and returned with the sumptuous carpets, furniture, and bric-a-brac with which they furnished their houses, would go scores of boys and young men to fight in a war for which little Mrs. Stowe's scribblings were helping create emotional fuel. Least of all could Lawrence have known that he, too, would leave this very town to enter that war and that his life would never be the same afterward.

But however well or slightly he may have known Harriet Beecher Stowe, his thoughts during the close of his Senior year were pretty thoroughly given over to his career and to Fanny Adams. He had decided that after his graduation at Bowdoin, he would enter the Bangor Theological Seminary to train for the ministry. He had also decided that he would marry Fanny Adams as soon as he completed that training, provided, of course, that she would have him and—such was the custom of the day—that her father would give his consent. "I know in *whom* all my highest hopes and dearest joys are centered," he told her. "I *know* in whom my whole heart can rest—so sweetly and so surely." To his great joy she accepted him.

Dr. Adams gave Lawrence less encouragement. He seems to have had no great regard for Lawrence at this time, and he knew his daughter, Frances Caroline, very well. She had, in reality, been adopted, being the daughter of Ashur and Amelia Wyllys Adams of Boston and a lineal descendant of Mabel Harlakenden, known in colonial days as the "Princess of New England" because of her blood relationship with so many of the royal families of Europe. Fanny, as everyone called her, was born on August 12, 1826, and was thus two years older than Lawrence. Orphaned when young, she was brought up by Dr. Adams. As he explained to a friend in later years, she was literally his cousin, but was very near to him and to his wife, Sarah Ann Folsom, as an adopted daughter, and always called them her father and mother.

Fanny was a complex person. She loved art and literature, and enjoyed to the full the attention she received from towns-folk as the Reverend George Adams' daughter and from the

Bowdoin community as an attractive girl. But, though bright
and vivacious, she could also be moody when not given her
way and when she thought herself neglected; then she would
often say things which she later regretted. There is little
doubt that her foster parents had spoiled her and less doubt
that because of her charm they could hardly be blamed. On
the other hand, neither Dr. Adams nor her cousin, Dora
Folsom, who lived in Hoboken, and with whom she corre-
sponded, was unaware of her deficiencies. When she was
either visiting relatives in Massachusetts or finishing her
education, her father begged her to "be prompt and business-
like in settling up your affairs and in getting away home: So
that Mr. Root may not be afraid to recommend you to some
situation. For I have my fears and doubts about you: see
if you can't shame them."

Dora Folsom was taken aback by Fanny's choice in clothes.
When Fanny wrote her, it was usually to ask Dora to buy for
her such items as mantilla trimming, silk ribbons, piping,
chemises, and lace drawers. Dora finally protested: "Do dress
simply as becometh a minister's daughter and one who ex-
pects to become the wife of a minister. You ought to be
willing to take advice on this subject and yield your feelings
on so *trifling* a subject, and in other points of view a most
momentous subject—as dress—to the feelings, the judgement,
the wishes of your friends. Beads and furbelows, and finery
. . . are very unbecoming one in your situation and your expectation. Your love for such things is a *weak* spot in your
character and you ought to fight against it." Poor Fanny!
She could scarcely be blamed for taking so long to reply to
such strictures that, on one occasion, Dora exclaimed, "What
a child you are not to send a line oftener!"

Undoubtedly Lawrence was completely unaffected by

Fanny's emotional flights, her lack of punctuality and efficiency, her extravagance and unconventionality, or any of her faults. He was too deeply in love with her. In the sentimental language of the day he burst out with this effusion, "May the sunshine but give growth and beauty to the twining tendrils of our hearts, and the storms only strengthen them and bind us closer."

He had in mind a specific storm, one hovering close at hand, namely, the disapproval of Dr. Adams. "Your father has not much faith in our relation," he continued ruefully; "he does not expect that much will ever come of it, or that it will last very long. I do not need to be told that. I *see* it plainly enough. The lack of interest he evinces shows that his opinion is the same as when he told me so frankly that he had no great confidence in the issue. Let it be so. I do not care for it in itself. The only trouble I have about it is that he does not seem to feel that I have much right to know of your affairs or to take much interest in you. As to this I simply say he has 'mistaken his man.' I am not so easily managed." Nor was he, as both Dr. Adams and Fanny, not to mention a host of other people, were to find out. But if Dr. Adams thought that Fanny's pledging herself to a man two years her junior and with at least three more years of study to complete before they could consider marriage was the height of unwisdom, he underestimated the strength of the devotion which both young people had for each other. When finally convinced of how they felt, he gave his consent, and became very proud of Lawrence. Likewise Lawrence eventually outgrew his resentment of Dr. Adams, and, forty years after he wrote his indignant letter to Fanny, he gave to the First Parish Church the handsome window in the chancel, back of the pulpit, in memory of his father-in-law.

His marriage deferred until he completed his ministerial training, Lawrence entered Bangor Theological Seminary in the fall of 1852. On the hill overlooking the bustling river port, the Seminary held high the twin lamps of learning and religious inspiration. Lawrence studied theology in Latin and church history in German. He also commenced a task which was to last for three years after he finished—six years in all: namely, the mastering of Arabic, Hebrew, and Syriac. To help finance his way, he taught German to classes of girls and supervised the schools in his home town of Brewer. He led the choir at Brewer and played the organ. He also alternated with two former schoolmates in teaching a Sunday School three miles away on the road to Ellsworth. In vacations he sometimes accompanied his father into the woods on Joshua's trips as a surveyor and appraiser of timber. One winter the two men carried out their inspection from the Penobscot to Rimouski on the St. Lawrence River, going all the way on snowshoes. Once there, Lawrence acted as interpreter for his father in Joshua's negotiations with the French Canadians. Finally he completed his course of study at the Seminary, wrote and delivered the four sermons required, and received, so it is said, "calls" from three churches.

Just as he was about to enter the Seminary in 1852 Lawrence had written Fanny, wondering what might take place before he finished his course there. One single portentous event occurred, his decision to present an oration at Bowdoin which, particularly in view of his graduate studies at Bangor, might earn him a Master of Arts degree from his old college. His oration was entitled, "Law and Liberty"; he analyzed their historical development, and demonstrated that law without liberty is tyranny and liberty without law is irresponsible and chaotic, and an easy and logical prey to would-be despots. The Bowdoin faculty and administration, then under President Leonard Woods, formerly a professor of Biblical literature at Bangor Theological Seminary, were deeply impressed. Accordingly they invited Lawrence for the academic year, 1855-56, to become an instructor in logic and natural theology, subjects taught in 1852 by Calvin Stowe who had moved on to his coveted professorship at Andover Theological Seminary. Lawrence promptly accepted the offer and celebrated by marrying Fanny Adams on December 7, 1855. Dr. Adams was in charge of the ceremony, which took place before the altar of the First Parish Church in Brunswick.

Lawrence remained at Bowdoin from the fall of 1855 to mid-summer, 1862. After he had taught logic and natural theology his first year, the professorship of rhetoric and oratory became vacant and Lawrence was promoted to it. He held the post until 1861, and spent an inordinate amount of time tutoring students. Possessing a fine sonorous voice himself, he firmly believed that every student should be required to have a course in voice culture, "as those who most need the benefit of it are not always those who voluntarily attend." He also believed that students should learn how to express themselves effectively in writing. In 1856 he said that he had read eleven hundred themes during the year which the students had to rewrite until they had attained an acceptable standard of proficiency. In the succeeding two years, he insisted that students should be given latitude in their writing, otherwise severe criticism might inhibit their development.

Such work as he was doing, if pursued indefinitely, can be slow death for even the finest of minds, and the long winter vacation of 1857-1858 he spent in research and the drawing up of a course of lectures. As he explained to a committee of the Board of Trustees, "the ordinary duties of the department are of such a nature as to require of the Professor a constant course of compensating and invigorating studies. And by embodying the result in the form of lectures, he may secure the desirable ends of awakening an enthusiasm in his pupils, and of keeping his own style free and his mind fresh and whole." Given the rather tedious nature of his duties, Lawrence was not regretful to be appointed professor of modern languages, a position which he held, on the records at least, from 1861 to 1865, and which had been originally established in 1829 with the appointment of Henry Wadsworth Longfellow, who subsequently left for wider scope and better pay at Harvard.

The Bowdoin College of pre-Civil War days was probably typical of most good liberal arts colleges of the era. It had a limited curriculum with stress on the classical languages and mathematics. Science was not ignored, but both science and modern languages received short shrift alongside those subjects considered as proper training for young men bound for theological seminaries, especially those of the Congregational persuasion. The president was convinced of the superior values of the English system of education, and while religious, and devoted to the cultural as well as the spiritual aspects of religion, he opposed the Congregational emphasis espoused by most of the faculty and alumni. He also abhorred the stern, parental role which a number of the professors wished him to assume.

To a considerable extent Lawrence hewed to President Woods' line rather than that of the Old Guard. He felt that socially students should be treated like adults rather than boys. He wanted them freed from the strait-jacket of regulations governing their intellectual and social life. "My idea of a college course," he said in 1859, "is that it should afford a liberal education—not a special or professional one, not in any way one-sided. It cannot be a finished education, but should be, I think, a general outline of a symmetrical development, involving such acquaintance with all the departments of knowledge and culture,—proportionate to their several values—as shall give some insight into the principles and powers by which thought passes into life—together with such practice and exercise in each of the great fields of study that the student may experience himself a little in all." Such a conception, common enough today, was hardly acceptable to most of his colleagues, and Lawrence found himself walking a pretty lonely path among a faculty distinguished in ability but possessing a narrowly circumscribed view of education.

He tried not to let his growing dissatisfaction with his college touch his marriage, something not too easy since Fanny was fond of Bowdoin herself and her father was an old-fashioned Congregationalist in whose opinion Lawrence was starting to reveal deplorable Unitarian tendencies. On October 16, 1856, a child was born to Lawrence and Fanny, a girl whom they named "Grace Dupee," but whom Lawrence often affectionately called "Daise." Lawrence may have wished for a son as his first-born, but if so, he soon lost any regret in the love he developed for his daughter, with whom he shared a bond of sympathy and rare understanding that lasted as long as he lived. Next a boy was born in 1857, but appears to have died in early 1858 despite the care of physicians and of Lawrence's mother who came down from Bangor to nurse the youngster. Fortunately another son was born who lived, Harold Wyllys, October 10, 1858. A fourth child also appeared, sometime in the early

1860's, but this one, like the second, did not survive. The arrival of these children seemed to fix even more firmly the love Lawrence had for Fanny. Once when she was visiting relatives in Roxbury and buying new clothes in Boston, he dreamed that she no longer cared for him and planned to leave him. He wrote her at once, hoping that she would not think the grief he felt "wild and insane" and that her visit would not be long. "Perhaps I am too much of a lover for a husband, as the world goes," he said, "but do forgive me, dearest, and lay it to my love and sorrow for you!"

While he was teaching at Bowdoin, he took great pleasure in the presence of his brothers, Horace and John, as undergraduates. Horace graduated with honors in 1857, received his Master of Arts degree, started brilliantly as a lawyer in Bangor, then died of tuberculosis on December 7, 1861. John finished at Bowdoin in 1859, also received his Master's degree, and, like Lawrence before him, entered Bangor Theological Seminary. During the Civil War he served with the Sanitary Commission and as a chaplain of the 11th Maine Infantry. In fact, his death on August 11, 1867, at Castine, Maine was caused by disease contracted while in service. The three older Chamberlain boys were together at Bowdoin, however, from 1855 to 1857, and, the family ties being very close, they saw a great deal of one another. In fact, it is possible—even probable in John's case—that Lawrence had the keen-witted Horace and the serious, affable John as students in class.

With the arrival of his children Lawrence felt the need to own his own house, and, in 1861, he acquired one just off the campus for $2500. It was built by a Captain Pierce in 1820, then bought by a man named Fales. The latter owned it when Longfellow brought his bride there in 1830 and passed what he was later reported to have said were the happiest years of his life. Subsequently it was acquired by the Reverend Roswell D. Hitchcock, who later became the president of Union Theological Seminary in New York. Lawrence bought the house from Hitchcock, with the assurance of the president of the largest local bank that he could have whatever money he needed to complete the purchase. After the war, he found the house too small for his many visitors, so he enlarged it in the rather unique manner of raising it off the ground and building another story underneath. Having twenty rooms thereafter, he threw open his doors, and through them came scores of distinguished men of the nation and of Maine. He entertained Generals Grant, Sherman, Sheridan, McClellan, Porter, Warren, Ayers, Griffin, and Howard. Senators, congressmen, and governors discussed the problems of the day within his walls: men like Charles Sumner, Carl Schurz, William Pitt Fessenden, Lot Morrill, William P. Frye, Eugene Hale, and James G. Blaine. Longfellow stayed there when he came back for the fiftieth reunion of his class in 1875 to deliver his famous poem, "Morituri Salutamus"; he wept when he saw his old room. There are very few houses in Maine that have seen more of the nation's great men as guests, but the tradition of such distinguished hospitality has been long discontinued since— unhappily—Bowdoin College does not own the residence.

But until the Civil War was over, Lawrence could not think of alterations in his house, for the conflict was beginning to take its toll of men and consciences, his own in particular. The great issues that disturbed the country and that led up to secession were felt less acutely at Bowdoin after the departure of the Stowes. In 1858, the college actually conferred the degree of Doctor of Laws on Jefferson Davis, the Southern leader in the Senate and former brilliant Secretary of War; this action decidedly embarrassed the college within two years. The bombardment of Fort Sumter and President Lincoln's call for volunteers sent a number of Seniors rushing to the colors, but the events of 1861 did not greatly upset the college, although it changed a number of habits—students were reported to be showing an unusual degree of attention to their studies! The real impact of the war began in 1862, and, from a total of approximately 1200 students and alumni, 290 Bowdoin men served in the Union forces during the conflict, a remarkable contribution and one proportionately greater, perhaps, than that from any college in the country.

As the national crisis deepened with Union defeats, Lawrence grew uneasy. He strongly disapproved of slavery on moral and religious grounds, but, if anything, he was more critical of secession as the abrogation of a government of laws which the Southern states had originally pledged themselves to sustain. Although he came greatly to admire the Southern officer and soldier, he denounced, as long as he lived, the South's withdrawal from the Union. He knew there were trustees and faculty colleagues who felt by no means so strongly about the war as he did, and the more he talked with his friends, the more the logic of his thinking turned him toward a personal participation in the conflict. He had, of course, his little family to consider, and there was within him a powerful aversion to the shedding of blood. He had a respect for all life as a manifestation of God; even as a boy hunting in the woods, while loving to stalk, he hated to kill. But neither concern for family nor compassion for life could prevail over the gradually mounting conviction that he must commit himself wholeheartedly to this struggle in which he saw the very citadel of civilization threatened, a respect for the laws of man and the laws of God.

People were disturbed at the possibility of his leaving. What Fanny thought is not known, but it is not difficult to imagine: rare is the wife who likes to see her husband go away to war. The Bowdoin people tried to persuade him to remain. At Bowdoin was where his duty lay, educating young men for the future, his colleagues said. Besides, if he was going to be an officer, he had had no qualifying experience, no military training at all save what he had received at Major Whiting's academy—he simply was not fit to command. And had he thought what "glory" would mean if he should be wounded, perhaps irremediably shattered? In its concern the college gave him a two-year leave of absence on the first of August, 1862 to travel and study in Europe. Presumably this extraordinary opportunity to pursue a course that, in the usual run of events, he would scarcely have dared to aspire to would wean him away from thoughts of war; it might even be the means of saving his life. These colleagues of Lawrence's, a number of them his old teachers, knew him better than he suspected; however they may have differed with him, they appreciated him too much to want to see him risk his life, and, knowing his scarcely restrained impulsiveness and his capacity for dedication to a task at hand, they feared the worst.

Lawrence was greatly tempted. He even tentatively accepted the leave of absence. Then his conscience proving too strong, he went to Augusta to see Governor Israel Washburn. The Governor and his very competent Adjutant General, John L. Hodsdon, were faced with pressure to raise troops as rapidly as possible, five regiments under President Lincoln's call of July 2 and eight under his call of August 4. Where to find capable commanders was a serious problem. But here was the professor of modern languages at Bowdoin offering his services, "a gentleman," said Adjutant General Hodsdon, "of the highest moral, intellectual and literary worth." Hardly a military recommendation, but Governor Washburn did not hesitate. Would Professor Chamberlain be interested in a colonelcy and the command of a regiment? Lawrence modestly disclaimed such an ambition at the moment in view of his ignorance of military matters. Instead, he would consider a lieutenant-colonelcy, a subordinate position but one in which he could master the art of command in war. The Governor promised to write him shortly.

Once his intention was learned at Bowdoin, Lawrence had to face severe faculty criticism. Unwilling to lose him, his colleagues strongly protested his lack of qualifications to Augusta. But Governor Washburn's need was too urgent for him to heed such a protest. On August 8, 1862, he wrote Lawrence tendering him a commission as Lieutenant Colonel of the new 20th Regiment Infantry, Maine Volunteers. Lawrence promptly accepted, said his "good-byes," and soon left for Camp Mason at Portland.

Thus began the active military career of one of the most remarkable officers and one of the hardest fighters ever to serve in any American army.

TRAINING CAMP TO FREDERICKSBURG

DEATH beat thunderously across the Antietam in Maryland as General George B. McClellan sent his corps in piecemeal attacks against Robert E. Lee's invading army. If Lee gave the Union general a fine opportunity to trap him in Sharpsburg between the Antietam and the Potomac, McClellan let so many opportunities slip out of his hand that he deserved defeat instead of the drawn battle that resulted on that hot September 17, 1862, the bloodiest single day's fighting of the Civil War. "Nearly all the Southern officers are gentlemen," a former Bowdoin student had written Chamberlain; they were "accustomed to command, and enforce obedience, and the men accustomed to obey or at least respect their superiors . . ." They could also fight, he might have added. But all their fine qualities as soldiers could not have availed at Antietam had McClellan made a concerted attack against Lee's inferior numbers instead of the three separate thrusts which Lee had trouble enough smothering. Even the seventeen-mile march of A. P. Hill's division from Harper's Ferry could not have saved Lee had McClellan decided to commit his big reserve, the Fifth Corps. And if he had given General Fitz-John Porter an order to lead his troops—many of them veterans—against the Confederates, Joshua Lawrence Chamberlain would have participated in his first real action.

37

Perhaps it was just as well for him, or at least for the 20th Maine, that the Fifth Corps remained largely inactive. After all, the 20th Maine had been mustered into service less than a month before. Although excited at the imminence of battle, Chamberlain must certainly have wondered how all these green troops—officers, as well—would have behaved if ordered into action. They were so new to military ways they hardly knew how to march.

But there were promising possibilities in these Maine men —this, Chamberlain realized full well. Foremost was their commander, Colonel Adelbert Ames, who had only recently graduated from West Point in June, 1861 but had comported himself so gallantly at the first battle of Bull Run that he was given the Congressional Medal of Honor. An ambitious young officer, Ames took one look at the men of the 20th Maine at Camp Mason and exclaimed, "This is a hell of a regiment!" He was correct, too. Drawn from many of the little coastal and inland towns and villages and therefore possessing a full measure of unsophisticated curiosity, independence of mind, and democratic manners, the nine-hundred-odd men of the 20th Maine were about as sloppy and unsoldierly as any body of men that ever dared call itself a regiment. Chamberlain noted, moreover, that, since they came from no one area, no mayor or civic organization had seen them off with bands and oratory, no flag had been presented to them, and they had no feeling of *esprit*. Yet there was a physical toughness about them and a willingness to "put out" that augured well if they could learn discipline and the mysteries of drill. Furthermore, they were volunteers, their ages running from 18 to 45, who had enlisted for three years.

The officers apart from Ames were likewise promising. Chamberlain realized painfully his own ignorance of military matters; after all, he had learned only the rudiments as a boy at Major Whiting's military academy. But now he drove himself hard to master this strange, new life. Charles D. Gilmore, the Major, had been a captain in the 7th Maine and possessed a large fund of common sense. So did Ellis Spear, commander of Company G and a school teacher from Wiscasset. Spear, a laconic, cautious optimist, was to have a notable career of his own in the war, and remained a life-long friend of Chamberlain. Captain Henry C. Merriam of Company H was also an unusual person, a Houlton man who was to continue in the army after the war, make important contributions to its development, yet fight for thirty years for proper recognition and win it only with the help of old comrades like Ames and Chamberlain. Also promising was a young non-commissioned officer, Sergeant Thomas Chamberlain, Lawrence's brother, who was to acquire a lieutenant-colonelcy before the war was over, then was to marry his brother John's widow, Delia, and reside in New York and Bangor. There was indeed good material in the 20th Maine.

Still, were the men ready to fight in this great battle across the Antietam? Chamberlain must have smiled ruefully at the very thought. The 20th Maine, after the most meagre introduction to military routine, had been mustered into Federal service as recently as August 29. It left Portland by train for Boston on September 3, and boarded the steamer *Merrimac*. After a dreadful experience with seasickness on the part of the country boys on its rolls, apprehension of destruction or capture by a Confederate privateer, and a moment of panic when a tier of bunks collapsed and everyone thought they had struck a rock, the regiment arrived safely in Alexandria on the 6th. The next day the troops swarmed into Washington and bivouacked near the Arsenal grounds on—according to

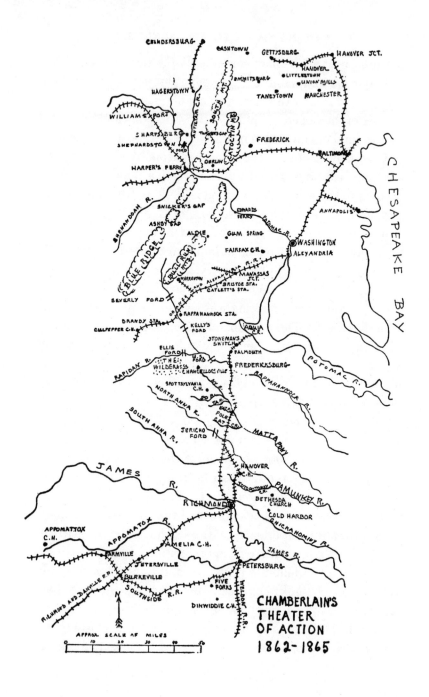

CHAMBERLAIN'S
THEATER
OF ACTION
1862-1865

Ellis Spear—"a downy bed of dead cats, bricks and broken bottles." After drawing arms and ammunition at the Arsenal the next day, they made such a mess of an attempted march-in-step to Fort Craig on Arlington Heights that people along the route—soldiers and civilians alike—howled with laughter and Ames, nearly apoplectic with rage and shame, told the men of the 20th to go home at once if they could do no better the next time.

Then on the 12th, having been assigned as one of the six regiments of the 3rd Brigade, 1st Division, Fifth Corps, the 20th Maine sweated its way with thousands of other men in blue toward Antietam. Sixteen miles it lunged forward, leaving hundreds straggling behind in the stifling heat. The next day, it made twenty-four miles, not bad at all for rookies with the leather still stiff in their new shoes and blisters making each step painful. Finally at nightfall on the 16th, they reached the middle ridge on the east side of the Antietam where they were held in reserve when the carnage started early in the morning of the 17th. Chamberlain on a horse had had it much easier than his men, but even he, hard fighter that he became, must have been grateful that the fumbling, inexperienced 20th Maine, though present, was not a participant in the dreadful battle of Antietam.

Chamberlain and the 20th received their "blooding" three days later. McClellan was so intimidated by Lee's bold stand that he was even more cautious in ordering a pursuit than was General Meade after Gettysburg the next summer. Lee was therefore able to execute a withdrawal across the Potomac without severe harassment. McClellan finally did send the Fifth Corps after him. At Shephardstown Ford Fitz-John Porter put several units over the river on the 19th, then withdrew all of them by the 20th as Stonewall Jackson hurried A. P. Hill to the high ground overlooking the Ford. Though the Union artillery prevented Hill's men from tumbling the bluecoats over the banks, it was a near disaster until the last Union troops splashed back to the Maryland shore.

The 20th Maine had received orders to cross to the Virginia bank, and no one had rescinded them. With Ames a stickler for obedience, the 20th waded into the river, plunging through the retreating troops. Confederates lining the bluff ahead fired into the blue masses filling the Potomac, while Union artillery, slamming away with shells that burst at short range, killed friend and foe alike. Later a number of angry Union infantrymen paid a hurried visit to the offending Union battery and silenced it in their own way. It was bad enough to be killed by the enemy.

Meanwhile, the 20th Maine had no sooner reached the Virginia shore than bugles on the Maryland side sounded a frantic retreat. Back went the regiment, the water jumping in hundreds of little spouts as the Confederates kept up an incessant fire from the bluff. No officer showed more conspicuous courage and calmness than Chamberlain. He sat on his horse in the middle of the Potomac apparently unperturbed, and, as the Fifth Corps historian noted, "was steadying the men through a deep place in the river, where several of the 5th New York were drowned in his presence." Of course, he made an inviting target. The Confederates missed him but shot his horse from under him, and Chamberlain returned to the Maryland shore as wet as any of his men. His steadiness, however, and that of the other officers paid off, for the regiment suffered only three casualties—wounds.

Within a few days President Lincoln gave the war a badly needed moral lift by issuing the preliminary Emancipation

Proclamation, which, together with Lee's failure to win at Antietam, helped dissuade the European powers, Britain and France in particular, from recognizing the Confederacy. The British government, regardless of its sympathy for the South, had no desire to identify itself with supporting slavery. Lincoln had long wanted a victory which could provide some semblance of reality for the Emancipation edict, to go into effect on New Years Day. Antietam was not what he had hoped for, but it had to do.

Then, on October 1, Lincoln arrived at the camp at Antietam Ford to talk with "Little Mac," this organizer of the army who loved it so dearly he did not seem able—or perhaps dare—to use it. Too long had McClellan been a victim of "the slows," as Lincoln described his deliberation, and on this visit the President spoke plainly about the popular general's "overcautiousness." Lincoln also reviewed the army. He was a guest at Fifth Corps Headquarters, and Chamberlain observed that "we had the opportunity to discern something more of that great spirit than was ordinarily revealed in those rugged features and deep, sad eyes." He added that the men conceived for the President "a sympathy and an affection . . . wonderful in its intensity." During the review, he noted how Lincoln's "earnest eyes" took in everything: "As the reviewing cavalcade passed along our lines, where mounted officers were stationed in front of their commands, he checked his mount to draw McClellan's attention to my horse, whose white-dappled color and proud bearing made me almost too conspicuous on some occasions."

Chamberlain and the 20th Maine spent the lovely month of October, 1862, training at the camp near Antietam Ford. Ames really went to work on his officers and men with school of the soldier, company drill, battalion maneuvers, loading and firing by the numbers, endless marching, continued lessons in military courtesy. The men grew so exasperated that Tom Chamberlain feared they would shoot Ames in the first battle (what war hasn't fathered such cherished thoughts among those exposed to the caustic comments of a drill instructor?). Personally Tom wished Ames would get a state's prison sentence or a brigadier-generalship. But somehow Ames made a disciplined regiment out of the 20th Maine, and Lawrence could write Fanny on October 26, "I believe that no other New Regt. will *ever* have the discipline we have now. We all *work*."

No man, with the possible exception of Ames himself, worked harder than Chamberlain. "I *study*, I tell you, every military work I can find," he wrote Fanny. "And it is no small labor to master the evolutions of a Battalion and Brigade. I am bound to understand *every thing*. And I want you to send my 'Jomini, Art of War'. . . . The Col. and I are going to read it." Every night, he would go to the Colonel's tent, or Ames to his, and Ames would pour into Chamberlain's mind everything of the art of war that he had learned at West Point and since then. Now as never before there was need to concentrate, to master much in little time; ignorance could cost lives as Chamberlain was learning by sad observation.

Unlike his brother Tom or the vast majority of officers and men in the army, he took easily to military life. Tom wrote their mother, "I wish you could hear Lawrence give off a command and see him ride along the battalion on his white horse. He looks splendidly." Tom also mentioned how well Lawrence said he felt, while Lawrence himself confirmed this in a letter to Fanny. He took special pleasure in his duties as field officer of the day for the brigade every third day when he had to make the rounds of the outposts and the advanced guards, which gave him "a fine chance," he told Fanny, "to ride over the country. I wish you could be beside me on some gentle palfrey plunging into some rich shaded valley, craggy defile, or along some lovely stream. Or perhaps, as a day or two ago, mount to the summit of one of these blue hills, whence you can see forty miles into Virginia—see the long lines of rebel fires miles away and villages and streams and bright patches of cultivated fields and on our own side the great battle field of Antietam—the hills trodden bare and the fields all veined with the tracks of artillery trains, or movements of army corps. I have enjoyed these rides much. Often I am 12 or 15 hours a day in the saddle."

Part of his enjoyment of this life originated in its contrast to the life he had left. As never before he had a sense of being appreciated for what he was as a man and what he could contribute as an officer. There were no professors to question the value of his ideas of educational reform or to ridicule him for leaving the wisdom and dignity of the academic world for the war. "I have my care and vexations," he admitted to Fanny, then added with some heat, "but let me say no danger and no hardship ever makes me wish to get back to that college life again. I can't breathe when I think of those last two years. Why I would spend my whole life in campaigning it, rather than endure that again. One thing though, I *won't* endure it again. My experience here and the habit of command, will make me less complaisant, will break in upon the notion that certain persons are the natural authorities over me." Two weeks later he said, "I feel that it *is* a sacrifice for me to be here in one sense of

the word; but I do not wish myself back by any means. I
feel that I am where duty called me. The 'glory' Prof. Smyth
so *honestly* pictured for me I do not much dread. If I do
return 'shattered' and 'good-for-nothing,' I shall think there
are those who will hold me in some degree of favor better
than that which he predicted. Most likely I shall be hit
somehow at sometime, but all 'my times are in His hand,'
and I can not die without His appointing. I try to keep ever
in view all the possibilities that surround me and to be
ready for all that I am called to."

How he missed Fanny—and she, him. She begged him
for a photograph of himself in uniform, but photographers
were not numerous at Antietam Ford and were seldom
around. "Does your innocent little head imagine that I could
get a *Photograph* (!) taken here? My stars! I fear you have
not a *high* ideal of my position. If we can get anything to
eat; or any thing to sleep on except the ground; or under,
save the sky; if we can find a bit of paper, or get a little
thimbleful of ink of a sutler; if we can see a house that is
not riddled with shot and shell, or left tenantless through
terror, or if we could get a glimpse of a woman who does
not exceed the requirements for *sweepers* in College, we
think we are in Paradise." She was "a very dear little wife"
to suggest that, since two colonels' wives were coming down
to stay with their husbands, she might come, too. This was
quite impossible: their husbands were stationed in permanent garrisons in the rear, while the 20th Maine was at the
front and his own abode "as shifting as the nighthawk's
flight." "My rubber blanket," he continued, "is not quite big
enough to accommodate ever so sweet and welcome a guest
on the rough hillsides, or in the drenching valleys that constitute my changing homes." At any rate, "You are coming

to Washington . . . this winter—you and Daise. I want you
to do every thing you wish, and go every where you like."
He dreamed of her and Daise and Wyllys constantly, and
he begged her repeatedly to write more often.

Chamberlain was not exaggerating when he spoke of his
uncertain residence. On October 27, McClellan began to
move the Army of the Potomac into Virginia. He felt that
if he slid along the eastern slopes of the Blue Ridge, occupying the mountain gaps, he could place his troops between
Lee and Richmond and thereby force Lee to fight on the
ground that he, McClellan, chose. The weather was magnificent and on no day more so than October 30 when the
Fifth Corps started for Snickersville, near Snicker's Gap,
where the 20th Maine bivouacked on November 2.

"What names they have here in the land of Rebeldom!"
Chamberlain laughed to Fanny in a letter on the 3rd. "Snicker's Gap! What an undignified name for a battle field. Yet
here we are, expecting a battle with the Rebels who are
just over the mountain at the other end of the Gap. We are
all in fine condition for a fight. To be sure our Regt. is now
reduced to about 550 [the effect of illness and disease, and
some desertions]. But what there are left are of the right
sort." There had been a brisk artillery skirmish on the afternoon of the 2nd, and Chamberlain expected action at any
time. The thought exhilarated him, and he wrote a long and
lively description of himself in the field: "Mr. Brown [proba-
bly John Brown, the Adjutant] says I am the most careless
and improvident fellow he ever saw—take no care of myself
at all—sleep on the ground when I have the whole Regt. at my
command to make a house for me. But I hate to see a man
always on the spring to get the best of every thing for himself. I prefer to take things as they come, and I am as well

and comfortable as any body, and no one is the worse for it. Picture to yourself a stout looking fellow—face covered with beard—with a pair of cavalry pants on—sky blue—big enough for Goliath, and coarse as a sheep's back—said fellow having worn and torn and ridden his original suit quite out of the question—enveloped in a huge cavalry overcoat (when it is cold) of the same color and texture as the pants; and ... wearing the identical flannel blouse worn at Portland—cap with a immense rent in it, caused by a picket raid when we were after Stuart's cavalry. A shawl and rubber talma strapped on behind the saddle and the overcoat (perhaps), or the dressing case, before—2 pistols in holsters. Sword about three feet long at side—a piece of blue beef and some hard bread in the saddlebags. This figure seated on a magnificent horse gives that peculiar point and quality of incongruity which constitutes the ludicrous. The Col. says the Regt. is recognized every where by that same figure. Rebel prisoners praise the horse and the sword, but evidently take no bang [sic] to the *man*."

The day before, the regiment had marched fifteen miles. The afternoon had been hot, but after sunset the weather changed abruptly: "A bitter cold northwester from the Blue Mountains tears down upon us. We bivouac as we can—some taking more pains and some less. I take my saddle for a pillow—rubber talma for a bed—shawl for a covering and a big chestnut tree for a canopy and let it blow. A dashing rain and furious gale in the night makes me put on a skull-cap (given me by the major) and pull the talma over me—head and all—curl up so as to bring myself into a bunch—and *enjoy it hugely*. I would confess to any body but you, that I was *cold*—feet especially. However I *enjoy* it I say and get up, (I don't say wake up) bright as a squirrel and hearty as a bear for a breakfast of salt pork, or hard bread; with, maybe, coffee with out milk and alas! without sugar."

He begged Fanny not to worry about him. "I am in the right place, and no harm can come to me unless it is wisely and kindly ordered so." She should try to "be happy—I should be perfectly so if I could see the dear ones under my little roof." In a letter on the following night, November 4, he told her again not to worry: "I want you to be cheerful and occupy your mind with pleasant things so as not to have time to grow melancholy. You mustn't think of me much. I am in earnest. Invite the Juniors over to spend the evening with some of the young ladies, as we used to, and keep up your character for hospitality and your spirits at the same time." She should not worry about his being wounded. Optimistically he said, "I expect to get some sort of a scratch when we 'go in,' but the chances are it will not be serious if anything."

Unknown to Chamberlain and the other officers of the 20th Maine, changes in the army command were now made that vitally affected the destiny of the Army of the Potomac. "Little Mac" was on the way out. Chamberlain had been wary of commenting about the army leadership in his letters to Fanny, because, he explained, "I don't know under what scrutiny the letter will pass before it gets to you." At the same time, he felt something was wrong: "We shall keep on fighting, I imagine, through the present Administration. I see no signs of peace. Good fighting on both sides, but while we will not be beaten, still something seems to strike all the vigor out of our arms just at the point of victory." President Lincoln decided that the chief reason for the Union's failure to drive home lay in the defects of General McClellan. Despite his large fund of military knowledge, his skill as an organizer, and his power to evoke the loyalty and love of his men, McClellan was cautious, hesitant, slow, ever fearful that Lee outnumbered him, conceited beyond measure, lacking in military but possessing an ambitious political imagination—the category of deficiencies could continue. Utterly disillusioned, Lincoln, on November 5, directed Secretary of War Edwin Stanton and Henry Halleck, General-in-Chief of the Armies, to remove McClellan. Two days later "Little Mac," to the grief of many soldiers, passed his command over to General Ambrose E. Burnside.

Burnside, a good friend of McClellan, had been a Regular Army officer who had resigned to manufacture firearms in Rhode Island and subsequently to hold an office in the Illinois Central Railroad. He had participated at First Bull Run, attained a fair degree of success in expeditions àgainst the coast of North Carolina, and handled a corps not too satisfactorily at Antietam. A large, powerful, energetic man, possessing little intelligence but a magnificent curl of whiskers sweeping from ear to ear via the upper lip over a shaven chin and throat, he had no real desire to command an army. The exigency of the situation, however, found the bluff, likable "Burn," as McClellan called him, in charge of the Army of the Potomac. Knowing that an aggressive move was called for, he proposed to march rapidly for Fredericksburg with a view to moving onto Richmond from that point. This would have the advantage of enabling the army to be supplied by the railroad running from the landing at Aquia Creek on the Potomac to Fredericksburg, though the railroad would have to be repaired because of its destruction by the enemy. There was, of course, the Rappahannock River to cross at Fredericksburg, but the engineers in Washington could furnish sufficient pontoons and bridge materials. Burnside also reorganized the army into Grand Divisions: the Right Grand Division, formed from the Second and Ninth Corps, under Major General Edwin V. Sumner; the Left Grand Division, consisting of the First and Sixth Corps, under Major General William B. Franklin; and the Center Grand Division, based on the Third and Fifth Corps, under Major General Joseph Hooker. Hooker, an ambitious, mercurial, back-biting officer but an aggressive fighter, had recently taken over command of the Fifth Corps with the summary removal of Fitz-John Porter on November 10 for having run into trouble with General John Pope at Second Bull Run back in the summer.

The 20th Maine had not known McClellan very well and so was not greatly upset by his departure; unfortunately it was to know Burnside too well by his deeds and few men who survived the experience "Burn" prepared for them at Fredericksburg were to have a more unpleasant impression of his generalship than Joshua Lawrence Chamberlain. Part of the trouble was not Burnside's fault: the all-important pontoons were hopelessly slow in arriving, and the success of Burnside's whole plan depended on its speed of execution. Although he might have got Sumner over the fords, the rain that began to swell the river might have made it difficult to pull Sumner back unless the pontoons appeared before Lee; hence Burnside sat and waited in front of Fredericksburg. Meanwhile, Lee arrived. Burnside should now have given up his plan altogether, but with the pontoons on hand at last, he decided to drive straight across toward the town. A small Confederate brigade held off his army of 116,000 until "Burn's" artillery pulverized the town and Union infantry flushed out the defenders. Then over the bridge went the army to contend against Lee's 72,000 dug in on high defensive ground. Particularly strong was his position on Marye's Heights protected by a stone wall, behind which defenders could stand in a kind of sunken road and keep up a continuous fire under almost complete protection. Burnside ordered Franklin to slash at Lee's right flank and roll it up, with Sumner driving through the left center at Marye's Heights. Hooker was to remain in reserve on the north bank of the river, prepared to throw his strength where needed.

On December 12 both attacking Grand Divisions moved across the river. The next morning artillery opened against Confederate positions through the heavy fog, Franklin went into action, and, about eleven o'clock, Burnside ordered Sumner's Grand Division to assault the Heights. The result was a bloody catastrophe; the Confederates controlled all approaches. Franklin, furthermore, let his Sixth Corps stand idle while his First was being badly mauled. His attempt to roll up the enemy right was therefore futile. The Confederates could now concentrate largely on Sumner, and the magnificent courage of his men simply could not accomplish the impossible.

Burnside, however, persisted in the criminal folly of blind assault. He called on Hooker, and into action went the 20th Maine and Lieutenant Colonel Chamberlain—but not immediately. The Fifth Corps, now under General Daniel Butterfield, who had formerly commanded the brigade to which the 20th Maine belonged, moved across the river. Chamberlain found the crossing itself a nerve-wracking experience: "The enemy's cannoneers knew the ranges perfectly. The air was thick with the flying, bursting shells; whooping solid shot swept lengthwise our narrow bridge, fortunately not yet plowing a furrow through the midst of us, but driving the compressed air so close to our heads that there was an unconquerable instinct to shrink beneath it, although knowing it was then too late. The crowding, swerving column set the pontoons swaying, so that the horses reeled and men could scarcely keep their balance."

Great was their relief when they reached Fredericksburg, although they knew they were shortly to be thrown into the furnace. The men unslung their knapsacks, leaving them with the quartermaster, then waited for the order to move out. Two brigades of the 1st Division were sent to the assistance of a hard-pressed division of the Ninth Corps. The 2nd and 3rd Divisions with a portion of the 3rd Brigade of the 1st Division, including the 20th Maine, moved to the assault. As Chamberlain said, "We were directed straight forward toward the left of the futile advance we had seen so fearfully cut down." Fences compelled the officers to send back their horses, and presently the regiment was picking its way over the dead and the writhing bodies of the wounded, who called out, "It's no use, boys; we've tried that. Nothing living can stand there; it's only for the dead." Chamberlain could well believe it, for, as the regiment moved out into an open field, he could see off to the right through the smoke a battery swinging into position to rake the regiment's front. "God help us now!" Adelbert Ames said to him. "Colonel, take the right wing; I must lead here!" And the line of blue, bearing its new state colors, advanced into the storm.

That unfaltering advance momentarily cheered the spirits of the regiment ahead of them, decimated and pinned down on the slope. Then the Maine regiment took these men's places and drove the attack nearer to the stone wall, "a sheet of flame," as General Humphreys, 3rd Division commander, described it. But raw courage could not avail that day. "We reached the final crest, before that all-commanding, countermanding stone wall," said Chamberlain. "Here we exchanged fierce volleys at every disadvantage, until the muzzle-flame deepened the sunset red, and all was dark."

That night was one that Chamberlain never forgot. Behind the slight crest within pistol shot of the enemy, the men made a ghastly bivouac among the dead. They had discarded blankets and overcoats in Fredericksburg, and now a bitter wind sweeping over the battlefield left them shivering with cold. They huddled close to the fallen for warmth and in many cases stripped the dead for their clothes. Chamberlain lay down between two men killed in the earlier assaults and rested his head on a third, pulling the flap of the last one's coat over himself. Now and then he would be startled by someone pulling the overcoat flap away and "peering, half vampire-like, to my fancy, through the darkness" then jumping away in fright as Chamberlain spoke to him.

But sleep would not come. From all over the muddy, bloody slopes of the hill rose a dreadful cacaphony of moans, shrieks, groans, and delirious mutterings from the wounded— some crying out for a surgeon, as many more begging to be put out of their misery, and all entreating to be given water. All this was more than the humanitarian in Chamberlain could bear. In the company of the Adjutant, John Brown, he went out onto the field, straightening limbs, bandaging wounds, holding a canteen to lips that drank greedily in an attempt to quench the feverish thirst that accompanies wounds, quickly writing down the last wishes of a dying man to send to some distant home. It was with deep relief that he discerned through the darkness a number of ambulances arrive on the far edge of the field with the litter-bearers bending over the fallen, holding half-covered lan-

terns or striking blue-flamed matches to see whether the
men were alive or dead.

Chamberlain now resumed his place of shelter among the
dead. But even now sleep would not come. The sounds of
the battlefield persisted, further depressing him as he thought
of man's inhumanity to man and its dreadful consequences.
Off to the right a loosened window-blind flapped in a battered brick house deserted except for a few despairing
wounded. It swung in a weird rhythm between the sash and
the wall, and to Chamberlain it seemed to say in a dark re-
frain that he ever after associated with that anguished night,
"Never—forever; forever—never!"

With dawn came a spattering of shots from the enemy,
then a storm of bullets and the deeper-voiced roar of cannon
as the Confederate artillery opened up with shell. The men
hugged the earth, and only by the most careful movements
could they load their muskets without being hit or at least
drawing the enemy's fire. Soon two to three hundred Confederates slipped from behind the stone wall to fire into the
left flank of the 20th Maine where the ground fell away.
Quickly the troops gathered the dead and built a breastwork of bodies into which bullets thudded all day, the men
still lying flat or, at most, crouching. To stand up, even to
raise one's head above the breastwork, was to die, as two
men found out.

Somehow they endured the day and, at night, received
orders to withdraw. First they scooped out shallow graves
for their own fallen with bayonets and fragments of shells
and carved the name and home of each on headboards
roughly fashioned from broken fence rails or musket butts.
Then, said Chamberlain, "We had to pick our way over
a field strewn with incongruous ruin; men torn and broken

and cut to pieces in every indescribable way, cannon dismounted, gun carriages smashed or overturned, ammunition
chests flung wildly about, horses dead and half-dead still
held in harness, accouterments of every sort scattered as
by whirlwinds. It was not good for the nerves, that ghastly
march, in the lowering night!"

Having arrived back in Fredericksburg, the 20th Maine
bivouacked in the streets, but there was little sleep the rest
of that night or the day following. Troops from all commands
were hopelessly intermingled. And into the tangled blue
masses came a storm of Confederate shells. In the late afternoon there was a rumor brought in by prisoners that Stonewall Jackson was about to whirl down upon the right of the
town and sweep everyone into the river. "No doubt he
could have done it," Chamberlain admitted. Lee, however,
still expected another attack, owing to his easy repulse of
Burnside on the 13th, and did not want to lose the advantage
of his position or expose his troops to the fire of Union
batteries across the river by moving toward the town.

With nightfall, the hopes of the Maine men that all
hazards for them were over for the time being were dashed.
The 20th Maine was sent out with two other regiments to
the extreme central front to cover some undisclosed movement of the army. The entire line was under the command of
Ames so that the command of the 20th Maine itself fell to
Chamberlain. The order was passed, "Hold this ground at all
hazards, and to the last!"

"Last of what?" Chamberlain wondered. Whimsically he
decided that no dictionary held that definition.

The men then set to work throwing up a protective mound
of earth between themselves and the enemy. The Southern
riflepits were so close that Chamberlain could hear enough

fragments of conversation to convince him the Confederates were about as anxious as his own men, who dared speak only in whispers. Presently Chamberlain crept along the line checking the alignment of his defenses. Noticing a fox hole being dug somewhat out of the alignment, he went up to the offender and muttered, "Throw to the other side, my man; that's where the danger is!"

"Golly!" the soldier replied, "don't ye s'pose I know which side them Yanks be? They're right onto us now."

In the darkness he had strayed over to the Confederate lines! Concealing his dismay, Chamberlain quickly pretended to be a Southern officer making the rounds. "Dig away then," he retorted, "but keep a right sharp lookout!" Then without lingering to consider the effect of his order or his accent, he walked swiftly away.

But he was not finished with being startled that night. The regiment had just completed digging in when there came a clatter from the left rear and a staff officer rushed up. "Where is the commander of these troops?" When Chamberlain acknowledged that he was, the officer shouted, "Get yourselves out of this as quick as God will let you! The whole army is across the river!"

For the moment Chamberlain was more startled by the man's voice than by the information. Everyone in the enemy picket line must have heard him, and the Confederates might attack in a matter of seconds.

"Steady in your places, my men," Chamberlain barked, "this is a stampeding coward."

When some of the officers came rushing up, he called out, "Arrest this man for a spy, and hold fast your lines!"

His voice, pitched in a tone to warn off the enemy as well as to calm his own men, could be heard the entire length of the 20th Maine battle line. Then Chamberlain stepped back and let the staff officer have the rough side of his tongue in a rebuke that reduced the astounded man to a whisper. He could only explain that he had had such difficulty getting up to the front that he had nearly gone crazy. Scarcely appeased, Chamberlain told him to get out of the way as fast as possible and he would not report him for such gross misbehavior.

Chamberlain now hunted up Ames. They decided to hold the line for a time, even to display a redoubled zeal. But this was just for appearances. Presently the odd-numbered men were to drop back and form a battle line a hundred yards or so to the rear. Then the even-numbered men were to withdraw through that line to a like distance behind, and the maneuver would be repeated.

The plan worked, although there were anxious moments when the Confederates were observed coming out of their trenches and following. Luckily they were both puzzled and nervous at closing in on the orderly retreat of the 20th Maine. Furthermore the night was so dark that they could not make out all that was happening in front of them. But just as Ames and Chamberlain began to think they could bring off their men successfully, the latter moving as quietly as possible in a stooping posture and with muskets at the "trail," a new enemy appeared. The night had been rainy until about midnight; then a bleak north wind broke up the storm into great black clouds. Suddenly as one half of the 20th Maine was passing to the rear through the other, the moon shone through a break in the scudding clouds. Its rays fell upon the polished musket barrels and revealed the entire regiment. A musket cracked in the distance, and as the men hit the earth, a scattering volley went over their heads. The officers now had to watch for the appropriate black cloud before ordering the withdrawal continued.

The retreat was an experience that none could forget—slipping back through the wreck of the battlefield with the dead everywhere—faces rigid and stark white in the moonlight, a furiously baying hound adding to the reality of the men being a fox to the pack, a mounting apprehension that they might reach the river too late. Finally they crept into the ruined town, its shell-torn houses deserted, yawning doors and broken window shutters banging about in the high wind, and again the dead lying across the door-stoops, on the sidewalks, and in the front yards. The 20th Maine had buried its own four dead and brought off those of its thirty-two wounded who could not walk. It had also carried back wounded men from other units, but, on reaching Fredericksburg, it discovered that almost everyone had left the town except a mass of the sorely wounded who could not be moved and a few devoted surgeons who decided to remain with them. The spectacle of so much suffering was too much for the regiment's assistant surgeon, Dr. Nahum A. Hersom of Sanford, Maine; he requested permission to stay behind to do what he could to ease the pain. "Sorrowfully but proudly we left him for his ministry of mercy," said Chamberlain. At last, just as it grew light, the regiment arrived at the bridgehead and passed over the pontoon floor which had been muffled with sod and brush so as not to disclose the withdrawal of the army. Hardly had the regiment reached the other side when the engineers let go the guy wires and started taking up the boats.

A cold December rain was falling again as the 20th Maine marched up the bank. Noticing the men's weariness, Chamberlain brought them to a rest-halt by the roadside. He was tired himself, and his cheek ached from a deep scratch. Wearily he slumped to the ground and leaned against a tree. He was deeply depressed by what had occurred. He could not, of course, ignore the feat just accomplished, that the army had recrossed the river without loss of men and without knowledge of the enemy. But as Chamberlain looked back over the river to those slopes blue with Union dead— "Death-gardens, haunted by glorious ghosts," he called them —he grieved at such evidence of "splendid but unavailing valor." From grief he passed to anger that Burnside had ever ordered the battle undertaken on the enemy's own terms. On the other hand, bad as the general battle plan was, Franklin had failed especially miserably; had he put his whole force of 60,000 men in on Lee's right, he could not have failed to roll up that flank. When his attack broke down, the burden fell upon those who were assigned to assault the stone wall, precisely where Lee was most strongly fortified and wanted the assault to come. Furthermore, the commander of the Center Grand Division, Hooker, had neither put his men into the attack in force, nor, linking with Sumner, concentrated on Lee's left above the town. Instead, as Chamberlain said bitterly, the components of the Center Grand Division "were sent by superior orders, in detachments, to support other commands, or as a 'forlorn hope' at various times and places. . . ."

A clip-clop of hoofs caused Chamberlain to look up. To his amazement, General Hooker himself came riding slowly by. Chamberlain had not seen Hooker for those three terrible days, and sight of "Fighting Joe" now made him furious: "he had no business to be where we were. We supposed he and our corps commander, Butterfield, were somewhere controlling and observing their commands."

"You've had a hard chance, Colonel," Hooker said in a kindly manner. "I am glad to see you out of it!"

Bitterness and fatigue made Chamberlain reckless. "It was chance, General; not much intelligent design there!"

"God knows I did not put you in!" Hooker retorted crisply.

"That was the trouble, General," Chamberlain shot back. "You should have put us in. We were handed in piecemeal, on toasting-forks."

This was plain talk. It was not every day that a lieutenant colonel told a major general and his superior officer to his face precisely what he thought of the general's tactics and intelligence. But neither was it every day that a lieutenant colonel would have been permitted to get away with such comments. Fredericksburg, however, had given Hooker a fright. He glanced at the rising ground across the river, the carpet of blue now dimly seen through the rain. "I never think of this ground but with a shudder," he said on visiting the battlefield after the war. Perhaps he realized the justice in the comment that the correspondent of the Cincinnati *Commercial* sent his paper, "It can hardly be in human nature for men to show more valor, or generals to manifest less judgment, then were perceptible on our side that day." Whatever his reasons, he remained silent—a most remarkable achievement for the proud, sharp-tongued Hooker. He nodded curtly to the weary lieutenant colonel of infantry, and rode on.

Had Chamberlain realized that in about six weeks the bumbling Burnside would be out and Hooker in as commander of the Army of the Potomac, he might have held his peace that dreary December day. But probably not: "Our dead . . . had died in vain," Chamberlain insisted angrily, and someone had to say something to someone responsible. Chamberlain might be slow to anger, thanks to his severe self-discipline, but, once roused, he could be awfully stubborn in defense of an ideal and loyal to those who rendered it a full measure of service and devotion.

CHANCELLORSVILLE TO GETTYSBURG

"ALAS my poor country!" wrote a former medical student serving with the 79th New York in the winter of 1863. "It has strong limbs to march and meet the foe, stout arms to strike heavy blows, brave hearts to dare—but ... have we no brains to use the arms and limbs and eager hearts with cunning? ... I am sick and tired of disaster...."

The young soldier was but expressing the thoughts of many in the Army of the Potomac, not the least of whom was Chamberlain. But the tragedy was that further disasters and humiliations were in store for that long-suffering army before it found itself at last truly victorious in battle at a little-known crossroads town in Pennsylvania. Several additional months were to pass even after that before it found a general who would lead it through the worst blood-letting of the war to ultimate triumph.

Even Chamberlain with all his ebullience could discover little to rejoice about during the winter of 1863. Winter quarters at Stoneman's Switch were not unpleasant but dull except for the incessant drilling and maneuvering on which Ames insisted and the discussion of strategy and tactics that went on between the two officers. Yet the dullness of camp was preferable to the experiences of the "Mud March" that Burnside ordered in January with a view to crossing the

63

Rappahannock and cutting Lee's communications with Richmond. The army moved out on January 20, but within a few hours a real January thaw set in with rain falling. By the next noon the whole army was stuck in the mud. Burnside, therefore, had to order the drenched, exasperated troops back to their camp, the 20th Maine returning on the January 24th.

The next day President Lincoln deprived Burnside, Sumner, and Franklin of their commands. Burnside had strongly recommended that Hooker be cashiered "as a man unfit to hold an important commission during a crisis like the present, when so much patience, charity, confidence, consideration, and patriotism are due from every soldier in the field." To Burnside's chagrin, notwithstanding the validity of his criticism of Hooker, President Lincoln promoted "Fighting Joe" to command of the Army of the Potomac. Ironically the President could say to Hooker in the same letter in which he told him of his promotion, "I am not quite satisfied with you"; and Lincoln mentioned both Hooker's habit of criticizing his superiors, thereby helping to undermine the confidence of the army, and his rashness. "Beware of rashness," Lincoln warned him, "but with energy and sleepless vigilance go forward and give us victories."

Although Hooker's appointment may have initially raised doubts in Chamberlain's mind, "Fighting Joe's" revival of the army's *esprit* found favor with him. And certainly Hooker's work was commendable: he had the old camp thoroughly cleaned up, unit kitchens and bakeries set up, and rigorous inspections instituted. Drill was intensified, and large details were set to work constructing corduroy roads and temporary bridges. The health of the troops improved noticeably, while Hooker's chief of staff, Dan Butterfield, raised troop morale by devising a system of corps badges, that of the Fifth Corps, worn on their caps by the 20th Maine, being a maltese cross. The grand-division status was dropped, and the army returned to the former corps organization. Among the personnel changes was the elevation of a tall, rather dour, unoriginal engineering officer to command of the Fifth Corps, General George Meade of Pennsylvania, more familiarly known as "the old snapping turtle." Of all the changes, socially the "Ladies' Days," for which General Daniel Sickles starred as an organizer, proved most popular with the officers.

Hooker also established a liberal system of leaves and furloughs, while toughening the policy on AWOLs, and Chamberlain was able to obtain a four-day leave in April. Where he spent his leave is uncertain but probably in Washington where Fanny could have joined him. At any rate he was on hand for "Fighting Joe's" great test, that test to which Lincoln alluded when he told Hooker and Major General Darius N. Couch, "I want to impress upon you two gentlemen—in your next fight, put in all your men."

Hooker's plan was comparatively simple, perhaps too simple against a soldier like Lee. Covered by cavalry, three Federal corps would march up the Rappahannock and cross above the confluence of that river and the Rapidan. They would soon be joined by additional troops when Lee was sufficiently distracted by a diversionary movement of three corps under rugged General John Sedgwick crossing below Fredericksburg, and Hooker would then sweep down on Lee from the direction of Chancellorsville. Meanwhile Major General George Stoneman was to take the Federal cavalry around Lee's flank and slash at his rear, destroying supplies and communications.

Unfortunately rain slowed the march as at Fredericksburg, and Lee divined the plan. Though outnumbered more than

two to one, approximately 130,000 to 60,000, he coolly
divided his army, using about one quarter to hold off
Sedgwick and another under his own command to demon-
strate in Hooker's front, while sending Jackson with half
the army in a wide turning movement to roll up Hooker's
right flank. Jackson slammed into the Eleventh Corps on
May 2 just as it was preparing supper. The surprise was
complete and the Union right collapsed, though Jackson
himself was mortally wounded by his own troops when
returning from reconnoitering his position. The battle continued until May 6, when Hooker, who had earlier been
stunned by a shell striking the pillar of the house against
which he was leaning and not by an excess of alcoholic in-
take as many believed, withdrew completely. Then it became
clear to all that Lee had won his greatest triumph.

Chamberlain's part in the battle had not been what he
expected or desired. An epidemic of smallpox, resulting
probably from poorly prepared serum with which the regiment was vaccinated at Stoneman's Switch, hit the 20th
Maine so hard that, on April 17, the surgeon, Dr. Monroe,
warned the Adjutant General of the danger of contaminating
the whole army. Ames reluctantly forwarded Monroe's message but succeeded in gaining for himself a detached service
post on Meade's staff and won promotion to a brigadier for
his effort in the battle. Chamberlain, not so fortunate in his
opinion, found himself in charge of a regiment ordered into
quarantine. The beginning of the Chancellorsville struggle
sent him hurrying to General Butterfield with a request
that the 20th Maine be permitted to fight. When the General
firmly refused, Chamberlain had a most un-Christian inspiration. Said he, "If we couldn't do anything else we would
give the rebels the smallpox!" Dan Butterfield, however,

was evidently not too impressed with such a modern and devastating conception of warfare, and, as one of the 20th Maine wrote, "to our great disgust . . . we were detailed to guard a telegraph line running from Falmouth to Hooker's headquarters." Until the evening of May 6, the regiment remained on duty, then returned to its old camp.

But as the 20th Maine guarded the wire, it was without its lieutenant colonel for part of the time. Unable to stay out of the fight personally, Chamberlain crossed the Rappahannock and was with General Charles Griffin's 1st Division of the Fifth Corps when that division became involved in a very sharp attack against General J. E. B. Stuart. Chamberlain rallied a number of the troops, but his horse was badly wounded and he soon found himself floundering around in the muck like the infantry. When the bewildered and angry troops scrambled back over the pontoon bridges in the driving rain, the Fifth Corps served as the rearguard. Chamberlain, on May 5 and 6, stayed long at the bridges, which threatened to give way in the freshet, steadying the men by his presence and his calm words. Engineering officers long remembered his effectiveness, while General Griffin was enormously impressed by his soldierly qualities and, when Ames was promoted to command a brigade in the Eleventh Corps, joined with Ames in recommending Chamberlain for the colonelcy of the 20th Maine. The promotion became effective on June 23, 1863.

Presently Chamberlain faced a serious morale problem. The 2nd Maine had been in the war since before First Bull Run and had a gallant record. Unfortunately a mix-up had occurred in signing the enlistment papers so that some of the regiment were in service for three years and others for two years. When the two-year men went home in May, the three-year men could not see why they should not be going home with most of their regiment and were in a mutinous condition. They refused to obey orders, and for three days no one assumed the responsibility for feeding them. A detachment of the 118th Pennsylvania with fixed bayonets brought them over to Chamberlain, whose orders from the corps commander, General Meade, were to "make them do duty, or shoot them down the moment they refused."

Chamberlain acquired a reputation during the war of being a severe disciplinarian but one who was also just, who looked after his men, who shared their hardships, who expected no feat of courage that he was not ready to participate in or even to lead. The result was that he had a magnificently trained and loyal command. Yet all his understanding of soldiers and their problems was put to the test in dealing with the angry men of the 2nd Maine, big men from the Bangor area who had got involved in a slam-bang fist fight with three other regiments during Burnside's "Mud March" and, according to one report, "cleared the field."

All his life Chamberlain stressed the importance of preserving the dignity of the individual. He did so now. He rode over to General Meade and asked permission to manage the men in his own way. His request granted, he sent the guard detail home and ordered food prepared for the hungry men. He had their names entered on the rolls of the 20th Maine and distributed them by groups to equalize the companies and particularly "to break up the 'esprit de corps' of banded mutineers." Then "I ... called them together and pointed out to them the situation; that they could not be entertained as civilian guests by me; that they were by authority of the United States on my rolls as soldiers, and I should treat them as soldiers should be treated; that they should lose no rights by obeying orders, and I would see what could be done for their claim." All but a half-dozen agreed to serve, and even a few of the recalcitrants were ultimately and at a timely moment to place their loyalty before their own grievances.

Meanwhile Lee prepared his invasion of the North. News from Vicksburg, where the whiskey-drinking, chain-cigar-smoking U. S. Grant had the elegant General Pemberton crowded into a tight corner, was discouraging, but Chancellorsville sent Southern morale rocketing upward. There appeared no end to what Lee and his troops could accomplish. An invasion of the North might be most desirable at this time. Hooker would be forced out of Virginia and the strain on the Confederate supply system relieved in Pennsylvania, a land teeming with food and horses. Furthermore, as Lee looked at the situation, there was more to be hoped for than mere military success. The peace party in the North might be invigorated, a point of view given encouragement by a great peace rally of 30,000 in New York City on June 11 under Horatio Seymour and Fernando Wood; certainly a Confederate victory would create an even greater demand for a negotiated peace. And there was always the possibility of European recognition of the Confederacy. Actually European recognition was never to be so close as in the summer and fall of 1862, but the South continued to hope that Britain and France would at last see the light. Lee therefore started his three large infantry corps of three divisions each northward. "Jeb" Stuart's cavalry division, which was given a surprising and punishing check by Federal cavalry under General Alfred Pleasonton at Brandy Station on June 9, was to act as a screen between Lee and Hooker, seizing the mountain passes and keeping the former supplied with intelligence of "Fighting Joe's" movements.

Hooker, who had to be persuaded by Lincoln that Lee's army and not Richmond was his proper objective, at last put his six small and one large infantry corps (the Sixth) on the road, with Pleasonton's cavalry fanning out to the west and north. Where he could catch Lee puzzled Hooker. Generally the Confederates were moving northward up the Shenandoah Valley just west of the mountain wall known as South Mountain. Hooker's troops pushed northward on the east slope of the Bull Run Mountains and the Catoctin Mountains. The Confederates clearly had the initiative, and there would be some hard marching before they could be challenged.

Chamberlain's regiment still belonged to the 3rd Brigade of the 1st Division, now under Brigadier General James Barnes. The brigade consisted of the 20th Maine, the 16th Michigan, the 44th New York, and the 83rd Pennsylvania. Commanding the brigade was Colonel Strong Vincent, an able, gallant officer to whom Chamberlain became strongly attached and for whose impoverished widow he did many acts of kindness in later years. Vincent, who had previously commanded the 83rd Pennsylvania, now moved the brigade upriver, Chamberlain first guarding United States Ford, then, for a week following June 6, Ellis Ford. On the 13th, the 20th Maine left for Morrisville, where Vincent's brigade took its position in the 1st Division's line of march. The next day, the entire Fifth Corps moved out, going as far as Catlett's Station, at which point the 1st Division joined the Corps. By rapid marching the Fifth Corps moved past Manassas Junction to Gum Spring and by way of Aldie to the Potomac River, which it crossed on a pontoon bridge at Edwards' Ferry. It bivouacked on Ballinger's Creek, near Frederick, Maryland, on June 27.

Chamberlain found the march an exasperating experience. The prospect of an action excited him, and for a while on June 15, during a halt at Manassas Junction, he thought there might be a Third Bull Run. On the other hand, the hard marching over dusty roads in heat that had become jungle-moist and stifling was wearing him down. For that matter, hundreds of soldiers were suffering from heat exhaustion, and, on the 17th, four soldiers in the 1st Division died of sunstroke. Chamberlain himself was ill on the night of the 20th and to his intense mortification lost an opportunity for a lively, little action on the 21st. "Jeb" Stuart had sought to control not only the passes in the mountains to the west but also in the Bull Run Mountains. This led him into conflict with Pleasonton's Federal cavalry which, on the 21st, was reinforced by the 1st Division of the Fifth Corps. Vincent's brigade succeeded in dislodging the enemy from a strong position on the Ashby Gap road, the 20th Maine losing one man killed and eight wounded. With the brigade back at Aldie on June 23, Chamberlain was sufficiently recovered to resume command of the regiment. Then, on the 26th, a day of drizzle, the Corps hit the road again, the 20th Maine ticking off twenty miles and crossing the Potomac that day and driving close to Frederick on the 27th.

At Frederick, where the Corps rested on the 28th, Hooker received the laconic order which removed him from command of the Army of the Potomac and gave that command to General Meade of the Fifth Corps. Once on the road, Hooker had not done badly, keeping his corps in liaison and maintaining his balance, ready to pivot if Lee should try to slip through the mountain walls. On the other hand, he was suffering from one of McClellan's faults, that of grossly overestimating the size of Lee's army despite the fact that reliable intelligence received on the 26th reported Lee across the Potomac with a force inferior in size to the Federal army. Hooker was also beginning to display the paralyzing hesitancy that had afflicted him at certain stages in the battle of Chancellorsville. Convinced that, despite his original instructions, he could spare no troops to cover Harper's Ferry and, at the same time, be ready to face Lee, he asked to be relieved of his command. Lincoln had had enough. Meade, a routinely competent brigade, division, and corps commander, a tenacious fighter possessed of a furious temper when roused —whether by the enemy or his own staff—and a man who minded his own business, was the choice of the President and Stanton for Hooker's successor.

Chamberlain never came to know Meade even after the war as well as he knew Grant, whom he liked and respected, or Sheridan, whom he respected but could not like unreservedly. Chamberlain was the principal speaker at the Meade Memorial Services on May 29, 1880 at the Academy of Music in Philadelphia, a ceremony attended by a distinguished audience that included General Winfield Scott Hancock, Sherman, and the then President, Rutherford B. Hayes. In Chamberlain's address, there were elements of a eulogy, and eulogies are invariably favorable. On the other hand, though he often became impatient with Meade, he appreciated the Pennsylvanian's sturdy character and utter devotion to duty. Meade was no Lee in ability and no McClellan in popularity, but he would do his very best at Gettysburg. That "best," however, would not have been enough if the bronzed, now lean-to-the-bone, sturdy-legged, often profane enlisted men had not begun to realize that, though leaders might come and go, it was they, the men in the ranks, who would have to do the fighting and win the battles.

Meade's orders were to cover Washington and Baltimore, and both cities as well as others in the North were in a state of alarm. As Lee's troops pushed up through the Cumberland Valley, seizing Chambersburg and Carlisle, hundreds of civilians fled eastward, taking what movables their wagons would hold, while others raced for the hills. Actually the Confederate occupation was about as orderly and considerate as any army has ever undertaken. Citizens were treated with courtesy, a Texan merely saying to a Pennsylvania woman who had defiantly pinned a United States flag across her front, "Take care, Madam, for Hood's boys are great at storming the breastworks when the Yankee colors is on them." Supplies were purchased with Confederate scrip, much to the wrath of Southern newspapers, which had hoped that their army would "bring the horrors of war to the homes of the Yankees—burn, destroy, devastate, and make them feel the ravages of war—in a word, treat them as enemies who have never spared us." The war, however, was still awaiting its Sherman phase. Meanwhile the Confederates continued to admire the yellow fields of grain, the thriving gardens, and the droves of fat cattle, and they lived higher than at any time during the war.

The only real worry Lee had was just where the Federal army lay at any particular moment. This was worry enough, however, and for his ignorance he could blame "Jeb" Stuart who had left off his screening operation, ridden south and east to get behind the bluecoats, captured at Rockville, nine miles from the District of Columbia, an enormously bountiful wagon train that thereafter slowed his movements, and got back to Lee by riding clear around Meade too late to make an effective contribution in the pay-off battle. But late on June 28 there turned up in Chambersburg the mysterious Harrison, favorite scout of the commander of Lee's First Corps, Lieutenant General James B. Longstreet. Not much is known about Harrison, but he hated Yankees and loved money, and was as adept at rifling the files of Secretary Stanton in Washington as in bringing in information of Federal army movements. He now told Lee of Meade's promotion and of the presence of three Federal corps in and about Frederick. Lee at once thought that Meade intended to push across South Mountain and cut his communications with Virginia, which had been in Hooker's mind but not in that of Meade, who was more concerned about Baltimore and Washington to the east than about Lee's communications in the west. Lee therefore decided to move east of South Mountain to protect his line of communications. General Richard S. Ewell of the Second Corps and General Ambrose Powell Hill of the Third Corps, strung out between Chambersburg and the Susquehanna River opposite Harrisburg, received orders rescinding an advance on Harrisburg. Lee at first thought of concentrating the army at Cashtown or Gettysburg as circumstances permitted, but intelligence received of the presence of Federal troops in Gettysburg decided him.

On June 26, at Hagerstown, Lee had talked with an old friend and veteran, Major General Isaac R. Trimble, a civil engineer. Speaking of the Federal troops, Lee said to Trimble, "When they hear where we are, they will make forced marches to interpose their forces between us and Baltimore and Philadelphia. They will come up, probably through Frederick, broken down with hunger and hard marching, strung out on a long line, and much demoralized when they come into Pennsylvania. I shall throw an overwhelming force on their advance, crush it, follow up the success, drive one corps back on another, and by successive repulses and surprises before they can concentrate create a panic and virtually destroy the army."

Lee's prediction was, in certain respects, amazingly accurate. Certainly the Federal corps were scattered and there was plenty of marching to do. On the evening of June 30 the First Corps under General John F. Reynolds was bivouacked five miles north of Emmitsburg, the Second Corps under Hancock at Uniontown, rash Dan Sickles' Third Corps between Emmitsburg and Tarrytown, where Meade had his headquarters, the Fifth Corps now under crusty George Sykes at Union Mills, "Uncle John" Sedgewick's big Sixth Corps at Manchester, the Eleventh under Oliver O. Howard of Maine north of Emmitsburg, and John S. Slocum with the Twelfth at Littlestown.

Full cavalry divisions were at Hanover and Manchester, while an under-strength division lay in Gettysburg itself under an alert, aggressive fighter, John Buford. Late that afternoon Buford's patrols had exchanged shots with a small column of Confederate infantry on the Cashtown road northwest of Gettysburg. Buford notified Reynolds, who informed Meade that Confederate infantry was swarming eastward through the gaps of South Mountain. The next day, July 1, was certain to be for both armies, but especially for Meade's scattered corps, a day of terrific marching. But would they be too broken with marching and hunger and demoralization to fight?

Meanwhile Chamberlain and his regiment had really been stirring up the dust of the Virginia and Maryland roads.

On June 26, the day the regiment crossed the Potomac, it marched twenty miles, and on the 27th it went the same distance again. On the 28th, the day that Meade took over command of the army, it gratefully rested. The 29th found it booting off eighteen miles, while by nightfall of the 30th it had driven twenty-three miles. The weather was hot and close, and the dust moved with the regiment in a long low-lying cloud that caked the men's faces and clothes and made them gasp for breath. By this time in their army experience most of the men knew enough about marching to keep up the pace. Furthermore Chamberlain had the knack of holding them together. He rested them frequently, and although he was often criticized for this procedure, it was presently noted that he always brought them in on time and in condition to fight. Nor did he waste their energy marching and countermarching to form camp. He would send an officer ahead to reconnoiter the ground, then, on the basis of the officer's report, he would decide the particular maneuver which would place the troops in the proper order for camp. His weary men never forgot such consideration.

On July 1, Chamberlain was ordered to move the 20th Maine to the van of the Fifth Corps. Everybody sensed that a clash was pending, though no one knew when or where, except that from somewhere off to the west came the muttering of distant thunder, yet too sharp and distinct and persistent to be thunder on this cloudless day. All day, however, as Chamberlain acknowledged, the regiment was "searching and pushing out on all roads for the hoped-for collision with Lee." Around noon the troops crossed into Pennsylvania with its great red barns and large stone houses, while cheers broke out from the long line of bluecoats, regimental bands began to play, and colors were unfurled in the motionless air. Near Hanover Chamberlain noticed corpses of men and horses where Brigadier General Judson Kilpatrick had hit "Jeb" Stuart sharply on the Confederate leader's great circuit which was to be completed at Gettysburg via Carlisle. Finally, about half-past four, the Corps halted, and the 20th Maine, having marched twenty-six miles, stacked arms for the nightly bivouac and scurried for water and fence-rails. But "the . . . fires had hardly blackened the coffee-dippers, and the hardtack hardly been hammered into working order by the bayonet-shanks, when everything was stopped short by whispers of disaster away on the left."

And near disaster it was as Chamberlain learned after a courier arrived from Meade to keep the Fifth Corps on the road. Buford's cavalrymen had valiantly held off Hill's Confederates on the Chambersburg road until Reynolds arrived with the Federal First Corps. When Reynolds was killed by a sniper, General Abner Doubleday, a division commander, took command until Howard appeared at noon with the Eleventh Corps. Howard put Doubleday with the First Corps, and gave the Eleventh to General Carl Schurz, whom he sent into the open fields north of the town when Ewell's corps was reported arriving along the Mummasburg, Carlisle, and Harrisburg roads. Schurz's lines were thin in the attempt to cover so much territory, and a wide gap existed between his left and Doubleday's right.

The relentless drive of the Southerners as Hill and Ewell threw in more brigades forced the Federals back. Finally the Eleventh Corps broke and streamed back through the town toward Howard's headquarters on Cemetery Hill. The retreat of the Eleventh exposed the right flank of the First, but the First was facing such superior numbers and was so badly mauled itself that the failure of the Eleventh only stepped up by a few minutes its own withdrawal. Doubleday now took the First back over the ridge where the Lutheran Seminary was located to Cemetery Ridge south of Gettysburg, his left flank covered by Buford's cavalry. Ewell, who was given a discretionary order by Lee to attack Cemetery Ridge, chose to interpret it negatively; Trimble was reported to have thrown away his sword in disgust rather than serve under him again. Meanwhile Hancock arrived with a written order from Meade to take command. Howard, his senior in rank, refused to relinquish the command, but let Hancock select the area from Culp's Hill to Round Top as the battle site. Though Hancock stabilized the lines, it is likely that only darkness and Ewell's decision not to attack prevented disaster. Colonel Freemantle of the British army, who was with the Confederates, said that on the night of July 1 their staff officers spoke of victory as certain and that the universal feeling in the Southern army was one of profound contempt for an enemy they had beaten so consistently.

Meanwhile "The General" was being blown shrilly by Fifth Corps bugles summoning the tired men back to the march. At six o'clock the Corps hit the road again, sixteen miles from Gettysburg. The rumors of disaster flitted owl-like in the gathering darkness. Chamberlain said that he could not quite believe them but that they deepened his mood.

It was a strange night, magnified and made mysterious not only by the shadows and the moonlight that shone through the cloud-breaks but also by the fatigue, the urgency, the sense that great events, as yet obscure and unfigured but portentous, impended in the pressing, relentless future known as "tomorrow." Somewhere up ahead, an officer thought he could inspire the men by telling them McClellan was in command again, and the news carried by mounted staff officers down the column touched off a brief wave of cheering for the beloved "Little Mac." More weirdly came the whisper that George Washington had been observed at sunset, riding over the battlefield of Gettysburg on a white horse. Ludicrous, perhaps, but fatigue plays odd tricks on the rational mind, and this was not the first, nor certainly the last, time that soldiers whose nerves and muscles have been stretched finely have seen occult symbols of great meaning to them, as if the powers of the other world were drawing near to assist them. "Let no one smile at me!" said Chamberlain when he repeated the story years afterward. "I half believed it myself!"

But all was not contrived or ghostly during that night march that was so long and vividly remembered. As the evening wore on, the clouds disappeared and the moon shone clear and bright. Theodore Gerrish of Chamberlain's regiment said, "The people rushed from their homes and stood by the wayside to welcome us, men, women, and children all gazing on the strange spectacle. Bands played, the soldiers and the people cheered, banners waved, and white handkerchiefs fluttered from doors and windows, as the blue, dusty column surged on." Chamberlain himself noted that young staff officers rode gallantly up to some of the girls who were waving their handkerchiefs and exchanged words of banter. Colonel Strong Vincent, Chamberlain's brigade commander, pulled out of the column to watch the brigade go by, removed his hat as the colors passed, observed the moonlight shining on the flags, the marching troops, the white dresses of the girls, and, turning to an aide, said that a man could do worse than die fighting under the colors here in Pennsylvania.

At about one o'clock the column halted by the roadside

for a rest of three hours; then assembled again at four o'clock without coffee or breakfast and marched the remaining miles to Gettysburg, halting a short distance from the woods skirting Culp and Wolf's Hill. After deploying with divisions abreast, the Fifth Corps listened to a written statement by Meade on the gravity of the situation. Then the 1st Division moved slowly across Rock Creek near the Baltimore and Gettysburg Turnpike and rested. In the distance could be heard an intermittent crackling of muskets and occasionally the muffled report of a cannon. But here in the orchard everything was peaceful. Some of the soldiers could not resist bathing in the creek, others went to sleep in the tall grass that smelled so pungently of penny royal.

Why Lee was so tardy in mounting his attack puzzled Chamberlain and the other Union officers as well as where, precisely, it would come. The delay has also puzzled historians ever since, though many tend to put the responsibility on Longstreet, Lee's First Corps commander. Longstreet, known aptly as "Bull" but more commonly as "Old Pete," was a powerful, robust man, utterly fearless. Between Lee and Longstreet a real affection existed—after as well as before the battle—though they had their tense moments. Between Longstreet and his troops a great affection also existed, and few commanders had the faculty of getting more out of his men. At the same time, Longstreet did not like to take unnecessary chances with his men's lives. In the late afternoon of July 1, as he listened to Lee expound his intention of hitting the enemy on the morrow along Cemetery Hill and the ridge extending southward if Ewell failed in his present attack, Longstreet strongly objected. He proposed instead that the army should move around Meade's left flank, thereby placing itself between Meade and Washington, and compel Meade to attack it in a position of the Confederates' own choosing. This was in line with Longstreet's thinking for weeks; he liked neither the idea of invasion, preferring a swift move to the west to save Vicksburg, nor Lee's desire for an offensive battle. He wanted, instead, another Fredericksburg. But Lee was adamant.

The next morning, when Lee hoped to attack, Longstreet's big corps was still moving up via the Chambersburg road. As it was, he had to leave George E. Pickett's division behind to watch the rear in Chambersburg, a task that should have been Stuart's had Stuart been available. The other two divisions, however, were large, five brigades each, and their commanders, Lafayette McLaws and John B. Hood, redoubtable fighters. Not until after eleven o'clock were these two divisions at full strength with the arrival of one of Hood's brigades under Evander McIver Law, a brilliant officer, principal of a military school in Alabama, and a future professor of history. Law's Alabamians had been on the road without a break since three in the morning, a great march of twenty-four miles in nine hours. Joshua Lawrence Chamberlain was to see that the Alabamians had little rest that day.

Lee proposed an attack in sequence from right to left. Longstreet was to move south, keeping well below Seminary Ridge to avoid detection from the Federal signal station on Little Round Top, then to swing onto the Emmitsburg road and roll up the Union flank. Once Longstreet committed himself, Hill was to smash at Cemetery Ridge while Ewell attacked Meade's right flank. Time was of the essence, but Lee seems not to have called a meeting of all his corps commanders simultaneously and given them specific instructions and a specific hour to open the attack. Instead, he conferred with them individually and relied on their discretion. This was complimentary to them, but it was already clear that Ewell was inadequate while Hill, a good division commander, was falling short of being a good corps commander. As for Longstreet, he was angry and hurt at Lee's rejection of his plan which he had put forward again in the morning, at Lee's giving direct orders to McLaws rather than through him, at Lee's reliance on his own staff officer's reconnaissance report which was insufficient and incorrect in details and on which Longstreet was to base the movements of his corps. Still, Longstreet finally got his big divisions in motion, though he disliked and disbelieved in his assignment.

Meanwhile Meade was making his own dispositions. The Twelfth Corps had arrived in the late afternoon of July 1, and it would have given Ewell a rough experience had he chosen to assault at any time after half-past four o'clock: perhaps he realized this. Meade stationed the Twelfth to the right of the First Corps on the very hook of the Union fish-hook formation. Until Sickles' Third Corps came up, Geary's division of the Twelfth was to occupy Little Round Top; afterward, Geary was to join the rest of the Twelfth on Culp's Hill. To the left of the First was Howard with the remnants of the Eleventh Corps. Then came Hancock's crack Second Corps, which by daylight of July 2 was on the field. Sykes' Fifth Corps was to be held in reserve until the Sixth Corps, making one of the great marches in American military history, should arrive.

Four remarkable developments occurred in the course of the morning and early afternoon of July 2. One was favorable to the Union: the arrival of the advance guard of the Sixth Corps at two o'clock, badly worn after its thirty-five-mile march from Manchester begun late the previous evening.

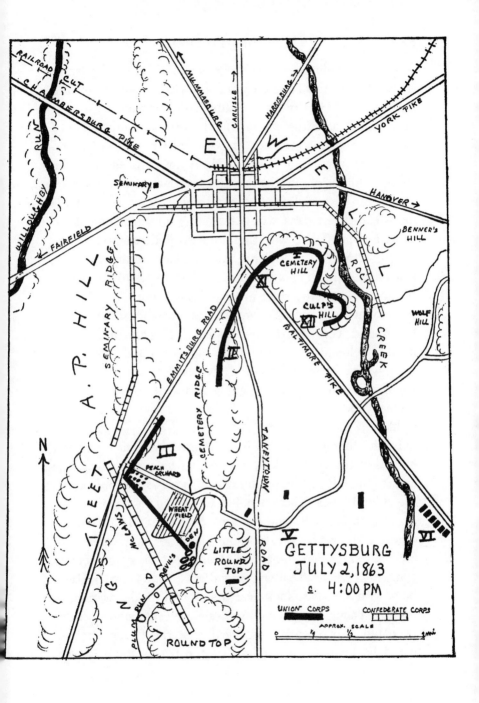

GETTYSBURG
JULY 2, 1863
c. 4:00 PM

A second development was Geary's unauthorized departure from Little Round Top for Culp's Hill without Sickles making any attempt to fortify Little Round Top. Southern possession of it would make the whole Union battle line impossible to hold, but for hours, except for a Signal Corps detail there, the Union army forgot it. The third development was the strange confusion in the cavalry command that induced Pleasonton to withdraw Buford's troopers who were guarding Meade's left flank without sending any detachments to replace them. There was, therefore, no Federal force to the left of Sickles' Third Corps, and Sickles became uneasy. Furthermore he did not like the fact that his part of Cemetery Ridge was scarcely a ridge at all and that there was too much space between Hancock's corps and his own for him to occupy the Round Tops. He began, instead, (the fourth development), to look with favor on the higher ground a half-mile west which extended from a rock-outcropping known as Devil's Den on his left along a series of low hills, little ravines, and patches of woods to a peach orchard on the right.

In the forenoon Meade had directed his son, a captain, to make sure that Sickles understood he was to hold the area to the left of the Second Corps as far as, and including, the Round Tops. Though polite to the young man, Sickles decided to talk with the captain's father. At Meade's headquarters, however, Sickles found Meade immovable. But Sickles was so persistent that Meade sent his magnificently competent chief of artillery, Brigadier General Henry J. Hunt, back with Sickles to look over the ground Sickles wanted to occupy. Though Hunt could see strength in the new position, he could also see a glaring weakness: the Peach Orchard could be hit from two sides and the troops there cut off.

When Sickles asked for permission to move to the position, Hunt said he had no power to authorize such a move but that he would report the situation to Meade. Back at head-quarters he had no sooner started to make his report than action elsewhere distracted Meade's attention.

Presently, feeling the absence of cavalry, Sickles threw a small body of U. S. Sharpshooters out on a skirmish line supported by an infantry regiment. When these uncovered a strong mass of Confederates in the woods west of the Emmitsburg Road, Dan Sickles made his famous decision. A New York lawyer and Tammany politician, Sickles had served as an Assemblyman at Albany, as first secretary of the legation in London when James Buchanan was the ambassador, and as a member of Congress. When he dis-covered that his wife had become the mistress of handsome Philip Barton Key, son of the author of "The Star Spangled Banner," Sickles shot him dead in Lafayette Square within sight of the White House, which Sickles, himself, had dearly hoped, one day, to occupy. In the resulting trial Sickles was acquitted on the grounds of temporary insanity, a plea urged by his lawyers, of whom one was Edwin M. Stanton, now Secretary of War. Sickles subsequently outraged the up-holders of the chivalric code by continuing to live with his wife. His private and political reputation made him unpop-ular with officers of the Regular Army; Meade, a model of rectitude, could not stand him. On the other hand, Sickles had not done badly in the war, though, unlike the cautious Meade, he had shown a disposition to make quick decisions and to take chances.

He did so now. One cannot say the decision itself was quick, but the chance he took was astounding. Between one and three o'clock he moved his entire Third Corps in battle order with his caissons and batteries of artillery rolling along, his flags streaming, and his drums beating, down the slope, across the level ground and up into his new position. Second Corps men watched in admiration and amazement. But Sickles was at last where he wanted to be, Brigadier General Andrew Humphreys' right division faced to the northwest, Brigadier General David Birney's left division extending from the Peach Orchard on the right to Devil's Den on the left.

Meade now called his corps commanders to a conference. When Sickles arrived, however, the sharp rattle of musketry and growing volume of artillery fire caused Meade to tell him not to get off his horse. He also ordered Sykes to get his Fifth Corps over to the left as quickly as possible. Then Meade followed Sickles back to his position. He was horrified to see Humphreys' position exposed to attack from three sides and Birney's left flank anchored only at Devil's Den instead of extending to the Round Tops, which were left completely undefended. When Sickles asked if he should withdraw, Meade agreed that he should do so immediately.

As Meade reined his horse's head about, Longstreet opened on the Peach Orchard and Birney's line with forty-six guns. It was too late now for Sickles to pull back, Meade shouted that he would send support from both the Second and Fifth Corps and tell Hunt to make available all the artillery Sickles asked for. He then rode back to headquarters, directing Brigadier General Gouverneur K. Warren, his chief engineer, to hurry to Little Round Top and take what measures were necessary to secure its defense.

Longstreet had been long getting into position, but this was not all his fault. Lee had specified no hour for a morning attack and had agreed to wait until Law's brigade was up. To move the two big divisions into attack positions without being observed from the Federal Signal Corps station on Little Round Top necessitated a march far in the rear of the Confederate lines. The map followed was faulty, the guide became confused, and it looked at one point as if they had been discovered. His temper growing short, Longstreet decided on a different route and countermarched his divisions, Hood's now becoming the leading division. One Confederate officer thought that two to three hours were consumed in the countermarch, while a recent estimate in a masterly study of the battle has the average soldier marching eight miles, much of it through woods, to the point of attack. Though Longstreet should have made a personal reconnaissance of the area in the morning, the duty of exploring the battle route was the cavalry's and Stuart was miles away.

Furthermore, to find Sickles in a position where they had anticipated no one was shocking to Longstreet's division commanders, McLaws and Hood. When scouts sent out by General Law reported that it would be an easy move to skirt the rear of Round Top, seize the entire Federal wagon train, and fall on Meade's left flank and undefended rear, Law eagerly went to Hood with the proposal that he do precisely that. Hood agreed with Law and hastened to Longstreet, entreating him to adopt Law's suggestion. Although this was what Longstreet himself had desired to do, he knew Lee wanted an attack up the Emmitsburg Road and that the hour was getting late for the corps attack in echelon that Lee had planned. Three times Hood made his request, and three times Longstreet insisted that Lee's orders had to be obeyed. The guns then opened up between half-past three and four o'clock, and, not long afterward, Hood ordered Law's brigade forward.

The regiment which ultimately took position on the right of Law's brigade was the tired and thirsty 15th Alabama under Colonel William C. Oates, and this regiment was to exert an all-important role in the destiny of Joshua Lawrence Chamberlain. Oates ordered two men from each of his eleven companies to fill the canteens of the regiment at a well near by. While the detail was at work, the attack order arrived and Oates was not permitted to wait for his water detail, which, on trying to rejoin the regiment, was captured. Though Oates was to swing between the Round Tops, a number of U. S. Sharpshooters from Sickles' command forced him to change his attack. Accompanied by a large part of the 47th Alabama, he went straight up the south and west sides of Round Top, dislodging the Sharpshooters but grieving to see his men suffering from exhaustion, heat, and, particularly, lack of water. He therefore gave them a ten-minute rest, while he looked down, charmed with the view, upon the undefended Little Round Top and the Union battle line beyond.

Within five minutes a staff officer, Captain L. R. Terrell, arrived. He told Oates that Hood had been wounded, Law had taken over the division, and Oates was to capture Little Round Top. Oates in turn told Terrell that a few cannon mounted on Round Top could command the entire battlefield. Terrell agreed that Round Top should be held but pointed out that Law's order had precedence. Oates then took his men down the slope of the hill, sending one company to the rear of Little Round Top to capture or destroy the Federal wagon trains parked perhaps eight hundred feet beyond. He now aligned the 15th and 47th Alabama for their assault on Little Round Top. If he had not been forced to rest his men for ten minutes on Round Top because of their lack of water, the course of the battle might have been vastly different; certainly Oates always thought so. Furthermore, Oates' ten-minute "break" made possible Chamberlain's day of glory.

Meanwhile, when Sykes got back to the Fifth Corps after the corps commanders' conference, he assembled the Corps at Pipe Creek, sending General Weed's brigade at once to join Sickles, then marching the Corps to the left. It was while part of the Fifth was on the road and part waiting to move out that General Warren observed a terrifying sight. What he had seen of Sickles' position and the skirmishing about it convinced him the Confederates were more heavily massed on the left than anyone suspected. Ordering a battery near the base of Little Round Top to pitch a shell across the Emmitsburg Road, he noticed "a glistening of gun-barrels and bayonets" among the trees as the Confederates looked in the direction of the shell. At once he sent for help to Sykes, who ordered Barnes, his 1st Division commander, to hurry a brigade to Warren. For some reason, Barnes could not be found, but Colonel Strong Vincent, who read the message, said he would take his brigade there without delay.

He had hardly finished speaking when Hood's division broke the end of Birney's line and overran Devil's Den. Evander Law's brigade, filling the air with the high-pitched rebel yell, came pounding along Plum Run toward Little Round Top. These were tough fighters, ranged from left to right: Law's 44th and 48th Alabama, the 4th and 5th Texas from General Jerome Robertson's brigade, and Law's 4th, 47th, and 15th Alabama. Although the 44th continued to clear Devil's Den and the 47th and 15th were still working their way down the slopes of Round Top, the imminence of the other regiments caused Warren to scurry frantically elsewhere for help, especially to Weed's brigade moving up to support Sickles' collapsing lines. Unless Union troops arrived from somewhere, Little Round Top would be captured, Meade's army flanked, and the battle catastrophically lost. Fortunately Strong Vincent was on the way if only he could arrive in time, and in his brigade was the remarkable Bowdoin College professor whose Maine regiment was for a few minutes at least, thanks in large part to his leadership, to determine the result of this greatest battle of the Civil War.

DAY OF GLORY
JULY 2, 1863

IT was the good fortune of the North that in Colonel Strong Vincent, just turned twenty-six, Meade had one of the finest officers in the Army of the Potomac. Even as Adelbert Ames had tried to turn the 20th Maine into a first-rate regiment, so Vincent had accomplished the same with the 83rd Pennsylvania, for which he had won McClellan's commendation. Unlike Ames, who was a West Pointer, Vincent was a graduate of Harvard and, in President Charles Eliot's opinion, "one of the manliest and most attractive persons that I ever saw." Chamberlain thought the world of him, and, like Chamberlain, Vincent had become a kind of model of the citizen-soldier. Furthermore he loved Pennsylvania with a passion, the great crisis of the war and of his life was now mounting on her soil, and he recognized it in his decisive response to General Sykes' order.

Vincent hurried his regiments to Little Round Top, crossed Plum Run on a crude wooden bridge, and turned onto a farm road that led to the base of the hill. "Here, as we could," said Chamberlain, "we took the double-quick." He did not like what he saw of the hill, an eminence strewn with great boulders, intersected with jagged ledges, bald on the top and with only a few gnarled trees straggling along the sides.

As Chamberlain's regiment, the last in line ascended the

lower gradient, Longstreet's batteries poured it on them. The air was filled with flying iron, branches of trees and splinters of rock. Chamberlain was riding with his brother Tom, who was, at the time, the regimental adjutant, and with his brother John, who was serving with the Sanitary Commission. Suddenly a solid shot swept close to the heads of the three brothers. "Boys," Chamberlain said, "I don't like this. Another shot might make it hard for mother. Tom, go to the rear of the regiment, and see that it is well closed up! John, pass up ahead and look out for a place for our wounded."

Vincent posted his regiments below the cap of Little Round Top in a right-to-left alignment facing west and south: the 16th Michigan, 44th New York, 83rd Pennsylvania, and 20th Maine. As Chamberlain came up the southern face, Vincent said to him, "I place you here! This is the left of the Union line. You understand. You are to hold this ground at all costs."

Chamberlain moved his men into position by what he acknowledged was a slow and uncommon maneuver on the order, "On the right by file into line." But it had the advantage of enabling the regiment as a whole to be facing the enemy as it came to a front and the individual soldier to start firing as soon as he reached his post.

Chamberlain was troubled by the realization that though he was "anchor man" on the Union army's left flank, his own regimental left flank was exposed. Hence he withdrew Captain Walter G. Morrill with B Company and ordered him up the valley to the left between the regiment and the eastern base of Round Top. He was to remain within supporting distance and to act as the situation might warrant. This left Chamberlain with 308 men in the line.

As Chamberlain studied Round Top, wondering what he would do if the enemy should drag a battery up its side,

Colonel James C. Rice of the 44th New York suggested that they take a look from his regiment's position at what was happening below. "It was a forewarning indeed," Chamberlain said. "The enemy had already turned the Third Corps left, the Devil's Den was a smoking crater, the Plum Run gorge was a whirling maelstrom; one force was charging our advanced batteries near the wheatfield; the flanking force was pressing past the base of the Round Tops; all rolling toward us in tumultuous waves." The great contest for possession of Little Round Top was about to begin; as the leading war correspondent of the New York *Times* wrote, "one of those mortal struggles rare in war, when the hostile forces, clenching in close contest, illustrate whatever there is of savage and terrible in battle."

Now the crash of artillery ceased as the Confederate gunners held off for fear of hitting their own men, but the musketry opened up as Vincent's right engaged the men in grey swarming up the slopes. Soon the action extended to the left, and the 20th Maine clashed hotly with the 4th Alabama, which was presently joined by seven companies of the 47th Alabama. Chamberlain moved quickly here and there as his attention was called by developments in the action.

Suddenly Lieutenant James Nichols of K Company, "a bright officer near our center, ran up to tell me something queer was going on in his front, behind those engaging us." Chamberlain sprang up on a rock in Nichols' company line. He was startled to see "thick groups in grey" moving between the Round Tops toward his left flank. This force was Oates and his 15th Alabama, five to six hundred men worn with marching and thirst but now eager to sweep away the thin line of blue that was the 20th Maine. Chamberlain saw clearly that if the enemy gained the regiment's rear, the entire brigade would be caught "as by a mighty shears blade, and be cut and crushed." Obviously Vincent's orders had to be interpreted liberally: the front had to be maintained but Chamberlain could not let the rear go uncovered.

Chamberlain became a great infantry officer, and among his valuable qualities were a kind of intuitive grasp of where an attack would come (a grasp based in good part on a knowledge of terrain, weapons and men) and a gift for improvisation in meeting emergencies. He summoned the officers commanding his companies and told them of his plan. The regiment was to maintain a hot fire in the front "without special regard to its need or immediate effect." While the right kept contact with the 83rd Pennsylvania, the men were to side-step to the left, gradually coming into one rank. At the extreme left of the front line stood a great boulder. Chamberlain placed the colors and the color guard there, then bent his line back to the left at a right angle, thereby covering twice the original front. The weakness was that the men were widely spaced and there were no supports. But at least neither the regiment nor the brigade could be surprised by a flank attack. He now awaited Oates' attack in the following formation by companies:

F D K I E
A
H
C
G

But while he completed his arrangements, the crescendo of musketry and wild shouting on the west slope of Little Round Top made him wonder whether Vincent could with-

stand the heavy Confederate assault there. Indeed the onrush
of the Texas regiments cracked the stout 16th Michigan
defense, and if Warren had not caught the attention of
Colonel Patrick O'Rorke, commanding the 140th New York,
the last regiment in Weed's brigade on its way to bolster
Sickles, Little Round Top might have been lost. On Warren's
promise to take the responsibility, the gallant O'Rorke, first
in the class of 1861 at West Point, took his regiment up the
hill at the double. There was no time to load muskets, no
time to fix bayonets. O'Rorke and the New Yorkers swept
down the hill in a headlong rush and halted the Texans by
the sheer weight of their bodies. Though O'Rorke and many
of his men were killed, they had saved the hill for the
moment.

In the meantime, Weed had brought the rest of his brigade
to Little Round Top and placed his men to the right of
Vincent. Then turning to give an order to Lieutenant Charles
E. Hazlett, whose men had manhandled two cannon into
place on the summit of the hill, Weed dropped dead from
a sniper's bullet fired from Devil's Den, which had finally
been secured by Robertson's Texans and Benning's Georgians,
both of Hood's Division. As Hazlett bent over Weed, a sniper
got him, too, and Warren was also wounded. It seemed that
no one could live on the summit of Little Round Top. But
with U. S. Sharpshooters now beginning to make life difficult
for the Confederate marksmen in Devil's Den, the cannoneers
of Battery D, U. S. Artillery, lineal descendant of Alexander
Hamilton's artillery company, stuck to their posts and hurled
shells into the Confederate reinforcements, while the battle
churned up and down the rocky hillside—a tumultuous blue-
grey line of shouting men, blazing muskets, vivid agony, and
death.

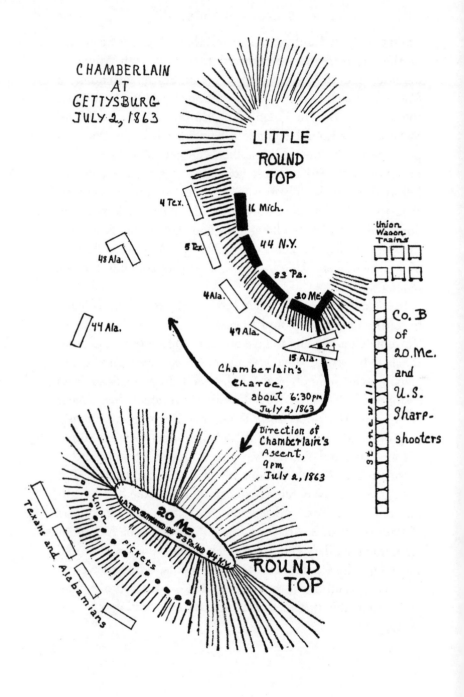

CHAMBERLAIN AT GETTYSBURG JULY 2, 1863

LITTLE ROUND TOP

4 Tex.

16 Mich.

5 Tex.

44 N.Y.

48 Ala.

83 Pa.

4 Ala.

20 Me.

44 Ala.

47 Ala.

15 Ala.

Union Wagon Trains

Co. B of 20. Me. and U.S. Sharp-shooters

Stonewall

Chamberlain's Charge, about 6:30 pm July 2, 1863

Direction of Chamberlain's Ascent, 9 pm July 2, 1863

20 Me. LATER REINFORCED BY 83 Pa. AND 44 N.Y.

Union pickets

ROUND TOP

Texans and Alabamians

In the end the control of Little Round Top was to be decided not by the bitterly engaged troops on the west slope but by Chamberlain and his little Maine regiment over on the other side of the hill. Oates' Alabamians assaulted not only Chamberlain's front but came tearing up on what they presumed was his exposed flank with the rush and energy of men who had just rested instead of troops who had been on their feet since three o'clock in the morning. Then, where there had been nothing except rocks and trees, a blast of fire leaped out at them. Staggered, they stormed up again on what was now the right and left fronts. "Again and again," said Captain Howard Prince of the 20th Maine, "was this mad rush repeated, each time to be beaten off by the ever-thinning line that desperately clung to its ledge of rocks." "The two lines met and broke and mingled in the shock," Chamberlain said. "The crash of musketry gave way to cuts and thrusts, grapplings and wrestlings. The edge of conflict swayed to and fro, with whirlpools and eddies. At times I saw around me more of the enemy than of my own men; gaps opening, swallowing, closing again with sharp, convulsive energy; squads of stalwart men who had cut their way through us, disappearing as if translated. All around, strange, mingled roar,—shouts of defiance, rally, and desperation."

There seemed to be no end to the furious battle. Men frantically tore the cartridges from their boxes, bit the caps, rammed the cartridges home with steel rammers that clashed in the heated gun barrels, then fired, their hands and faces turning black with burning powder. For a while, said Theodore Gerrish, "Our line is pressed back so far that our dead are within the lines of the enemy." Oates thought his Alabamians had penetrated the Maine defense five times, but somehow the Northerners found strength enough to hurl his men back: ". . . five times they rallied and charged us," he admitted. "If I had had one more regiment," Oates said, "we would have completely turned the flank and have won Little Round Top, which would have forced Meade's whole left wing to retire." Throughout his life he never ceased to deplore that he had not been supported. But to Chamberlain and his hard-pressed men it looked several times as if Oates with the 15th and 47th had enough and more. Chamberlain had almost everyone in the line—his sick, cooks, bandsmen, pioneers, provost guard, even two mutineers from the old 2nd Maine who had been prisoners; only the hospital force remained aloof, and they had grim work of their own to do.

Once during the melée he experienced a dreadful moment: "I saw through a sudden rift in the thick smoke our colors standing alone. I first thought some optical illusion imposed upon me. But as forms emerged through the drifting smoke, the truth came to view. The cross-fire had cut keenly; the center had been almost shot away; only two of the color-guard had been left, and they fighting to fill the whole space; and in the center, wreathed in battle smoke, stood the Color-Sergeant, Andrew Tozier. His color-staff planted in the ground at his side, the upper part clasped in his elbow, so holding the flag upright, with musket and cartridges seized from the fallen comrade at his side he was defending his sacred trust in the manner of the songs of chivalry. It was a stirring picture—its import still more stirring. That color must be saved, and that center too."

Chamberlain sent his adjutant, brother Tom, and an orderly, Sergeant Ruel Thomas, to fill that gap by pulling men over from neighboring companies or contracting the salient. The fighting was so heavy he began to wonder if they would get back alive, but they came out with scarcely anything more than a scratch.

A lull now occurred as the Confederates drew back to regroup, and Chamberlain took advantage of the moments to gather his dead and wounded. As he walked over the field, he came across a young man, George Washington Buck, who had been a sergeant at Fredericksburg but whose commanding officer had taken away his stripes back at Stoneman's Switch for his refusing, when sick, to perform a menial personal service for a bullying quartermaster, who was eventually to spend several years in the Maine State prison for attempting to rob a bank. Buck had torn his shirt away from his chest which was covered with blood from a mortal wound. "Tell my mother I did not die a coward!" he whispered. Chamberlain quickly told him he was promoting him at once to a sergeant, and had him borne from the field. The sights Chamberlain saw as he continued his inspection were dreadful, dead men contorted into grotesque postures, wounded men writhing, blood trickling down the rocks and gathering in little pools. For that matter, he had barely missed death himself. A soldier of the 15th Alabama saw him standing behind the center of his line and recognized, by Chamberlain's uniform and actions, that here was a great prize to be put out of the way. As the soldier wrote him, years afterward, "I rested my gun on the rock and took steady aim. I started to pull the trigger, but some queer notion stopped me. Then I got ashamed of my weakness and went through the same motions again. I had you, perfectly certain. But that same queer something shut right down on me. I couldn't pull the trigger, and gave it up,—that is, your life. I am glad of it now, and hope you are." Yet Chamberlain had not escaped unscathed: blood dripped from his right instep where a rock splinter or piece of shell had penetrated, and he had a contusion on his left leg where his sword scabbard was smashed against it by a Minié ball.

But if Chamberlain's command had lost heavily, so had Oates'. "My dead and wounded were then nearly as great in number as those still on duty," Oates said. "They literally covered the ground. The blood stood in puddles in some places on the rocks." Several of his company officers were down. He saw his brother John die. Losses, however, did not deter those tough Alabamians, whom Chamberlain came greatly to admire. The 15th and 47th reformed, and this time it was now or never.

Chamberlain ordered his men to make every shot count, for his command was now paper-thin. Every man was in the line who could carry a gun, even the walking wounded, including "one fine young fellow, who had been cut down early in the fight with a ghastly wound across his forehead" but who returned with a bloody bandage around his head. As Chamberlain studied the battle situation, "The formidable Fifteenth Alabama, repulsed and as we hoped dispersed, now in solid and orderly array—still more than twice our numbers—came rolling through the fringe of chaparral on our left. No dash, no yells; no demonstrations for effect; but settled purpose and determination! We opened on them as best we could. The fire was returned, cutting us to the quick. The Forty-Seventh Alabama had rallied on our right. We were enveloped in fire, and sure to be overwhelmed in fact when the great surge struck us ... Already I could see the bold flankers on their right darting out and creeping catlike under the smoke to gain our left, thrown back as it was. It was for us, then, once for all."

It did not seem possible to Chamberlain that he could

withstand another shock like this one rolling up the hill. One half of his left wing was down—in fact one-third of the regiment was just behind the line dead or so badly wounded as to be out of action. Furthermore, Chamberlain's anxiety was increased by the great roar of musketry on the other side of the hill. Bullets from the Confederate assault there fell into Chamberlain's left rear so that he thought that Little Round Top was now about surrounded and only a desperate chance left to avoid defeat or death. He urgently requested of Captain O. S. Woodward, commander of the 83rd Pennsylvania, at least one company as a reinforcement. The 83rd could spare not a man, but Woodward agreed to extend his regiment farther to the left.

Then Chamberlain heard a frightening demand from his own men. "Ammunition!" they shouted. With sixty rounds to a man they had expended more than twenty thousand bullets. They reached frantically for the cartridge boxes of wounded comrades but found little left. Anxiously they turned to Chamberlain.

What to do now? As Chamberlain phrased it, "My thought was running deep." Despite Vincent's last order, to hold his ground was to invite disaster: in his present condition—one-third of his men out of action and the remainder out of ammunition—the enemy would have hit with a force "which we could not probably have withstood or survived." As he looked at his men grabbing the hot barrels of their muskets and preparing to use the butts as clubs, he saw the futility of it all. Desperate though the chance, he decided to counter-attack. Calling Captain Ellis Spear to him, he told him that he wanted Spear to take the bent-back left wing and sweep down the hill to the right. Then as he limped over to instruct Captain A. W. Clark of Company E to hold that extreme right flank company tightly against the 83rd Pennsylvania and thus prevent the enemy from breaking through, Lieutenant Holman S. Melcher of Company F, the color company, asked if he might go forward and bring in some of the wounded.

"Yes, sir, in a moment! Take your place with your company," Chamberlain replied. "I am about to order a 'right wheel forward' of the whole regiment."

He moved to the colors, all eyes upon him.

"Bayonet!"

The men rose with a shout, and the steel shanks of the bayonets clashed on the musket barrels. Sergeant Tozier raised the colors; the line quivered like sprinters on the mark. Then with the enemy only thirty yards away, young Melcher leaped out in front, his sword glittering in the slanting sunlight. "Come on! Come on! Come on, boys!" he shouted. Tozier dashed toward him. And with a wild yell the regiment flung itself down the hill, Ellis Spear's left wing whirling the enemy out of the rocks and soon fighting its way abreast of the right.

The Confederates recoiled, so bewildered they did not know whether to fight or surrender. At the onset, one Confederate officer fired a Navy Colt's pistol at Chamberlain's face, then handed over his sword in submission as Chamberlain's own sword pinked his throat. Chamberlain gave the surrendered sword to the non-com at his side but kept the pistol. Many in the first Confederate line tossed their weapons on the ground and held their hands up. Others were taken in fierce combat.

The 20th Maine swept forward like a reaper. A second line, composed of men from both the 15th and 47th Alabama, tried to make a stand near a stone wall. For a moment it looked as if they might succeed. Then a line of blue infantrymen rose from behind the wall and more than sixty rifles cracked in volley. This was Walter Morrill's B Company that Chamberlain had detached to guard his flank and a number of U. S. Sharpshooters whom Oates had driven off Round Top.

Attacked in front and rear, Oates gave the order to retreat, but he scarcely anticipated the panic that swept over his men: ". . . we ran like a herd of wild cattle," he admitted.

And after the fleeing Confederates charged the 20th Maine, bayonets flashing in the westering sun; Chamberlain was determined to make the most of his psychological surprise. Lieutenant Colonel Bulger of the 47th Alabama surrendered and Colonel Powell of the 4th Alabama was taken, badly wounded. Knots of the 4th and 5th Texas put up resistance, but these, too, finally surrendered or fled as the 20th Maine, "swinging," said Chamberlain, "like a great gate on its hinges, . . . swept the front clean of assailants."

It was with great difficulty that he halted his men when he reached the front of the 44th New York. Many of them declared they were "on the road to Richmond" and did not want to stop. Chamberlain, however, felt that he had gone far enough. He had only about two hundred men now, while the Texan regiments were rallying over on his right as were the Alabamians on his left who had fled up the slopes of Round Top. It was a tribute to the discipline of his men and the respect in which they held him that he finally got them into good order and withdrew to his original position.

Chamberlain and the 20th Maine had clearly saved the hill at what Colonel Rice of the 44th New York, succeeding the mortally wounded Vincent as brigade commander, called "the most critical time of the action." Entering the battle with 358 riflemen, the 20th Maine had 90 men wounded and 40 who were killed outright or who died of wounds. At the same time the regiment had inflicted even heavier casualties upon the enemy in dead and wounded and had captured nearly four hundred prisoners. It was a magnificent feat of arms, rarely if ever surpassed in the importance of its accomplishment by any regiment in American military history. And much of the success was directly attributable to Chamberlain's brilliant, imaginative leadership. Colonel Oates of the 15th Alabama said later, "There never were harder fighters than the Twentieth Maine men and their gallant Colonel. His skill and persistency and the great bravery of his men saved Little Round Top and the Army of the Potomac from defeat. Great events sometimes turn on comparatively small affairs." One of the "small affairs" in Oates' opinion was the loss of his own men's water bottles which obliged him to rest his thirsty troops on the summit of Round Top for ten fateful minutes, the margin of time by which Vincent had occupied Little Round Top before the Confederate assault.

Hard as they had fought, Chamberlain and his men had one more astonishing feat to perform before the day ended. A Texas orator eulogized after the war that the Texans with Hood had been victorious on every field "until God stopped them at Little Round Top." Possibly surmising that God might continue to aid them if they tried hard themselves, Chamberlain and Colonel Rice conferred in the early evening about the possibility of securing Round Top. The battlefield to the west and northwest was fairly quiet where Sickles, after horrible fighting in the Peach Orchard and the Wheatfield, let alone Devil's Den, had been forced to retire to his original position of the morning. To the north and northeast, action still blazed furiously as the Confederates stormed vainly against Culp's Hill. What both Rice and Chamberlain feared was that the Confederates might now do what Oates had originally wanted to do: emplace artillery on the summit of Round Top and enfilade the entire Federal defense. Colonel Joseph Fisher had come up in support of Rice with a brigade of Pennsylvania Reserves from General Crawford's 3rd Division of the Fifth Corps. At dusk Rice asked Fisher to seize Round Top. For some reason, Fisher declined, so Rice directed Chamberlain to go.

Although fresh ammunition had still not arrived, Chamberlain took out his two hundred men again in extended order and in one rank, with bayonets fixed. It was now nine o'clock, and practically dark under the trees with their summer foliage. Chamberlain felt that to go up the mountain with only the bayonet was hazardous but that, without the means to fire, his troops would expose neither their movement nor their few numbers. Yet as they climbed over the steep and jagged surface of Round Top in an order that became even more extended because of the nature of the terrain, the enemy could not help hearing them. Chamberlain in turn could hear the enemy falling back. When near the crest, the Confederates opened with a scattering fire that mortally wounded one of Chamberlain's officers. The 20th Maine then rushed the crest, capturing two officers and a half-dozen enlisted men in the ascent.

Chamberlain now drew his little command together in a solid front, and, after placing them in a strong position among the rocks, sent back to Rice for ammunition and reinforcements, He was especially concerned about his right flank which was so close to the Confederates that he could hear their movements and their conversation. These were

troops of the 15th and 47th Alabama whom Oates was trying
to form into a line of resistance.

In a half-hour two of Fisher's regiments, which had found
a wood road up the mountain, clumped and crashed through
the underbrush near Chamberlain's right. Thinking they
might be the enemy, Chamberlain readied his men for a
desperate fight. But Oates had heard them, too, and the
brisk fire his troops opened on the confused Reserves sent
them scurrying back down the mountain side, or, as Chamberlain kindly expressed it in his report, the action "disheartened the supports themselves, so that I saw no more
of them that night."

Realizing that in his isolated position his troops were
vulnerable in the event that the enemy should attempt to
envelop his right, Chamberlain quickly detailed a picket line
on the front and left and withdrew the rest of his troops
to the lower ground near the base of the mountain. He then
hurried a messenger to Rice with a request that the 83rd
Pennsylvania come up in support. Rice sent him not only the
83rd and supplies of ammunition but, shortly afterward, the
44th New York as well. Chamberlain then scrambled back
up the mountain, sent out a strong picket line, and ordered
the other troops to rest on their arms.

But he had little sleep that hot, sticky night. He had the
picket line relieved every two hours and reports delivered
to himself every half-hour. Despite their exertions of the
previous day, the pickets grew adventurous. Slipping down
the mountain, they discovered that the enemy had withdrawn to a line near the foot of Round Top. When they
were close enough to see the Southern camp fires and hear
voices, they withdrew. As it happened, they had appeared
near the 4th and 5th Texas, and the Texans, hearing them,

sent out a guard detail to see if they were friends or foes. Halted and challenged by a Maine picket to identify themselves, the Texans answered, "Friends!" When they were then told to come right along, and did so, the Texans found themselves facing a line of leveled muskets. This little strategy continued until the 20th Maine had bagged twenty-five prisoners from the 4th Texas. More might have been taken if someone down at the left had not given the order to fire; and the silence was shattered by a flurry of musketry. Daylight brought sharp skirmishing at the foot of Round Top, and Chamberlain lost another officer.

By nine in the morning, Fisher's men finally having arrived, Chamberlain received orders to withdraw and go into reserve with the rest of Rice's brigade in support of the left center of Meade's main line of resistance on Cemetery Ridge. This position placed them to the left of Lee's great effort of the afternoon, when General George Pickett with the cream of the Virginians and North Carolinians made his gallant, futile effort to crack the center of the Union line. Though the 20th Maine was not actively engaged, it was under heavy artillery fire during Lee's attempt to knock the Union batteries out of action before Pickett swept forward in the most picturesque and fateful movement of the war.

All that day, Chamberlain was the recipient of congratulations. When he was relieved from his assignment on Round Top and rode off at the head of his battle-scarred and blood-stained little regiment, the brigade commander, Colonel Rice, rode over and grasped him by the hand. "Colonel Chamberlain," he said warmly, "your gallantry was magnificent, and your coolness and skill saved us." Rice, though an intense, emotional officer, was yet, in Chamberlain's opinion, "as brave and true a man as ever went 'booted and spurred' from the field"; he was also generous. In his official report of the brigade's action, while mentioning the resourceful defense arrangements on Little Round Top which Chamberlain "wisely determined," Rice said that his order to Chamberlain to advance and take Round Top "was promptly and gallantly executed by this brave and accomplished officer." After commending Chamberlain, his brother Tom, and a number of officers from the other regiments in the brigade "for their gallant conduct in battle," Rice added, "Especially would I call the attention of the general commanding [General Barnes, 1st Division] to the distinguished services rendered by Colonel Chamberlain throughout the entire struggle."

Chamberlain's seizure of Round Top was especially gratifying to the Fifth Corps Commander, Sykes, who was responsible for that sector. He considered the achievement "one of the most important of the day." Such praise was not unwelcome to Chamberlain, but, as he whimsically wrote Fanny, he was trying to "bear it meekly."

Adelbert Ames, now a brigadier general who commanded a division in Howard's hard-luck Eleventh Corps and who had covered himself with glory, was delighted when he heard of what his old regiment had accomplished. He scribbled a note to Chamberlain: "I am very proud of the 20th Regt. and its Colonel. I did want to be with you and see your splendid conduct in the field. My heart yearns for you; and more and more, now that these trying scenes convince me of your superiority. The pleasure I felt at the intelligence of your conduct yesterday is some recompense for all that I have suffered. God bless you and the dear old Regiment." Later he paid the regiment a visit and complimented his old command. A Maine corporal dryly considered this worth recording in his diary since it had been Ames who had originally been so disgusted with the 20th Maine that he had urged the men to desert and go home.

The battle of Gettysburg, filled with more "ifs" than any single great conflict in American history, has been refought in articles and books almost literally from the time the guns ceased firing. There are innumerable heroes and villains, depending on one's prejudices. Dan Sickles, who lost a leg in the battle, has been praised for his courage and criticized for his rashness. There are those who have condemned Meade's irresolution and those who have lauded his firmness, even as there have been the defenders and critics of Longstreet and Stuart and the great Lee himself. Certainly there was enough glory to go around, whether to officers like General Warren, who saw the importance of Little Round Top, Colonel Vincent who occupied the hill in time, Colonel Oates who assailed it so valiantly, or to the enlisted men of both armies, of whose courage and dogged fighting and endurance it would be difficult to say too much.

Likewise to single out a specific area in which fighting occurred and insist that the battle was won or lost here may be unfair. It could have been won or lost at numerous places and times during those three days, particularly on the first two. But, so far as the Union cause is concerned, it would be hard not to recognize considerable justice in the evaluation of the historian of the Fifth Corps: "Historians have exhausted themselves in describing the actions of the 'Peach Orchard' and the events of the third day at Gettysburg. Great stress has been laid upon the results of Pickett's charge, while famous pictures have presented that scene to the gaze of the American public; but the truth of history is, that the little brigade of Vincent's with the self-sacrificing valor of the 20th Maine, under the gallant leadership of Joshua L. Chamberlain, fighting amidst the scrub-oaks and rocks in that vale between the Round Tops on the 2nd of July, 1863, saved to the Union arms the historic field of Gettysburg. Had they faltered for one instant—had they not exceeded their actual duty—while the left of the Third Corps was swung in the air half a mile to the right and front of Little Round Top, there would have been no grand charge of Pickett, and 'Gettysburg' would have been the mausoleum of departed hopes for the national cause; for Longstreet would have enveloped Little Round Top, captured all on its crest from the rear, and held the key of the whole position."

Nearly fifty years after the conflict, Chamberlain made one of his numerous visits to the battlefield. It was now in good part a neatly laid-out park interlaced with avenues and studded with monuments. He walked up to Little Round Top, where his services had won him a Congressional Medal of Honor, where the Alabama men—"none braver or better in either army" in his judgment—had been "victims of a surprise, their quick and mobile imagination." He stood upon the crest, looking down at the rocks where Vincent and O'Rorke, Weed and Hazlett fell, and especially where his own beloved officers and men of the 20th Maine perished. It was near dusk, and Chamberlain sat down on the summit. Overcome by his memories, he mused until the sun went down behind the hills to the west and darkness mantled the slopes. And it seemed to him in his mystical mood as if, with the coming of night, he were surrounded by a radiant fellowship of the fallen, the young men who did not know "what were their lofty deeds of body, mind, heart, soul, on that tremendous day." He saw the earth itself as treasuring something infinitely more precious than graves. But these hills of Gettysburg which had witnessed such valor and sacrifice "shall hold the mighty secret in their bosom till the great day of revelation and recompense, when these heights shall flame again with transfigured light—they, too, have part in that adoption, which is the manifestation of the sons of God."

Whew! I'm exhausted!

GETTYSBURG "PURSUIT"
TO PETERSBURG

"WE are fighting gloriously," Chamberlain wrote Fanny the morning after Pickett's charge. "Our loss is terrible, but we are beating the Rebels as they were never beaten before. The 20th has immortalized itself."

Like so many others in the Army of the Potomac, as well as President Lincoln and Secretary of War Stanton, Chamberlain did not consider the battle ended. Now that Lee's army had shot its bolt, he expected an aggressive advance by Meade. After all, the Confederates had suffered severely, too, and Meade had the Sixth Corps, big, now rested, and virtually untouched, to be the spearhead of a counterattack at Gettysburg or of an aggressive pursuit that might smash Lee with his back to the Potomac as McClellan should have done ten months ago after Antietam. But to Chamberlain's disappointment, as to Lincoln's, the prospects of a brilliant victory vanished with Meade's resolve to rest the army.

While the rains started to fall on the 4th and Lee began his withdrawal unopposed, Rice took the brigade on a reconnaissance over to the Peach Orchard, even as far as Willoughby Run. Once returned, Chamberlain marched the regiment to Little Round Top to bury his dead. This was a sad if proud duty, but one that Chamberlain's regiment insisted on carrying out after every battle in the war. A marker made of an ammunition box with the soldier's name and home carved on it was placed at the head of each soldier's grave. Chamberlain never forgot the men who died on that hillside or their families. Later the bodies were removed to the National Cemetery, but Private Theodore Gerrish, who became a minister, regretted that they had not been left where they fell. After the burial, Chamberlain went to look after his wounded, whom he had originally placed in the houses of citizens east of Little Round Top. The artillery barrage preceding Pickett's charge had necessitated their removal to less adequate if safer shelter two miles away, and Chamberlain found his brother John deeply distressed that a number of the men were partially exposed to the weather. Chamberlain gave what comfort he could to them.

Late the following afternoon, July 5, he led his troops out onto the Emmitsburg Road in a downpour as Meade started his infantry south in a leisurely pursuit—if it can be called that—of the fast-moving Lee. Though the President and General Halleck kept prodding him to push forward and battle Lee before the Confederates could cross the Potomac, Meade was wary. He regarded Lee's army as still able to fight an effective battle, which indeed it was, but, if its morale was still high, it was short of supplies, inferior in numbers to Meade, and the river it must cross was rising in the torrential rains. Meade intended to swing south to Frederick, then west and northwest over the Catoctins and South Mountain and past the old battleground of Antietam to wherever Lee planned to cross the Potomac—Williamsport, as it turned out. But whereas Lee was driving hard, despite being encumbered by a long wagon train of wounded, Meade's pursuit was cautions. The march schedule of Chamberlain's regiment gives some idea of this: ten miles on July 5, one mile on the 6th, eighteen on the 7th, twelve on the 8th, and about eight on the 9th. Despite the rains, the Catoctin Mountains which they crossed on the 8th, and South Mountain which they traversed on the 9th, the pace could hardly be considered swift when one thinks of the pre-Gettysburg marches.

By now, even moving as cautiously as he had, Meade was close to Lee's entrenchments, and on July 10, having crossed the Antietam, Chamberlain lost two killed and six wounded and missing in a brisk skirmish. One of the four prisoners of the 2nd Maine still refusing to do duty changed his mind that day; he was one of those killed, and Chamberlain cleared the man's record. The next three days the troops inched forward, Meade unwilling to assault Lee. Finally, on July 14, after a night of cloudbursts, the army discovered that Lee had withdrawn across the Potomac.

After moving into Williamsport on the 14th, Chamberlain marched to Berlin on the 16th, where he bivouacked until the following afternoon. He took advantage of the rest to write Fanny a long letter. On the 10th, the day the skirmish had occurred, the brigade had been drawn up in review to listen to an announcement that Colonel Vincent had been promoted to a brigadier general. Everyone cheered lustily, not knowing that Vincent had already been dead for two days. Now the brigade learned of his death, and the shock was great. "I grieve for him much," Chamberlain said. He told Fanny he was going to write Mrs. Vincent, and he hoped she would write, too. A few hours after he had finished his letter, he took the regiment out again in the futile maneuvering of the Army of the Potomac that finally ended for the

20th Maine on August 7 when the regiment assumed the task of guarding Beverly Ford on the Rappahannock.

Chamberlain soon came down with malaria, an affliction fairly common in the army that August. He therefore went home on sick leave for about two weeks, and his reunion with his family was rapturous. Furthermore, he found himself recognized by the towns-folk as a genuine hero, which embarrassed him as much as it pleased him that he was not forgotten. The days at home, however, were all too few. When he was ready to return, Fanny packed a box of food and included several jars of sweet pickles for which he had a fondness. His train was late in getting into Boston, and in his rush to catch the New York train, he was forced to leave the box behind. This naturally did not please Fanny, as he presently learned. He therefore replied playfully, "Ah, rogue, you scold me about the sweet pickles ... but would you have me 'lug' that big heavy thing all the way to the Rappahannock, weak as I was?"

He may have arrived back at camp without the sweet pickles, but he found something waiting for him even sweeter. As a result of General Barnes being wounded at Gettysburg, General Charles Griffin was again given command of the 1st Division of the Fifth Corps. When Colonel Rice, in charge of the 3rd Brigade after Vincent fell, was promoted to brigadier general and given another command, Griffin insisted on having Chamberlain, and only Chamberlain, for the 3rd Brigade. He even rejected a number of other officers proposed. On August 24, 1863, therefore, Chamberlain was posted to command of the brigade, a joyful duty he immediately assumed on his return. Private Gerrish of the 20th Maine said that "Colonel Chamberlain had, by his uniform kindness and courtesy, his skill and brilliant courage, endeared himself to all his men. . . ."

Chamberlain's friends worked hard to have him made a brigadier general that late summer and fall. Their representations to Secretary Stanton and Senator Fessenden of Maine were strong, particularly those from Generals Ames and Rice. The latter put the case plainly to Fessenden: "My personal knowledge of this gallant officer's skill and bravery upon the battlefield, his ability in drill and discipline, and his fidelity to duty in camp, added to a just admiration for his scholarship, and respect for his Christian character, induces me to ask your influence in his behalf." Speaking of the second day of the battle of Gettysburg, Rice said, "History will give credit to the bravery and unflinching fortitude of the 20th Maine Volunteers more than to any other equal body of men upon the field. . . . The conduct of this Regiment at the battle of Gettysburg has rendered, for all time, the prowess of the arms of your State imperishable: conduct which, as an eye-witness, I do not hesitate to say, had its inspiration and great success from the moral power and personal heroism of *Col.* Chamberlain."

But Chamberlain's promotion languished. Perhaps Fessenden did not prod Stanton enough, or Stanton may have resented any prodding by Fessenden, who had not hesitated on occasion to criticize Stanton's department. Had Chamberlain become active in his own behalf, as so many officers were, he might still have obtained the promotion, but, throughout his life, Chamberlain was reluctant to push his personal advancement. The result, therefore, of all the energetic endeavors by his friends was a cold shoulder by Washington.

It is unlikely that such treatment greatly distressed Chamberlain; he was pleased with the brigade command, and his letters to Fanny reflect his cheerfulness. "How I wish I could sit with you and Daisy at some communion table," he said on August 31, "if we could only get rid of the association of formality, and factitious if not forced feeling—lugubriousness instead of solemn joy. How happy such a season would make me." "Oh, ho! you want to be *liked*," he jested tenderly; "Well, that will do—a girl that is loved so much that she longs to be liked! And did you ever think of that word *like*—it carries an idea of things reciprocally befitting— of a certain agreeableness—of similarity—*like*ness in fact . . . If I might be so bold, I do *like* you for I *am* like you. Sufficiently unlike for all practicable purposes (and some impracticable ones!) and all the more 'like' for being not the *same*."

Nearly a fortnight later the cheerful, even playful, mood persisted. "Fan, you pretty butterfly, how you do spell," he laughingly chided her; " '*advise*,' you ask for; '*bussiness*,' inadvertent no doubt. And then—don't think I would care how an angel spelled a loving word to me—'dreamyly.' You darling, sweet girl, it is dreamily. How are your pretty roly-poly horns, or 'rats'—or whatever you call the puffs of hair I plague you about?"

More seriously, in this letter he sounded the same optimistic and fearfully mistaken note shared by so many in the North after Vicksburg: "This war, I suppose you can see, is rapidly coming to a close issue, and the *heavy fighting* is nearly over. *We* may see one or two battles more like Gettysburg, though many doubt even that." He dreamed one night that many of the officers' ladies were coming to camp, "and

I was all excitement to have you come." Then he added, prophetically, "But I suppose we shall have something else upon our hands before a great while."

"Something else" did happen. With Longstreet's corps sent south and the Federal Eleventh and Twelfth Corps also detached to Tennessee, Lee finally lunged across the Rappahannock. Meade quickly retreated to Catlett's Station along the Orange and Alexandria Railroad on October 13 and to Centerville on the 14th. The three rear corps of the Army of the Potomac, the Third, Fifth, and Second (the rear guard), were directed to keep in contact. About noon on the 14th, Griffin's division, which was rearmost in the Fifth Corps' line of march, had broken ranks near Bristoe Station to eat. But Chamberlain's brigade had hardly blackened their coffee pots over the fires when shells started dropping among them from the west and a Confederate skirmish line appeared. Instantly Chamberlain pulled his troops into formation, but word reached Griffin to keep the division on the move, so, to everyone's surprise, the Fifth Corps avoided the battle. The result was that the Second Corps, that day under Warren, was left to fight A. P. Hill's big corps alone. At length, Sykes, the Fifth Corps commander, after forming a battle line near Manassas, backtracked to assist Warren. By the time he returned, Warren had handsomely beaten back the enemy. A general battle never came off, Meade evidently thinking the two corps of Hill and Ewell too strong for him to attack.

When Meade subsequently discovered that Lee was falling back toward the Rappahannock, he decided to force a passage across the river. Hence he sent "Uncle John" Sedgewick, in command of his own Sixth Corps and the Fifth as well, to Rappahannock Station where Sedgewick proposed on November 7 to clear the north bank of the river on which the Confederates were heavily entrenched.

Actually this was one battle that Chamberlain probably wished himself out of since he was suffering from a recurrence of malaria and had chills, fever, and nausea all day. General Griffin himself was absent with illness and General Bartlett had taken over the division. The Fifth and Sixth Corps were advancing along the Orange and Alexandria Railroad, the Fifth to the left of the tracks. The main attack was delivered by the Sixth Corps, which was spiritedly aided by about eighty volunteers from the 20th Maine under Captain Walter G. Morrill, who won the second Medal of Honor to be claimed by the regiment. In the battle, which ended in a smashing little victory for the Army of the Potomac, Chamberlain was directed to hold his brigade in readiness for action on the left of the 1st Division. As at Gettysburg there were no troops to his own left, so he threw out two companies to guard against a surprise flank attack. Two of his regiments took an advanced position strongly supporting the skirmish line, and in making a reconnaissance of his front, Chamberlain had his horse again shot from under him. By this time he must have started to wonder how long it would be before some sniper would elevate his aim a little.

Chamberlain sent in his brigade report on November 10 from a bivouac near Kelly's Ford on the Rappahannock, and it was his last report for some time. The brilliant sunshine and wine-like weather of the 6th and 7th had given way to snow on the 8th, which was followed by cold, bitter winds. That night, when the brigade was ordered across Kelly's Ford toward the Rapidan, Chamberlain slept in the snow. The result was a violent malarial recurrence complicated by what appears to have been pneumonia. He collapsed soon after he signed his report on November 10.

Informed of the gravity of Chamberlain's condition, General Bartlett sent him off to Washington by the first train to leave, which happened to be a freight train of "empties." Attended by faithful orderlies, Chamberlain thus rode into the capital in a car ordinarily used for hauling cattle. He was taken to the Officers Hospital at Georgetown Seminary, and for a while it was "touch-and-go" whether he would survive. It was his good fortune, however, to have a very competent army nurse, Mary Keene, whose devotion to him he never forgot. Later, after she had married and was widowed, he helped her obtain a pension. Fanny came down from Brunswick, and Chamberlain felt that there were worse afflictions than illness since it brought Fanny and him together for a longer period than at any time since he entered the army.

While he was in the hospital, an assistant surgeon of the 15th New York Cavalry was brought in as a patient, one J. H. Robinson. Despite the doctors and the ministrations of his wife, Jennie, Robinson died in February. On Memorial Day, 1888, Jennie Robinson wrote Chamberlain from Syracuse that she would never forget the kindness he had shown both of them during her husband's illness. She heard him speak that Memorial Day night and was overjoyed when Chamberlain remembered her. She asked if her daughter, who had never seen her father, could meet him. Naturally he assented, and when her daughter asked for a photograph, Chamberlain gallantly sent her one. In the course of his life, many people besides the Robinsons felt grateful to Chamberlain for acts of kindness which may have come naturally for him to perform but which they never took for granted or forgot.

By January, 1864, Chamberlain had made such rapid progress that he was given light duty, being appointed to a general court martial which heard cases in both Washington and Trenton, New Jersey. For that matter, Lieutenant Colonel Gilmore of the 20th Maine was also in Washington that winter on similar duty, and Major Ellis Spear took over the regiment. Chamberlain did not object to this work so long as it was still winter and there was no action on the Southern front. Fanny continued with him for much of the time.

But in the spring when he observed many of his friends returning to camp and the heavy blue masses of troops and long trains of canvas-backed wagons moving South, he became restless. The new commander of the armies, U. S. Grant, evidently meant business. Certainly he wanted a lot of troops and supplies for whatever he had in mind. Furthermore, to the gratification of many of the officers and men in the Army of the Potomac, he had kept Meade on as that Army's commander while he assumed responsibility for the overall direction. After all, Meade had many good military qualities and could really put up a fight if someone else made the principal decisions.

Chamberlain assumed that he would have no difficulty in returning to the front. As Fanny wrote home from Washington on April 14, after Chamberlain had conducted her over the battlefield at Gettysburg, "They are almost through with the court here, [and] in a few days L. will go to the Army." But the court adjourned only to meet at Trenton, and on the 25th Chamberlain wrote from Trenton, requesting permission to rejoin his command. Meanwhile he fretted in wild impatience as on that beautiful May 4, with the dogwood blossoms white against the new green of the Virginia woods, Grant's troops, stripped to the essentials as the Army of the Potomac had never been before, crossed the Rapidan and, on the day following, opened the great and dreadful campaign in the Wilderness. As word of the hard, nasty fighting in the woods and underbrush appeared in the newspapers, Chamberlain wrote the Adjutant General's Office again, on May 9, explaining, "At the time I was placed on this duty, I was under medical treatment in Georgetown, D. C. My health will now, in my opinion, permit my resuming active duty; and never before having been absent from my command in time of an active campaign, my anxiety to be in the field is very great." It is always difficult to deny the request of an officer who wishes to sacrifice a safe and comfortable duty for the real mission of a soldier. The Adjutant General's Office quickly processed his papers and sent the militant professor back to his most unacademic duty in Virginia.

He soon discovered that although Grant had not achieved the success against Lee in the Wilderness for which he had hoped, this time there was no drawing back. Instead Grant slid to the southeast, crossing the rivers of big and little dimensions and severely testing Lee, yet never quite succeeding in tearing open the Confederate defenses. Over the Rapidan, the Ny, the North Anna, the Pamunkey, Totopotomoy Creek, and the Chickahominy he went, and as he lunged to the left, Lee slid quickly to the right to meet him with an impregnable line of entrenchments. The North heard of terrific battles at Spottsylvania Court House, Bethesda Church, and Cold Harbor. Grant, however, was determined to wear Lee down regardless of his own losses.

When Chamberlain arrived at Spottsylvania only to find General Bartlett leading his old brigade, he cheerfully took over command of the 20th Maine again. The 20th gave him a rousing welcome, but he was scarcely back with his old friends when Bartlett became ill and Chamberlain resumed command of the brigade. And almost at once, on May 22, he was in action again at Pole Cat Creek.

This action was not much of an affair, but it was typical of many such actions during that campaign, and typical, too, of the imaginative way Chamberlain fought. With the 3rd Brigade in the van of the Fifth Corps, Chamberlain left Spottsylvania on the morning of the 21st, bivouacked near Bowling Green at night, then pushed cautiously toward the North Anna the next day as it became evident that the Confederate rearguard was not far ahead. At noon of the 22nd, Griffin detached the 118th Pennsylvania, the famous Corn Exchange Regiment of Philadelphia, to assist Chamberlain, who was ahead of the column with a few scouts and a skirmish line examining every angle from which the enemy might launch an attack.

Suddenly a cannon boomed, and a pillar of white smoke rose from a wooded crest in front. Instantly Griffin halted the division. After a moment's consultation with him, Chamberlain swiftly moved the brigade into a field to the right, hoping to take advantage of the cover offered by a patch of woods to catch the enemy unseen. He ordered that the first men to strike the battery should ignore the cannoneers and kill the horses so that the enemy could not save his artillery. But when the 20th Maine and 118th Pennsylvania were nearly up to the woods and on the flank of the battery, skirmishers from the latter regiment encountered a small, narrow but deep stream known as Pole Cat Creek. As the line halted and Chamberlain learned the reason, his eye fell on a heavy plank fence on the near side of the stream.

"Take the fence along with you, my men," he shouted; "throw it in, and yourselves after it!"

As one of his men said, "It was done with a will: one jump to mid-stream, with the planks for a pontoon, and we were over."

But the movement had attracted the enemy's attention. One gun fired a canister shot at the charging troops, while the entire battery got away. Though Chamberlain felt chagrined at losing such a prize, he had cleared the way, and the Fifth Corps marched on.

A bizarre little incident occurred immediately after the dislodgement of the enemy battery. The Pennsylvania officer in charge of the skirmishers, Captain Walters, saw a Confederate major on a grey horse holding his hand to his ear and leaning forward in a manner of concentrated attention. Partly deaf, perhaps partly blind, he had obviously neither heard nor seen Walters or the advancing troops. As Walters circled about to cut off the officer's retreat, Chamberlain observed the little tableau. In the words of an eyewitness, "He [Chamberlain] dare not speak a word to halt the line or caution quiet. But as he raised his hand and turned toward the troops, his countenance and his gesture seemed to communicate what he desired." Walters, his pistol out, now grasped the major's reins and demanded his surrender.

"Not so, sir, you are my prisoner," the major said, reaching for his carbine.

"Touch that and you die," Walters barked.

Slowly, painfully, the major slid out of his saddle. He gave up his carbine but angrily plunged his sword into the ground, breaking it off at the hilt. As the shaken officer was taken back past the troops, his face had turned so ashen that "its absolutely colorless hue" was much talked about.

The next day Chamberlain crossed the North Anna at Jericho Ford. He was to hold an interval between two divisions of the corps and to protect their flanks. Under heavy fire he stood far in front of his men whom he ordered to keep down. When his officers begged him to take cover, he said that he was in no more danger than anyone else and that it was necessary for him to be where he was in order to know what was going on and how to meet it.

Likewise in the fighting of June 2 and 3 at Bethesda Church, three miles north of Cold Harbor where the Second, Sixth, and Eighteenth Corps lost 12,000 casualties in a brief, futile, frontal attack, Chamberlain showed the same coolness in executing commands and the same disregard of peril. General Bartlett had returned to take over the brigade, so Chamberlain was back in command of the 20th Maine. He was withdrawing by the right flank to move to the left when Bartlett earnestly asked him if he could fight his men by the rear rank. Chamberlain replied that he could fight his men any way. Bartlett doubted as he watched the maneuver that it had ever been effected with more skill and rapidity by any command under fire. At the same time Chamberlain so exposed himself that a couple of burly sergeants actually took him by the arms and forced him to share their shelter. As it was, one shell struck a tree just above his head and showered him with debris.

This was the last time he had direction in action of the 20th Maine as its regimental commander, for General Warren reshuffled his Fifth Corps. On June 6, Chamberlain was appointed to command of the new 1st Brigade of Griffin's division, a brigade of six Pennsylvania regiments, of which

five were of veteran status and one was brand new. Warren
also tried again on the same day to get Chamberlain promoted to brigadier. He said, "Col. Chamberlain is one whose
services and sufferings entitle him to the promotion and
I am sure his appointment would add to my strength even
more than the reinforcement of a thousand men." This was
strong praise, but recommendations forwarded by Generals
Griffin, Barnes, and Bartlett contained similar sentiments.
To have Regular Army officers give such support to a
Volunteer is indicative of the respect in which they held him.
Griffin, a rugged fighter himself with a formidable chin and
mustache and an incongruously high-pitched voice, once
said that it was a magnificent sight to watch Chamberlain
in battle dashing from flank to flank and personally leading
the assaults in front of his troops.

But this type of leadership, as offered by any one officer,
could last only so long in a war as fierce as the 1864-stage
of the American Civil War. Since his campaign opened,
Grant had lost nearly 60,000 casualties, almost as many men
as Lee had in his army. Though Grant had replacements
which Lee lacked, it was clear that he simply could not fight
it out on that line all summer despite his proud statement.
He therefore hopped his army across two unbridged rivers,
the Chickahominy and the James, in an extraordinarily skillful and well concealed move that lasted from June 12 to
June 16. His objective had long since become not the capture
of Richmond but the destruction of Lee's army. To pull that
army away from its powerful position, however, Grant proposed to jump these rivers and come in on Richmond from
the rear at the railroad-and-supply center of Petersburg,
where the flashy, dressy little fighter, General P. G. T.
Beauregard, kept watch with a garrison of second-line troops.

If his move succeeded, not only would Grant cut off Lee's supply connections with the Shenandoah Valley and the Deep South, and take Richmond as well, but he would also force Lee out into the open where his own superior numbers would count.

Timed to synchronize with Grant's Wilderness campaign had been a drive against Beauregard by troops led by the political general most loathed by Southerners and detested by many Northerners, Benjamin F. Butler, whose daughter Adelbert Ames married. Although Butler started well, he soon slowed down, thereby permitting Beauregard to counterattack so successfully that he had Butler trapped in a peninsula between the James and the Appomattox Rivers until Beauregard pulled back when Grant poured his big army across the James. Beauregard sent frantically to Lee for help—Lee, who, for once, was really surprised. Even Lee's own pickets had not observed Grant's stealthy withdrawal from the lines. Grant had, at last, a real opportunity, but to capitalize on it, his corps had at once to assault the Petersburg defenses; everyone knew that within hours after the Union troops formed before the town, Lee's veterans would be hastening into the Petersburg lines.

As had happened so many times before, the Union generals were hesitant and unsure. Petersburg, which could have been captured on the night of the 15th, was harder to get to on the 16th as Beauregard built new interior defenses. Fumbling into awkward positions, maintaining wretched liaison, failing to coordinate their objectives and their attacks, the leaders of five Federal corps, with powerful units of those corps in position, missed a superb opportunity to overwhelm Petersburg on the 17th. The troops had actually cracked the lines, and Beauregard, fighting desperately, thought the last hour of the South had struck. But there was no follow-through with darkness. In the night Beauregard retired to within gunshot of the town; if he could hold out but a few hours more in the morning, Lee's troops would be up. Realizing that time was running out, Meade ordered a general assault at dawn on the 18th. The assault broke down as the Federal troops encountered difficult ground, particularly a railroad cut, and sharp fire from Beauregard. Had they persisted, however, particularly Warren with the Fifth Corps, they would have smashed the defenses and Grant would have had Lee out in the open where he wanted him. Not until late afternoon, again at Meade's insistence, did the Union commanders get their attacks again under way. By this time, Lee's field army had arrived, the odds of eight-to-one in favor of the blue evaporated, and the struggle in Virginia went on for almost another year.

Notwithstanding Lee's arrival, the afternoon attacks on June 18 were strongly pressed and by no subordinate officer more strenuously or courageously than by Chamberlain. The Fifth Corps had to get across several ravines and the Norfolk Railroad cut. Griffin's division bore the burden of the attack, with the main effort being carried by the brigades of Chamberlain and General Jacob B. Sweitzer; the 3rd Brigade was to be used generally in support. The point of attack of Chamberlain's 1st Brigade was known as Rives' Salient, which could only be reached by sweeping across open ground commanded by rifle and cannon fire directly and enfiladed by artillery fire from Fort Mahone, later fittingly called "Fort Damnation."

In the early morning attack by the Fifth Corps, Chamberlain had dashed ahead with his brigade and captured a strongly defended position from the Confederates which was subsequently given the name "Fort Hell." The Confederates having withdrawn their guns, Chamberlain sent for three batteries from the 9th Massachusetts. For cover and maximum effectiveness he dug gun platforms so low on the crest that the gunners laid the gun muzzles on the grass. He was in an exposed position far in advance of the main army and did not like the situation. Had the entire Fifth Corps kept its attack moving, the enemy defenses might have been carried, but, with a halt called by the command and no orders reaching him to withdraw, he was left in a position on which the enemy could concentrate at will. Nor could he help observing the tide of reinforcements the enemy was receiving with the arrival of Lee's army.

While Chamberlain was making preparations to hold the crest, a staff officer unknown to him brought him verbal orders to charge the Confederate defenses, two to three hundred yards in front. Chamberlain could scarcely believe his ears. His lone brigade to carry out such an assignment? He was so disturbed at the impending sacrifice of his men that he sent back a note in which he stated his position, precisely, baldly, and boldly:

I have just received a verbal order not through the usual channels, but by a staff officer unknown to me, purporting to come from the General commanding the army, directing me to assault the main works of the enemy in my front. Circumstances lead me to believe the General cannot be aware of my situation, which has greatly changed within the last hour.

I have just carried an advanced position held by the enemy's infantry and artillery. I am advanced a mile beyond our own lines, and in an isolated position. On my right is a deep railroad cut; my left flank is in the air, with no support whatever. In front of me at close range is a strongly entrenched line of infantry and artillery with projecting salients right and left, such that my advance would be swept by a cross-fire, while a large fort on my left enfilades my entire advance, as I experienced in carrying this position. Along my front close up to the enemy's works appears to be bad ground, swampy, and boggy, where my men would be held at a great disadvantage under a severe fire.

I have got up three batteries, and am placing them on the reverse slope of this crest, to enable me to hold against an unexpected attack. To leave these guns behind me unsupported, their retreat cut off by the railroad cut—would expose them to loss in case of our being repulsed.

Fully aware of the responsibility I take, I beg to be assured that the order to attack with my single Brigade is with the General's full understanding. I have here a veteran Brigade of six regiments, and my responsibility for the welfare of these men seems to warrant me in wishing assurance that no mistake in communicating orders compels me to sacrifice them.

From what I can see of the enemy's lines, it is my opinion that if an assault is to be made, it should be by nothing less than the whole army.

This was a hard day for Meade as commander of the Army of the Potomac, and he was in a furious temper. Grant's great move across the James was being nullified by the difficulty of Meade's getting his corps commanders to bring off an effective concerted attack. The corps which had seen the least action in recent days had been the Fifth, and both Grant and Meade wanted Warren to push this attack hard. But Warren, whose independence of mind often exasperated the two generals, hated frontal assaults and their lavish expenditure of life. It was probably in his anguish at knowing time was short that Meade, to spur Warren on, ordered

Chamberlain forward. His message of protest and explanation overruled, Chamberlain was instructed to step off the attack with Sweitzer's brigade to his left—too far to the left to be of truly effective assistance.

When confirmation of the verbal orders arrived, Chamberlain opened fire with his battery, Captain John Bigelow's cannoneers trying to aim their pieces so as to have their shot hit the enemy's heavy guns slantwise and knock them off their trunions. Then Chamberlain formed the brigade into two lines. The men were ordered not to stop and fire since this would slow their approach and expose them longer, but to try to carry the defenses with the bayonet. Earlier in the action at "Fort Hell," Chamberlain, once again, had had a horse shot from under him, this time by a cannon ball. Still, Chamberlain went into action. As he explained, "It was a case where I felt it my duty to lead the charge in person, and on foot."

The defense was bitter, and casualties were heavy. The color bearer shot dead at his side, Chamberlain picked up the flag himself—a red maltese cross on a field of white—and raced forward in the face of a fire so fierce that men leaned into it as they would toward a heavy wind. Presently he came to the spongy ground just under the slope leading to the enemy's works. Fearing his men would be caught in the soft, sticky ground, he glanced back at them and ordered them to oblique to the left. His voice drowned in the roar of battle, he half turned and, waving the colors and his sabre to attract their attention, pointed both in the direction he wanted the brigade to move.

Then it happened—long delayed, often threatening, at last succeeding. While he was still in this half-turned position, a Minié ball slammed into his right hip joint, passed through his body, and came out behind the left hip joint. The colors were jolted from his hand, but the sabre remained fast. Unable to move his feet and unwilling to fall, he thrust the sabre into the ground and rested both hands on the hilt. "Break files, to pass obstacles!" he called out to the troops, standing, if anything, a little straighter than usual in a desperate effort to conceal his condition from them. He was the obstacle, and, neither of his lines noticing the blood spurting from both his sides and reddening his pantlegs and boots, the troops parted for him and dashed on, some of them getting to within twenty feet of the entrenchments before enemy fire cut them down.

With the men past him, his bodily weakness proved stronger than his will. The loss of blood brought him down at first to his knees, then to his elbows, and at last, like a crumpled sack, to the ground.

Though sorely hurt, he still thought of the battle. Two of his aides, Lieutenants West Funke and Benjamin F. Walters, raced toward him and carried him back out of point-blank range. He ordered one of them to run back and tell the senior colonel to take over the brigade, while he directed the other to hurry support to Bigelow's guns, which were threatened by an enemy force pouring out of the entrenchments.

Shortly afterward, during a lull, Bigelow swept the field with his glasses and noticed the shoulder straps in the dust. Instantly he sent out four men with a stretcher. But Chamberlain remonstrated, begging them to remove others worse off than he. They stood their ground: their orders were to bear him off the field. Just then a big shell from Fort Mahone landed close, half burying all of them with pebbles and dirt. Thereafter the bearers wasted no more time parlaying with a wounded colonel. Digging themselves out, they placed him on the stretcher and hurriedly carried him behind the guns. Later he was brought three miles to the rear to a field hospital. Thinking his time had come, he bade a last farewell to Funke and Walters and expressed the hope that the brigade would not be permitted to lose the good name it had acquired that day. That the battle of the day was lost and that Petersburg would remain in Confederate hands were all too clear to him and hard enough to bear.

As they examined his wound, the doctors were anything but optimistic. The single-shot, muzzle-loading rifle of those days, a primitive weapon indeed alongside the army rifle of today, was yet a potent weapon. Along with the new rifled cannon, the rifle was outmoding the tactics which were used through most of the Civil War and which were based on the short-range, smooth-bore musket. Frontal assaults were becoming about as lethal to the attackers as they were in 1914. The rifle fired a Minié ball, a soft-nosed leaden bullet that was potentially deadly at a half-mile, and actually a dreadful killer at 250 yards. When it hit a man, it did not make a neat, little hole like a modern steel bullet; it struck at high velocity, then tended to expand like a dum-dum bullet and made a ghastly aperture. The Minié ball that entered Chamberlain's right hip, severed arteries, nicked his bladder, and fractured the pelvic bones before it tore its way through his left hip. The reports from the first surgeons who examined him were so discouraging that Tom Chamberlain rounded up two surgeons of Chamberlain's former brigade, the 3rd, Drs. A. O. Shaw of the 20th Maine and M. W. Townsend of the 44th New York, and the three men groped through the darkness to reach the field hospital. At once Shaw and Townsend joined the staff there in trying to save the suffering man; Abner Shaw, in particular, was a magnificent young surgeon. Once, however, the doctors left off their work—with so little chance to save Chamberlain, why cause him such agony in the little time remaining to him? But Chamberlain was still game, so the surgeons turned to their task again; and it was reported that "This time good fortune rewarded intelligent persistence, severed parts were artifically connected, and to the great joy of patient and surgeon, there was a possibility of recovery." Actually the surgeons performed what came to be regarded as a miracle of medical science, which was hardly an exaggeration considering the bullet's effect, the crude facilities of the day, and the working conditions. In fact, the wound, the operation, and the recovery were regarded as so unusual as to be worth recording in the official medical and surgical history of the war.

It had been a near thing, and Chamberlain's superiors were convinced his death was certain. Many of them visited him during his time of agony, including Griffin and Warren. Both officers had previously recommended his promotion, and Warren now made strong verbal representations to Meade, followed by a written request. Grant, however, took the matter entirely out of their hands and acted independently of Washington. As he said in his *Memoirs,* "Colonel J. L. Chamberlain, of the 20th Maine, was wounded on the 18th. He was gallantly leading his brigade at the time, as he had been in the habit of doing in all the engagements in which he had previously been engaged. He had several times been recommended for a brigadier-generalcy for gallant and meritorious conduct. On this occasion, however, I promoted him on the spot, and forwarded a copy of my order to the War Department, asking that my act might be confirmed without any delay. This was done, and at last a gallant and meritorious officer received partial justice at the hands of his government, which he had served so faithfully and so well."

The "on the spot" which Grant mentioned was not quite that immediate. He was enormously impressed by what Chamberlain had done and seems to have spoken around Army Headquarters of issuing a special order for his promotion. When Chamberlain's superior officers visited the hospital, they mentioned Grant's intention, which naturally encouraged Chamberlain. The next day, although the operation had been a success, even the doctors wondered whether his constitution was strong enough to withstand the shock and loss of blood. Believing the wound mortal, Warren reminded Meade in an official telegram on the 19th of Chamberlain's previous recommendations. He added, "He [Chamberlain] expresses the wish that he may receive the recognition of his service by promotion before he dies for the gratification of his family and friends, and I beg that if possible it may be done. He has been sent to City Point." Meade at once forwarded the telegram to Grant with an earnest endorsement of the recommendation. Grant wasted no time. On June 20, he issued Special Order Number 39, in the first paragraph of which he appointed Chamberlain a brigadier general "for meritorious and efficient services on the field of battle, and especially for gallant conduct in leading his brigade against the enemy at Petersburg, Va., on the 18th instant, in which he was dangerously wounded. . . ." The promotion was to rank from June 18, and the Senate, in executive session on June 27, confirmed Grant's action. It has often been remarked that this was the only promotion Grant ever gave on the field of battle.

On the 19th, Chamberlain had indeed been sent to City

Point, as Warren mentioned to Meade. Warren directed Dr. Townsend of the 44th New York to accompany Chamberlain and detailed eight litter bearers to carry the wounded officer the sixteen miles to City Point, an exhausting assignment for all concerned. That Chamberlain survived the trip was a marvel in itself, but he had a tremendous will to live. At City Point he was taken aboard the hospital transport *Connecticut* and brought to Annapolis, where he was placed in the Naval Academy hospital.

When he was well enough, two items constituted his favorite reading matter. One was the special order with his promotion notice. The other was his obituary released by the army to the New York newspapers. He was indeed to die of his wound—the initial statement from the surgeons was right, after all—but when he was eighty-five instead of not quite thirty-six.

NAVAL HOSPITAL TO WHITE OAK ROAD

CHAMBERLAIN'S recovery from his wound was at first slow, then very swift. For days he lay at the point of death and for weeks suffered from convulsive chills and fever. From mid-August on, however, his recuperation was so remarkable that in September he talked of returning to the front, and Fanny, who had spent a large part of the anxious summer weeks with him, knew better by now than to raise serious protests. He began to send off a stream of letters in acknowledgment of the solicitude expressed by so many friends at his condition. Adelbert Ames, who had feared the "streak of daylight" through Chamberlain might unfit him for active outdoor duty, declared himself happy to hear that Chamberlain was "about to take the field." As an aside, Ames thought Chamberlain a very lucky man in another respect, too: for being "married to the woman, of all the world, that you most admired and loved."

But even the affection he bore his family could not hold Chamberlain back from what he regarded as his duty. The glamor of war had long since passed for him—he had witnessed too much horror and had suffered too excruciatingly himself to be beguiled by its trappings. If he never lost his love of military pageantry, he was able to distinguish between it and war itself. The latter he wanted to help terminate, though he could see values in it.

The finish, moreover, as November came around and Chamberlain reported for duty, was not far off; this was clear to most people. Although a stalemate existed in the lines before Petersburg despite vigorous local actions, the ghastly failure of Burnside's great mine, and the everlasting sniping, there was good news elsewhere. Sheridan had ruined the Shenandoah Valley, Sherman had captured Atlanta and was on his devastating march to the sea, while on November 8 the North had reelected Abraham Lincoln over the one-time glamourous McClellan, thereby underwriting a war to the bitter end. All in all, by mid-November, 1864, it was becoming clear that the dreadful sacrifices of the spring and summer had not been entirely in vain. To be sure, Hood was loose in Tennessee with a large army, but Union forces were present in sufficient strength to contain him, even eventually to defeat him.

When Chamberlain reported, he was again assigned, on November 19, to command of the 1st Brigade, 1st Division, Fifth Corps. Why he was permitted to rejoin is something of a mystery since he was still unable to walk any real distance or to ride a horse. But perhaps the reason went beyond a friendly doctor's closing an understanding eye to his real condition. It was in the very spirit of the man who had identified himself so closely with that massive collective entity, the Army of the Potomac. "This army—but what army?" Chamberlain asked himself. "Is this identity a thing of substance, or spirit, or of name only? Is this the army which bright as its color thronged the bridges of the Rapidan on that May morning . . . and vanished into the murk of the Wilderness?" Obviously not: too many had died, their places often taken by men who were volunteers in name only, who received bounties or who were drafted. There seemed to be "some slackening of the old nerve and verve, and service was sustained more from the habit of obedience and instinct of duty, than with that sympathetic intuition which inspires men to exceed the literal of orders or of obligations." Yet even these men had become seasoned soldiers, and many of them had also made the same sacrifice as the original volunteers. The Army of the Potomac, different though it was, and weaker in some respects, was still a disciplined army, and, in Chamberlain's opinion, discipline was "the soul of armies"; in fact, "taken in the long run, and in all vicissitudes, an army is effective in proportion to its discipline." The Army of the Potomac, however, was held together not only by discipline but also by "strength of great memories, pride of historic continuity, unfailing loyalty of purpose and resolve." Men staked their lives on the ultimate victory of a great cause. Chamberlain's own return to the army is understandable in this context only, and it truly represented a triumph of the spirit.

His brigade was not the solid phalanx of Pennsylvania regiments that he had commanded in June. Instead he found himself at the head of only two regiments, though these were quite large, the 198th Pennsylvania under Brigadier General Horatio G. Sickel and the 185th New York under Colonel Gustave Sniper. Both Sickel and Sniper were able and courageous soldiers, but both had ranked Chamberlain as colonels, and had they not been generous and realistic as well, the situation could have been embarrassing. Fortunately, as Chamberlain acknowledged, they accepted the new relationship with "sincerity and utmost courtesy."

On December 7 the Fifth Corps started on a great raid

along the Jerusalem Plank Road, destroying the Weldon Railroad for forty miles south of Petersburg. The Corps soon learned the Sherman technique of railroad destruction: heaping up the ties, burning them, placing the rails on the blazing piles, then twisting the steel into fantastic shapes. Rain and sleet followed by icy weather made everyone uncomfortable, especially Chamberlain. His task was initially one of guarding the destroyers. Later, on the way back, the troops stumbled onto an impressive store of applejack, and he was chiefly busy rounding up drunken soldiers. Those few days of campaigning, however, were more than his body in its weakened condition could tolerate. He finally succumbed to pain and the persuasions of his friends and went north on sick leave.

This time he was hospitalized in Philadelphia, where the surgeons insisted that for him to resume active duty in view of the nature and condition of his wound would be folly. Word of their judgment got around, and it is said that he received many attractive offers of positions in civil life. But Chamberlain had no intention as yet of leaving the service. Under surgical treatment and rest, his wound improved so encouragingly that one day he quietly left the hospital and returned to the front after a month's absence, just too late to become actively involved in a Fifth Corps encounter with the enemy at Hatcher's Run.

With the arrival of March, the great campaign to finish off the Confederacy received its final polishing as a plan. As never before, the North had the numbers and the matériel, and, as never before, Grant intended to apply the pressure on Lee's hungry, shabby, thinly spread troops. Lee's escape route was via the Southside and the Richmond-Danville Railroads which crossed at Burkeville, toward which Sherman was to start driving from Goldsboro, North Carolina, on April 10. Meanwhile Grant would extend farther to the west for the double purpose of seizing the Southside Railroad and forcing Lee to defend it. This would leave Lee's lines around Petersburg and Richmond so thin that at an appropriate moment they could be stormed. If Lee should still succeed in withdrawing his army down the railroads, he would run into Sherman at Burkeville, where, caught between Sherman and Grant, he would be destroyed. It was a simple strategy, the North had the means to make it work, and Lee could only retard, not prevent, its operation. Though Lincoln hoped there would be no more bloodshed, both Grant and Sherman were agreed that a final bloody battle was likely before the war ended. An attempt by Confederate General John B. Gordon to break through the Union lines at Fort Stedman on March 25 had been effectually smothered after an initial success—Lee's last real offensive thrust. Then, with General Edward D. C. Ord's Army of the James beginning to move south and west around the Army of the Potomac on March 27 and thousands of other troops being withdrawn from the trenches and started in the same direction at 3:00 A.M. on March 29, Grant opened the last campaign.

This campaign called for close cooperation between corps commanders and the breezy, hard-driving Westerner, General Philip H. Sheridan. On the 29th, he was to cross Hatcher's Run with nearly ten thousand cavalry and pass near Dinwiddie Court House. From here he would dash northward, cut the Southside Railroad, and get to the right and rear of the Confederate lines. The Second Corps under General Humphreys, as soon as Ord's troops took its place in the entrenchments, was likewise to cross Hatcher's Run, on which Humphreys should base his right flank while his left kept touch with the Fifth Corps. The Fifth, which was to cross Hatcher's Run, too, was not to go beyond the junction of the Vaughan and Quaker Roads until the Second Corps was in position. Then it was to advance toward the enemy by the Boydton Plank Road which joined the more southerly Vaughan Road at Dinwiddie Court House.

Lee was not caught asleep. He sent General Richard H. Anderson with Bushrod Johnson's division and Henry Wise's brigade to the extreme right of the entrenchments along the White Oak Road. George Pickett's division was also ordered to the western end of the lines, while General Fitz Lee was directed to move immediately to Five Forks and, assuming command of all cavalry, together with infantry supports, attack Sheridan.

At daylight on March 29 the Fifth Corps moved toward the Confederate right, Griffin's division in the lead, and Chamberlain's brigade at the head of the column. Shortly after noon, Griffin ordered Chamberlain up Quaker Road from its junction with Vaughan Road, Meade and Warren meeting at the junction and following the troops to where the Confederates had destroyed a bridge spanning Gravelly Run, one of the innumerable streams intersecting this swampy forest land. Chamberlain found the enemy entrenched on the north bank. Since there was no alternative but to wade the stream, he mentioned to Griffin his plan of placing Sickel with half the 198th Pennsylvania below the ruined bridge to open with a heavy fire while Major E. A. Glenn with the second battalion in skirmish order and Colonel Sniper of the 185th New York immediately behind forded the stream. Griffin agreed and directed General Gregory of the 2nd

Brigade to support Chamberlain on the left and General Bartlett to hold himself ready to assist as circumstances should require.

Chamberlain then gave the signal, and the 1st Brigade dashed through the stream, waist high in water, and struck the enemy's right flank obliquely. The Confederates fell back under the impetuous attack for about a mile up Quaker Road to the Lewis Farm. Reinforced at this point, they poured

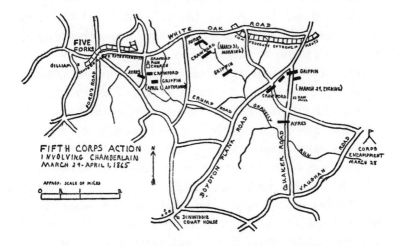

FIFTH CORPS ACTION
INVOLVING CHAMBERLAIN
MARCH 29-APRIL 1, 1865

APPROX. SCALE OF MILES

a withering fire into Chamberlain's troops. Chamberlain, however, kept his line moving in an envelopment that drove the enemy into the woods where a heavy body of Confederates was massed behind a breastwork of logs and earth. Enemy resistance now became so fierce that the bluecoats retreated. The Confederates then sallied out, and a desperate struggle took place until the arrival of reinforcements permitted Chamberlain to drive them back again. Afterward he withdrew to the Lewis Farm to reform. Prisoners told him that the Confederate command was determined to hold this position since it covered the junction of two roads they simply had to control, the White Oak and Boydton Plank Roads.

Chamberlain now regrouped. He gave the right of the line to Sickel and the left to Sniper on each side of the road. Then he took Glenn's battalion straight up Quaker Road to a sawdust pile where a mill had once stood; the pile was the very center of the enemy's advanced line of resistance. Though the Confederates laid down a hot fire, Chamberlain ordered his men not to stop and return the fire but to get in close and use the bayonet. Sharpshooters in the treetops galled them, but soon the troops drove home their charge in a furious melée of stabbing and shooting.

As the volume of fire increased, Chamberlain's horse dashed far ahead of the charging column. When Chamberlain tried to check him, he reared. At that moment a bullet aimed at the rider ripped through the big neck muscle of the horse and hit Chamberlain just below the heart. It tore his sleeve to the elbow, bruised his left arm, and no doubt would have killed him had it not been partially deflected in its passage by a leather case of field orders and a brass-mounted hand mirror in a breast pocket. On its new course, it slid around two ribs and left through the back seam of the coat. After that, it smashed the holstered pistol of one of Chamberlain's aides and knocked the man clean out of the saddle.

The blow halted the horse and stunned Chamberlain, who fell forward on the animal's neck. To General Griffin, who rode up quickly, Chamberlain looked like a dying man. "My dear General, you are gone," he said in a kind voice, putting a steadying arm around his brigadier's waist.

But as Chamberlain clawed his way back to consciousness, he heard not only the General's voice, sounding thin and far away, but also the high, keening rebel yell, near and menacing. He raised his head and saw to his horror that a yip-yipping grey mass had broken the entire right of his line. "Yes, General, I *am* gone," he gasped, and spurred away from the astonished Griffin.

He was a strange and ghastly, yet inspiring sight. He had lost his cap in his momentary faintness, and his hair and face were covered with his horse's blood, while his tattered coat and arm were smeared with his own. Officers and men stared in amazement as he galloped to rally his line. To many he was unquestionably a dying man on his last mission, and someone again sent a wire to the New York morning papers of his death.

Dashing among the retreating men, he begged, exhorted, and threatened. By the sheer force of his personality and the spectacle of unquenchable courage he presented, he got them to halt, face about, and reform again to confront the grey wolf-pack. Down at the right Sickel had rallied a group by the time Chamberlain arrived. Then the dauntless Sickel went down with a horribly shattered arm, followed quickly by his young major, Charles I. McEuen, a favorite of all, who was shot dead in his saddle. Panic now gave way to anger, and the 198th Pennsylvania whirled back over the field and chased its pursuers right over the breastworks. Chamberlain spurred back at once to the tumult at the saw-dust pile, while, to his astonishment, troops of both armies cheered him. "I hardly knew what world I was in," he said.

But once he was back at the sawdust pile, his horse, Charle-magne, nosed to the earth from exhaustion and loss of blood. Instantly Chamberlain leaped off, sent him to the rear, and plunged forward into the maddened struggle. When he reached the front, a sudden enemy lunge left him isolated from his own troops and surrounded by men in grey and butternut who lowered their muskets, locked bayonets about him, and demanded that he surrender.

For a moment he had a dreadful vision of what it meant to be a prisoner. Then realizing that in his hatless, tattered, mud-caked appearance he resembled no spruce Yankee officer, he saw his chance. "Surrender?" he shouted in a fruity Southern accent. "What's the matter with you? Come along with me and let us break 'em." With his one good arm he gave a slight flourish with his sword in the direction of his own troops. And the Confederates, completely duped, followed him—to be taken prisoner themselves.

One of those strange battle lulls now occurred, and a curious and admiring crowd gathered around the exhausted Chamberlain. Then up walked Major Ellis Spear of the 20th Maine. Spear, who kept a watchful eye on Chamberlain whenever that was possible, looked very mysterious, and reaching into his breast pocket as if to present a brevet's commission, produced instead a flask of rare wine which he invited Chamberlain to sample. Gratefully Chamberlain took the Jamaica-ginger-shaped bottle and drank—perhaps, indeed, more than courtesy demanded, for as he passed the bottle back and his friend held it up to the light, he observed the "melancholy, martyr-like look" on Spears' face.

Then the lull passed, and the battle flared fiercely on the left where the 185th New York under Sniper, who had driven to the edge of the woods, was being pressed back to a line perpendicular to the original position along the road. Someone found a horse for Chamberlain, a mud-spattered white one, and the dazed officer rode furiously down to assist the hard-fighting Sniper. More than ever, Chamberlain looked like "Death on a pale horse."

He found the situation so desperate that he sent for help

to General Gregory of the 2nd Brigade. But Gregory was slow in getting into position because of the woods and the streams his troops had to cross. Fortunately Griffin was quick to perceive the danger. His face pale and anxious, he rode up to Chamberlain and said, "If you can hold on there ten minutes, I will give you a battery."

As Griffin, who loved his artillery, went galloping back for the guns, Chamberlain dashed over to Sniper. There was a crest in his rear behind which he had intended to reform should he be driven farther back. Now he wanted to save the crest for the guns and felt that, to keep the enemy from seizing it, he had no choice but to counterattack and drive the enemy back toward the woods. Besides, his men were getting short of ammunition; to have them continue on their present basis was to invite disaster. He shouted to Sniper so that all would hear, "Once more! Try the steel! Hell for ten minutes and we are out of it!" Then he led them back against the enemy in a surprise charge that saved the knoll. As the men hit the earth, he told Sniper that once the guns were up he intended to charge the woods.

Finally—it seemed eons to him—Battery B of the 4th U. S. Artillery arrived under Lieutenant John Mitchell. "And now they come—," Chamberlain said, "B of the 4th Regulars, Mitchell leading with headlong speed, horses smoking, battery thundering with jolt and rattle, wheeling into action front, on the hillock I had been saving for them, while the earth flew beneath the wheels,—magnificent, the shining, terrible Napoleons."

Mitchell smiled slightly at his appearance, but Chamberlain could see nothing funny in the situation.

"Mitchell," he barked, "do you think you can put solid

shot or percussion into those woods close over the rebels' heads, without hurting my men?"

"Yes, Sir! if they will keep where they are."

"Well then, give it to them the best you know. But stop quick at my signal, and fire clear of my men when they charge."

He stepped back, and the battery went into action. He found the whole situation "splendid and terrible: the swift-served bellowing, leaping big guns; the thrashing of the solid shot into the woods; the flying splinters and branches and tree-tops coming down upon the astonished heads."

But the enemy retaliated with a charge on the left flank of the battery, where the 185th New York, some of the men without a cartridge left, were putting up a terrific fight. Mitchell went down, but his guns continued, now firing canister.

Chamberlain, looking ghastly and swaying in the saddle, had posted himself near the guns and was directing the defense when Griffin galloped up. "General, you must not leave us," Griffin cried out. "We cannot spare you now."

"I had no thought of it, General," Chamberlain replied.

Then he saw to his relief that Griffin had brought help: the 189th New York from Gregory's 2nd Brigade and the 1st and 16th Michigan and the 155th Pennsylvania from Bartlett's 3rd Brigade. Throwing these regiments into line, Chamberlain charged the woods, capturing the breastworks, and sent the enemy flying up the road to his main position near the junction of the Boydton Plank and White Oak Roads. Griffin now pulled Chamberlain's own brigade back to the Lewis Farm, sent Gregory to occupy the captured position, and ordered Bartlett to a position near the road junction.

Chamberlain had had quite an afternoon. Until the reinforcements had arrived, he had tangled for two hours with four brigades of General Anderson's corps numbering more than 6,000 officers and men. Although in this severe action at different times he had had both flanks turned and his center broken, he had triumphed. His own brigade, even with Mitchell's battery thrown in, amounted to barely 1700, of whom he lost about 400 killed and wounded in the action. Yet he had inflicted casualties as large, captured upwards of 200 prisoners, and cleared the way for a grand attack on the White Oak Road. All told, it had been a remarkable example of inspired leadership. After the battle, Warren met him and said pleasantly, "General, you have done splendid work. I am telegraphing the President. You will hear from it."

Chamberlain, however, had little desire to think at this time about rewards. He looked in on his wounded in the old Quaker meeting house and said what he could to cheer them. He rode over the battlefield, still murky with battle smoke and thickening with mist, and gazed with somber eyes at the dead. These and the wounded had been men made in the image of God and marred by the hand of man. But if so marred, had it been in the name of God? Why? And who was answerable? For the moment the theologian replaced the soldier; the uneasy, restless conscience challenged the ruthless commander. "Was it God's command we heard," he brooded, "or His forgiveness we must forever implore?" He came upon young McEuen's body, "where God's thought had folded its wing," and knelt beside it before the burial detail arrived.

Then he rose, spoke to several of the wounded, and suddenly discovered "brave old Sickel lying calm and cheerful, ... refusing to have more attention than came in his turn." Chamberlain sat down beside him to cheer him as best he could. But Sickel, who could still smile despite his pain, thought Chamberlain needed the comforting rather than himself. "General," he whispered, "you have the soul of the lion and the heart of the woman."

"Take the benediction to yourself," Chamberlain replied gently; "you could not have thought that, if you had not been it."

Later he watched, in the darkness, the burial parties at work, the dim moving forms weirdly illumined and magnified by the hovering lanterns and reminding the troubled commander of the veiled and hooded figures in a procession of the "misericordia." A dismal rain began to fall, the cosmos weeping, as it were, for the sins of men. Deeply oppressed, he retired to the Lewis house, and, by the light of a sputtering candle, sat down to one of the saddest tasks of his life— to write a letter of consolation to Doctor McEuen of Philadelphia who had laid his hand on Chamberlain's shoulder and commended his only son to the General's care.

The next day, a day of rain, the Fifth Corps rested, and, on March 31, it expected to do likewise since the arrival of Grant's early morning order that, because of the rains, the troops should remain pretty much where they were. At the same time, it was clear that Grant wanted Warren to obtain control of the White Oak Road in his front. In fact, if by a reconnaissance Warren thought that he could secure and hold the road, Meade directed him, through General Alexander Webb, his chief of staff, to make the attempt notwithstanding the order to suspend operations.

A report by Brigadier General Romeyn B. Ayres of the 2nd Division confirmed Warren in his resolve to get hold of White Oak Road, using Ayres' division in attack and the 3rd Division under Brigadier General Samuel W. Crawford in support. Chamberlain was surprised at Warren's decision in view of a despatch from Grant to Sheridan, a copy of which Griffin had shown him the night before and in which Grant spoke of a possible attack on Warren in the morning. But with the arrival of morning and still no attack, Warren prepared to move against the White Oak Road position. This was hazardous in any case, and more so after word came from Grant to Meade that no help on the flank could be expected from Sheridan, who was now facing the Confederate cavalry at Five Forks and Pickett's division of infantry, which was deploying along the White Oak Road as far as Five Forks. Warren, however, wisely placed his divisions in echelon rather than in line and moved forward.

Unfortunately for Warren, no less a personage than Robert E. Lee himself was with General Anderson that day, and Lee was determined to cover Pickett's advance toward Dinwiddie Court House and prevent any penetration of the gap between Anderson's right and Pickett's left. Lee therefore directed Anderson to throw four brigades against Warren. They struck Ayres' division on both flanks and in the center without warning and with such force that his troops broke and ran right through Crawford's division, which was in support behind it. It was as if someone had pushed the panic button, for many units of both divisions were soon but a mass of demoralized, frightened soldiers splashing through a branch of Gravelly Run to reach safety behind the lines along the Boydton Plank Road.

Back in reserve, many of Griffin's division had spread their blankets and spare clothing out to dry in the warm spring sun that had broken through at last and were boiling late morning coffee. Chamberlain himself was lying on a heap of straw trying to ease the pain caused by the accumulation of wounds, old and new. Suddenly the roar of battle burst about them and a disorganized mass of soldiery headed toward them. Instantly bugles screamed, and the men grabbed their rifles. But Griffin had his eye on the fugitives. "For God's sake, let them through, or they will break our line!" he shouted.

Quickly he formed his division, leaving gaps for the fleeing men to run through, and Chamberlain and Bartlett opened with artillery and a sharp musketry fire on the pursuers. Then Griffin and Warren left off their work of reforming the fugitives and came galloping down to Chamberlain on the left, deeply mortified.

"General Chamberlain, the Fifth Corps is eternally damned," Griffin growled.

"Not till you are in heaven," Chamberlain shot back pleasantly.

But Griffin did not smile. "I tell Warren you will wipe out this disgrace, and that's what we're here for."

"General Chamberlain,"—it was Warren, and his voice had a strangely compressed tone as he struggled for control— "will you save the honor of the Fifth Corps? That's all there is about it."

Chamberlain looked now at the dark, slim Warren with his Indian-like face and his lank, black hair, and now at Griffin with the ramrod back and the big mustache. He liked them both, but they were asking a lot. He expected an attack at any moment on his left flank; his thin, little brigade had borne the brunt of the action two days before; and this was one of his bad days—his left arm was in a sling, and his ribs were stiff and sore from the previous action, while his abdomen ached and burned from the Petersburg wound. He realized that Warren's appeal deserved a chivalrous response, but he simply could not make it. Instead, he suggested Bartlett, whose 3rd Brigade was the largest in the division and had scarcely been engaged the other day.

But Warren shook his head.

"We have come to you; you know what that means," he said pointedly.

"I'll try it, General," Chamberlain said. Then, remembering how Rives' Salient might have been taken in the first attack the year before had he not been halted by Warren, he added, "only don't let anybody stop me except the enemy."

Warren looked at the branch of Gravelly Run, sixty feet wide and four to five feet deep.

"I will have a bridge ready here in less than an hour. You can't get men through this swamp in any kind of order."

But Chamberlain knew that an hour's delay would give the enemy so long to entrench that he would lose heavily in the assault. "It may do to come back on, General [but] it will not do to stop for that now," he said bluntly. "My men will go straight through."

He then took his brigade across the stream, half the units covering the advance of the attacking battalions, while the latter waded through water waist-high and held their cartridge boxes on the bayonet sockets. Once across, Chamberlain swept the bank clear, Gregory's brigade now coming up on his right, the 3rd in reserve and Ayres' division moving up on his left rear. Units of the Second Corps on his far right also heavily engaged one of the four Confederate brigades. Though he encountered a hot fire, Chamberlain swept through the woods and semi-cleared land for a mile. Then as he burst out into a field which was intersected by enemy breastworks supported by a line of battle along the edge of the woods at the far end, an order to halt arrived from Warren, who wanted to make a personal reconnaissance.

This was the very kind of obstacle that had frustrated Chamberlain at Rives' Salient and which he had wished removed as a condition for making this present assault. Impatiently he rode back to Warren and Griffin and explained the situation in polite but forthright language. He had already recovered more than the ground lost by the 1st and 2nd Divisions, and the question was whether to take the White Oak Road or not. Certainly he could not remain where he was, for the enemy would soon attack him. If to go forward was dangerous, to withdraw would be equally costly to many men. Therefore, why not attack? He would put Gregory's brigade in the woods on his right arranged by battalions in echelon by the left which would enable Gregory to hit successively in the flank any attempts to strike Chamberlain's own right. When Gregory was well advanced, Chamberlain would assault the works strung across the field.

Both Warren and Griffin gave their approval, and Chamberlain at once informed Gregory and his own officers. He also gave them instructions which indicate a mind not dedicated to a routine military practice that accounted for so many casualties in the Civil War. Many officers, ignoring the long-range destructive power of the modern rifle, still insisted on charges in close order, with reliance on the bayonet; the result was often a slaughter. While Chamberlain continued to believe in the bayonet, which his troops generally used with effectiveness, he disliked a close-order charge over a long distance. If he had once believed in this, he had learned better, particularly since now he had over three hundred yards to go before reaching the breastwork. He said that he wanted rifles at the shoulder until near enough for a rush. But in the entire approach he wanted an open front, a loose-order arrangement with little attention to rank or alignment. With troops thus spaced, casualties would be kept down. He thus anticipated a procedure not generally pursued until the machine gun necessitated its adoption in modified form in World War One. Still, as Chamberlain acknowledged, "Had I known . . . that General Lee himself was personally directing affairs in our front, I might not have been so rash, or thought myself so cool."

Presently Gregory's guns in the woods opened a roaring barrage, the bugles sounded the charge, and Chamberlain rode out to the front of his command on his battered Charlemagne. "He had been shot down in battle twice before," said Chamberlain; "but his Morgan endurance was under him, and his Kentucky blood was up."

Notwithstanding arrangements, the cutting power of the rifles was deadly, and the troops broke into a run to close quickly with their owners. The 185th New York went over the breastworks at a bound. The 198th Pennsylvania on the right encountered heavy artillery fire and, for a moment, wavered. Chamberlain instantly called on Gregory's infantry. Thus supported, the 198th swarmed back over the breastwork, captured a large part of the 56th Virginia Regiment, and, linking up again with the 185th New York, drove the enemy three hundred yards across the White Oak Road to his main entrenchments. The entire charge, intelligently planned, ably led, and handsomely executed was, in the words of Confederate General Eppa Hunton, whose own brigade received its brunt and retreated, "one of the most gallant things I had ever seen."

Chamberlain's performance on this day, if less sensational than on the 29th, had been remarkable; actually he should have been back in a field hospital instead of up at the front. The action to secure the White Oak Road revealed not only the rare quality of personal leadership he always manifested, but, in addition, a degree of organizational skill in the management of large bodies of troops in action (Griffin let him direct Gregory's brigade as well as his own) that gave some indication of how effective a division or perhaps a corps commander he might have become had he secured recognition sooner or the war have lasted longer. He had clearly become the brigadier in the Fifth Corps that Warren depended on to accomplish whatever was especially difficult or hazardous. It was no fault of his that Grant gave scant attention in his *Memoirs* to either the action on the Quaker Road or the White Oak Road and singled out no one for special mention. But that is another story, one involving Grant, Meade, Warren and Sheridan, particularly the latter two.

For the moment, however, Chamberlain had won for Warren an objective that Grant, originally, had wanted very badly, a lodgement on the White Oak Road. It seemed to Chamberlain and the Fifth Corps officers that, with both the Second and Fifth Corps close to the enemy's lines, if Sheridan could have disengaged himself at Dinwiddie Court House and have dashed up with a division of cavalry between the Fifth Corps and Five Forks, a large part of Lee's army could have been destroyed and the end brought much sooner to its realization. But the roar of action in Sheridan's direction just now roused both curiosity and apprehension; after all, the left flank of the Fifth Corps was exposed. Furthermore, for some strange reason the waves of sound seemed to be receding toward Dinwiddie. What could have happened to Sheridan? It was becoming evident that the great objective, the destruction of Lee's army, was, for the present, to be put aside. As Chamberlain expressed it, "... another, and by far minor, objective interposed. Instead of the cavalry coming to help us complete our victories at the front, we were to go to the rescue of Sheridan at the rear."

That movement, with its ultimate results, was to plunge Chamberlain squarely into the middle of one of the great personal tragedies of the war, to reveal him again in the stress of emergency as one of the finest combat generals in the Union army, and to lead him to perhaps the greatest honor of his career.

☞ ☞ ☞ VII ☞ ☞ ☞

FIVE FORKS TO APPOMATTOX

THE battle of Five Forks, referred to even by Southerners as the Waterloo of the Confederacy, was a decisive battle in that it forced Lee to evacuate Petersburg and Richmond and to attempt a withdrawal that he hoped would effect a junction with General Joseph Johnston's army in North Carolina. But Five Forks was also one of the most confused battles of the war, and, partially because of the confusion, it brought about the downfall of General Gouverneur Kemble Warren at the hands of Phil Sheridan. Chamberlain, fond of Warren and respecting Sheridan, found himself not only taking an active part in this important crossroads battle but also serving as an unwitting agent (and our chief source of information) in the crisis of the famous Sheridan-Warren controversy.

The controversy has consumed thousands of printed pages since it occurred; it poisoned the life of an accomplished officer with a fine record; and it set an uneasy precedent for the removal of army officers. When Grant sent Sheridan to destroy the Southside Railroad and sever Lee's communications with the South, Lee foiled Sheridan by despatching General Anderson's corps which, with Confederate cavalry, drove the Union cavalry back to Dinwiddie Court House. On March 30, a day of rain during which General Griffin congratulated Chamberlain's brigade for its gallantry and firmness on the Quaker Road the previous afternoon, Sheridan rode over to see Grant at the latter's headquarters south of Gravelly Run.

Sheridan's mission was to ask for the Sixth Corps to break the enemy's right. Grant, however, said that because of the condition of the roads Sheridan would have to use cavalry alone. Besides, the Sixth was miles to the east in the Petersburg trenches and would take too long coming into action. Disappointed, Sheridan returned, visiting Warren on the way, and discovered that the Confederates, reinforced by Pickett's division, were entrenching along the White Oak Road to Five Forks. He again asked for the Sixth Corps; Grant now offered him the Fifth, but he declined. Sheridan explained later that he had nothing against Warren, whom he knew but slightly, or the Fifth Corps; rather that he knew the Sixth Corps very well, having compaigned successfully with it in the Shenandoah Valley. The fighting that the Fifth Corps heard late on March 31 after Chamberlain had crossed the White Oak Road was from Sheridan and Pickett sharply engaged at Dinwiddie Court House and Five Forks. Foiled in his attempt to smash Pickett, Sheridan still saw an opportunity to do so if Grant would let him have the Sixth Corps. The request being impracticable, Grant again offered him the Fifth, which, by this time, Sheridan was ready to accept. Accordingly, late in the afternoon of the 31st, Meade directed Warren to move to Sheridan's support.

The Fifth Corps was one of the crack corps in the army, but it was definitely different from the others. Fitz-John Porter had originally led it, and, based on General Sykes' division of Regulars, it acquired very early a reputation for being a well-disciplined, well-drilled, "spit-and-polish" out-

fit that endeared it to McClellan's heart. Though Porter and
McClellan were long since gone from the field and the last
of the old Regulars had been buried at Gettysburg and in
the Wilderness campaign, the Corps still retained an un-
mistakable flavor of the Regular Army. For example, Tom
Chamberlain, when a private, would never think of sitting
down in his brother Lawrence's presence without the latter's
permission. Most of the higher officers were West Pointers
or at least Regular Army—Griffin and Ayres were Mexican
War veterans and artillerists, while Crawford had been with
Major Anderson at Fort Sumter and was, of all things,
originally an army surgeon! Warren had graduated second
in his class at West Point and had become an army engineer.
This corps was very methodical and precise in its preparations. If it lacked something of the dash of the Second Corps
and the rough-and-tumble, get-up-and-go attitude of the
Sixth, still it could march and hit very hard, it had a great
reputation for tenacity, and it possessed fighters like Chamberlain and Bartlett, an old Sixth Corps man, who were fully
as aggressive as any in the army. Warren, formerly of the
Second Corps himself, wrote Chamberlain after the war
that he considered the Second, Fifth, and Sixth Corps by
far the best in the army, and he named them in that order.
The great misfortune of the Fifth Corps in the latter part of
the war was its early association with McClellan, which made
it no favorite with the War Office people or the Western
generals like Grant and Sheridan. Fifth Corps officers even
believed their promotions were slower to come through than
those in other corps because of this antagonism. Hence,
despite Phil Sheridan's statement that he had nothing
against the Fifth Corps, the association was not likely to
be happy.

Bangor Theological Seminary. From an early photograph.

Bowdoin College, Brunswick, Maine, 1860.
First Parish Church is at extreme left.

Marye's Heights, Fredericksburg.
The 20th Maine attacked at the extreme left.

The Stonewall, Marye's Heights, Fredericksburg, where the Confederates stopped Chamberlain and the 20th Maine. The photograph was taken from inside the Stonewall after Sedgewick's successful attack in the Chancellorsville campaign.

Little Round Top, Gettysburg, showing stone defense works at southern end occupied by brigade to which Chamberlain's regiment belonged.

Little Round Top, Gettysburg, as seen in a contemporary Brady photograph. There appears to be no contemporary photograph of the spur where Chamberlain's regiment fought, but according to Frederick Tilberg, Park Historian, the above photograph was taken from a point 100 yards northwest of Chamberlain's position.

Rives' Salient, Petersburg, from a photograph taken in 1865. Chamberlain was severely wounded, June 18, 1864, attacking over the open area in the left background.

Ruins of Fort Mahone—"Fort Damnation." Cannon in these works enfiladed Chamberlain's attack on Rives' Salient.

Joshua L. Chamberlain as a brigadier general after his recovery from his Petersburg wound.

Surrender of Lee's troops at Appomattox. No photograph of the surrender appears to exist. The above is a sketch of the surrender as described by Chamberlain to the artist, J. R. Chapin. Chamberlain is the central figure in the mounted group on the left.

Joshua L. Chamberlain in the 1890's.

Harold Wyllys Chamberlain, Bowdoin, 1881

Courtesy of Miss Rosamond Allen

Grace Chamberlain Allen. Photograph taken about 1906.

From the Arthur T. and David T. Parker Collection, Bowdoin College

The Chamberlain House, Brunswick, Maine.

Joshua L. Chamberlain at the age of 83.

Before Meade's directive arrived, and while Chamberlain was standing outside his own headquarters listening to Sheridan's battle, Warren came up to him and asked him if he thought the sound was approaching or receding. Chamberlain replied that he thought it was receding toward Dinwiddie. To Warren's question of where the duty of the Fifth Corps lay in the absence of orders Chamberlain said that since Grant was looking out for Sheridan, he would probably send units of the Second Corps rather than the Fifth in view of the now-known fact that Lee himself was confronting the Fifth. On the other hand, Chamberlain pointed out, the Fifth Corps would probably be blamed for not sending assistance to Sheridan.

"Well, will you go?" Warren asked.

"Certainly, General, if you think best," Chamberlain replied, "but surely you do not want me to abandon this position."

With Griffin coming up, Warren asked him to send Bartlett's 3rd Brigade to harass the rear of the troops attacking Sheridan.

As Griffin went to hurry Bartlett on his way across country along a wood road, Chamberlain and Warren crept forward on hands and knees to the extreme picket line. A sudden stir of activity along the line brought such a discharge of Confederate cannon and musketry that they could see the enemy was massed in considerable strength. Later Chamberlain put his troops in bivouac, uneasy about the situation with only his and Gregory's brigades available. Both brigadiers were on the picket line all during the evening.

Meanwhile Warren became the recipient of as confusing a batch of directives as was ever issued by an American army headquarters. As Chamberlain indicated subsequently, there were simply too many commanders in the field with overlapping authority—Grant commanding all the armies; Meade in charge of the Army of the Potomac, which was divided by Ord's Army of the James; and Sheridan commanding the cavalry and now getting the Fifth Corps. Orders from Grant and Meade to Warren, though their headquarters were side-by-side, were so contradictory that it is a wonder Warren kept his head at all that night.

Orders for the 1st Division in particular were baffling. Warren was to hurry a brigade to Sheridan, and he had already sent Bartlett's. The brigade was to go by the Boydton Plank Road instead of the road nearest the fighting; Warren therefore sent off three regiments under General A. L. Pearson by the Boydton Road. He was then ordered to dispatch Griffin's entire division by the same road. Since Griffin's division was now scattered, he put Ayres' division on the march. Next he was ordered to hurry the divisions of Ayres and Crawford the way Bartlett had gone and to be sure to have Griffin take the Boydton Plank Road. But since Ayres had already started on the Boydton Road, Griffin and Crawford were to take Bartlett's route. This last order really fouled up the situation because Griffin, acting according to instructions, had already ordered Bartlett to withdraw and join the rest of the 1st Division on the Boydton Road.

All this was complicated enough, but that evening within two hours Warren received further orders involving his corps that must have set his head to spinning. Grant ordered him to dig in where he was along the White Oak Road and fight the next day. Grant then ordered him to fall back to the Boydton Plank Road and hurry a division by that road to Sheridan. At this point Meade jumped into the ring with instructions for Griffin to take the Boydton Plank Road and

Ayres and Crawford to follow Bartlett's route across country to the Crump Road and fall on Pickett's rear. This order would have reversed the direction for Ayres and Crawford that Grant had indicated in his second order. Meade then proposed sending Ayres and Crawford ten miles around by the Quaker Road with instructions to forget about attacking the Confederate rear. Warren was thus asked to do what Stephen Leacock's mythical rider did—to jump on his horse and ride off at once in all directions! Finally, however, the Fifth Corps got underway in the darkness, Ayres' division by the Boydton Road and Griffin and Crawford by Bartlett's wood road. Small wonder, in view of such confusing and contradictory orders, that when Chamberlain's brigade met Bartlett's returning along the mucky wood road and told the weary men they would have to go back again without rest or rations, the 20th Maine and other veteran regiments loosed a storm of sulphurous language which, as Chamberlain expressed it, "could be conjectured only by a veteran of the Old Testament dispensation."

Grant had also further complicated the situation for the Fifth Corps. He informed Sheridan that the Corps was now no longer responsible to Meade but to Sheridan himself. "When news of this leaked out," Chamberlain said, "we kept our heads and hearts as well as we could; for we thought both would be needed." Such information to Sheridan was not in itself irregular; quite the contrary. But when Grant also notified Sheridan that the Corps would reach him by midnight, thus giving the energetic cavalryman the hope of an early morning attack, Grant was stretching the limit of reasonable expectation. The Fifth Corps had seen considerable action on the 31st and was tired from the marching and counter-marching during the night. The roads were like pudding, and the men's clothing was plastered with the sticky, red Virginia mud, while the artillery sank to the wheel hubs. Furthermore, the disengagement operation from the White Oak Road without the enemy's suspecting what was going on was delicate and took a long time. Orders had actually to be whispered. Worse still, the bridge on the Boydton Plank Road over Gravelly Run had been destroyed by the Confederates, a piece of intelligence evidently unknown to Grant, and the stream, swollen to three times its normal size, could not be forded by infantry. Warren's engineers, working swiftly and efficiently, tore a house to pieces to bridge the stream, but it was two o'clock in the morning before troops could cross it.

Chamberlain met Sheridan as the sun was coming up. Saluting, Chamberlain said, "I report to you, General, with the head of Griffin's Division."

Sheridan returned his salute, then challenged him. "Why did you not come before? Where is Warren?"

"He is at the rear of the column, sir."

"That is where I expected to find him," Sheridan growled. "What is he doing there?"

"General, we are withdrawing from the White Oak Road, where we fought all day. General Warren is bringing off his last division, expecting an attack."

At that moment Griffin came up, and Chamberlain was glad to retire. He noted that, ironically, his troops were on the very ground the enemy had occupied the night before when the arrival of Bartlett's brigade in their rear had led the Confederates first to think Warren's whole corps was at hand and then to withdraw to Five Forks where they were now entrenching.

As the divisions waited on the road from Dinwiddie Court

House to Five Forks—waiting for the cavalry, this time, to complete a reconnaissance at Five Forks, Griffin came over and joined Chamberlain sitting by a brook. He said that Sheridan was irked because of a reproof from Grant for not having done more the previous day and that Grant had given Sheridan the power to remove Warren from command of the Fifth Corps if he was dissatisfied with Warren. Both Griffin and Chamberlain sympathized with Sheridan but were anxious for Warren, and made up their minds to do their best this April Fool's Day to make things turn out right. They knew that although Grant had once considered giving Warren the Army of the Potomac if Meade should be killed, he had long since changed his mind. They knew that he was suspicious of Warren from those May days in the Wilderness when Warren had put his troops into battle in slow and piecemeal fashion. They knew also that the cantankerous Meade was likewise displeased with Warren for the latter's conduct after arriving before Petersburg. It seemed to Chamberlain that the fates had marked Warren and perhaps the Fifth Corps for some sort of final disaster. The meeting of Warren and Sheridan had been civil but scarcely more. Chamberlain wished that the distracted Warren had been warmer in his manner toward Sheridan, "for a voice of doom was in the air." Chamberlain found himself thinking that friends sometimes hurt one more than enemies, and wondered when this long delayed action would begin.

For that matter Sheridan was wondering the same thing and getting impatient. His cavalrymen were containing Pickett, but they needed infantry to complete the job, and the infantry was here if Warren would ever get it moving. Actually it was noon before the entire Fifth Corps was up. The men were tired, sluggish, and out of sorts. Chamberlain's brigade was lucky; having been first on the field, it had had several hours of rest. Between two and four o'clock the Corps formed, Sheridan restless and uneasy and apprehensive that his cavalry would run out of ammunition. Warren said he could not advance before four o'clock but he would be willing to go at any time with what units were available and let the rest follow. Sheridan thought Warren apathetic, which Chamberlain knew to be untrue, and when the cavalryman said it looked as if the sun would go down before the battle began, Warren piqued him by remarking that "Bobby Lee was always getting people into trouble."

Meanwhile Sheridan collected Warren's general officers and explained the plan of attack. With his sabre he drew a diagram in the soil. The cavalry was to divert the enemy on his right front while the Fifth Corps slipped around and hit the Confederates on their left and rear. At the extreme left of their line, the Confederates were bent sharply back in a "return," as it was called, for one hundred and fifty yards in order to protect their flank. Ayres' division was to strike the angle of the "return," while Crawford and Griffin were to sweep to Ayres' right and fall upon their rear. Chamberlain thought the diagram "perfectly clear . . . a splendid piece of tactics. . . ."

Then as four o'clock arrived and the Corps began its march, a diagram from Warren arrived which surprised Chamberlain. It showed the entire Corps, stationed oblique to the Gravelly Church Road, hitting the enemy's main line of resistance before a single brigade touched the White Oak Road. Instead of Ayres striking the angle, Crawford's division was shown pointing toward it, whereas Ayres, if he swung to the left as directed, would hit the enemy not from the rear as Sheridan had planned but from the front over in the

Union cavalry sector. To make matters more confusing, the
order accompanying the diagram was pretty much as Sheridan had wanted it. Chamberlain rode over to Griffin for an
explanation. Griffin replied, "We will not worry ourselves
about diagrams. We are to follow Crawford. Circumstances
will soon develop our duty." Puzzled, Chamberlain returned
to his and Gregory's brigades—both under his command this
day—and reflected that no doubt the enemy was "Susceptible

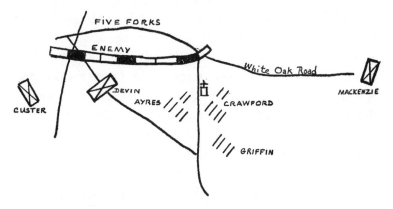

WARREN'S DIAGRAM OF APRIL 1, 1865

to discovery, whatever might be true of roads, diagrams, or
understandings." Certainly there appeared to be little agreement. Had Sheridan misunderstood the information given
him by his reconnoitering cavalrymen? Had these scouts
themselves been mistaken? Had Warren misinterpreted
Sheridan?

But Chamberlain had little more time for reflection, for
the Fifth Corps with Ayres and Crawford abreast and Griffin
in support soon struck the White Oak Road. To everyone's
surprise there was almost no opposition—the Corps had

marched about a half-mile east of where it should have been, leaving Sheridan's dismounted cavalrymen to the west to fight alone. What was worse, Crawford soon encountered a thin line of dismounted Confederate cavalrymen who put up enough of a fight for him to think this was the real thing. Not a bright man despite his lofty air and conscious gentility, given to the punctilious and literal obedience of orders that often saved him from the criticism of his commanding officers, Crawford went smashing off through the woods and getting farther and farther away from where he should have been and being followed by Griffin. Ayres also missed his objective, but since he was on the left and closer to where the Union cavalrymen were engaged, he heard the fighting. A competent old-army Regular, he pivoted at a ninety-degree angle to come back upon the Confederate entrenchments. Sheridan was with his division and kept hurrying the Union skirmishers into contact with the enemy.

Meanwhile as Warren raced ahead to get Crawford and Griffin's divisions back into the fight, Chamberlain took the initiative himself. Hearing Ayres sharply engaged somewhere on the left, he informed Bartlett, then took his own and Gregory's brigade by the left flank to Ayres' assistance. Griffin saw him, waved him on, then rode toward Warren and Bartlett. At the head of a gully, Chamberlain formed a battle line, opened fire, and led his men in. Once the battle was joined, he spurred over toward Ayres. On his way he met Sheridan astride his black horse, Rienzi, and wearing a frown almost as dark.

"By God, that's what I want to see!" Sheridan bellowed. "General officers at the front. Where are your [other] general officers?"

When Chamberlain replied that Warren was in the field to the north and that he himself had come to help Ayres by Griffin's order, Sheridan nodded vigorously and barked, "Then you take command of all the infantry round here, and break this damn. . . ."

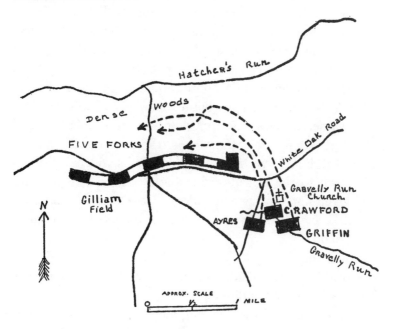

THE MOVEMENT AS EXECUTED

Chamberlain was off before Sheridan even finished his order. He rounded up scattered groups of bewildered men. One soldier he found hiding behind a stump, grimacing at the bullets hitting close. "Look here, my good fellow," Chamberlain called out, "don't you know you'll be killed here in less than two minutes? This is no place for you. Go forward!"

"But what can I do?" the man protested, echoing the feeling of the individual soldier in any war who has become separated from his outfit. "I can't stand up against all this alone!"

"No, that's just it," said Chamberlain. "We're forming here. I want you for guide center. Up and forward!"

Chamberlain quickly formed on the man a line of two hundred fugitives whom a staff officer led into the fight. As Chamberlain observed later, "My poor fellow only wanted a token of confidence and appreciation to get possession of himself. He was proud of what he did, and so I was for him."

Chamberlain now saw Ayres' 3rd Brigade under General Gwyn emerging from the woods, the men excited and in good line, but Gwyn himself apparently bewildered. Galloping down to the brigade, Chamberlain asked him if Ayres had given him any specific orders. "No, General," Gwyn replied, "I have lost Ayres. I have no orders. I don't know what to do."

"Then come with me," Chamberlain said. "I will take the responsibility. You shall have all credit. Let me take your brigade for a moment!"

Chamberlain led the cheering men in beside his own brigade, which was about ready to link up with Ayres. Suddenly Sheridan reined up alongside him, wild with anger. "You are firing into my cavalry!"

"Then the cavalry have got into the rebels' place," Chamberlain replied boldly. "One of us will have to get out of the way. What will you have us do, General?"

"Don't you fire into my cavalry, I tell you!" Sheridan stormed.

Chamberlain was exasperated at the fiery little man. As he explained later, "I felt a little left out in the cold by General

Sheridan's calling them 'my cavalry,' as if we were aliens and did not belong to him also; but, whosesoever they were, I could not see what business they had up here at the 'angle.' This was our part of the field. The plan of the battle put them at the enemy's right and center, a mile away on the Dinwiddie Road and beyond."

Just then Ayres came up, and Sheridan turned his anger from Chamberlain to the division commander, accusing him of the same offense. But Ayres had a quick temper, too, and replied crisply, "We are firing at the people who are firing at us! These are not carbine shot. They are minié-balls. I ought to know."

Ayres and Chamberlain, however, adjusted their firing so that they would not be shooting at each other or the presumed cavalrymen of Sheridan, and when they had done so, Griffin appeared.

"We flanked them gloriously!" Sheridan called out to him.

But Griffin had business elsewhere and soon left Chamberlain alone with Sheridan. The bullets were whistling so close that Chamberlain became disturbed for Sheridan's safety. Yet when he asked him not to stay in such an exposed place, Sheridan "gave me a comical look, and answered with a peculiar twist in the toss of his head, that seemed to say he didn't care much for himself, or perhaps for me, 'Yes, I think I'll go!' " And away he went, right into the controversial cross-fire, clenching his fist and shouting to the troops, "Smash 'em! Smash 'em!"

Away Chamberlain flew, too, swinging his troops to the right and down the rear of the entrenchments. Portions of two enemy regiments surrendered to him after hand-to-hand fighting, but Chamberlain had no time to feel exultant. Part of Bartlett's brigade which had now come into the fight was

in trouble, including the 20th Maine. Chamberlain ordered
Gregory's brigade to Bartlett's assistance, then turned to his
own left center where the redoubtable Glenn with a battalion
of the 198th Pennsylvania was meeting fierce resistance.
Promising Glenn a colonelcy if he could take the breastwork,
Chamberlain saw the battalion bound over the entrenchments
in an overwhelming wave. But his delight turned to horror
when Glenn was mortally wounded. "War!" Chamberlain
groaned in despair, "nothing but the final, infinite good, for
men and God, can accept and justify human work like that!"

To this grief was added a different kind of tragedy. Captain
Brinton of Griffin's staff dashed up and asked if he knew that
Griffin now commanded the Corps. Then into Chamberlain's
astonished ears he poured the amazing story. Warren had
finally caught up with Crawford and turned him toward the
battle. Actually in coming in as late as he did, Crawford
captured hundreds of Confederates fleeing to the rear. But
when Warren's chief of staff informed Sheridan, the cavalryman shouted, "By God, sir, tell General Warren he wasn't
in the fight!" Coming across Griffin, Sheridan said, "I put
you in command of the Fifth Corps!"

Appalled, Chamberlain soon found himself alongside Sheridan, who snarled at an officer who dared take time to report
the capture of three guns, then shouted to a crowd of gawking
soldiers, "I want you men to understand we have a record to
make before that sun goes down, that will make hell tremble!
—I want you there!" Then with Griffin and Chamberlain following, he leaped his horse over a breastwork. Chamberlain's
horse was struck again but kept going.

They were beyond the Forks now, but sharp fighting was
still going on. Ayres had just joined the group when Sheridan

said, "Get together all the men you can and drive on while you can see your hand before you!"

At Griffin's direction, Chamberlain assembled the 1st Division on the White Oak Road. As his bugler sounded the brigade calls, Warren appeared, riding slowly. Chamberlain explained what he was doing, and Warren replied, "You are doing just right, but I am not in command of the Corps." Sad for him, Chamberlain left to bring the division into the Gilliam field on the enemy's right. When the division was checked, Griffin ordered one of Crawford's colonels to assist. The colonel hesitated momentarily, then grasped his regimental colors and led his regiment forward. Instantly Warren snatched up his own Fifth Corps flag and galloped to the colonel's side. The two officers spurred right over the smoking entrenchments into the startled enemy. With the bluecoats pouring in behind them, the enemy resistance collapsed, and five thousand prisoners were captured.

As Warren rode slowly off the field, a staff officer handed him a confirmatory field order. By the light of the dying sun he read: "Major-General Warren, commanding the Fifth Army Corps, is relieved from duty and will at once report for orders to Lieutenant-General Grant, commanding Armies of the United States. By command of Major-General Sheridan."

His face stricken, Warren approached Sheridan and asked if now he would not reconsider his order. Sheridan, the fury of battle still in him, glared. "Reconsider. Hell! I don't reconsider my decisions. Obey the order!"

Nor did he ever reconsider. Nor did Chamberlain and the officers and men of the Fifth Corps ever forgive him for what they considered an unjust act made cruel by his refusal to reconsider it. A military court which Warren had pled for finally met and two years later, in 1882, after an enormous

mass of testimony, substantially vindicated him. By the time
the findings were promulgated in War Department orders,
however, the man whose career was damaged by Sheridan's
impulsive act and who had lived for so long under a cloud
was three months in his grave.

At the same time, Chamberlain admitted that he liked
Sheridan's style of fighting. Up to this point the army, said
Chamberlain, had gone into a battle with dogged resolution
and little flare, and when they won a vital point, the men
entrenched, a procedure Grant sanctioned. But Sheridan did
not entrench: "He pushes on, carrying his flank and rear with
him,—rushing, flashing, smashing." Chamberlain liked this
way of fighting—it was the kind at which he himself excelled.
Sheridan, indeed, had become Grant's driver, a tremendous
embodiment of will and energy. The Army of the Potomac
was a good army and deserved better of its commanders. As
a distinguished historian of the war has so aptly said, ". . . the
underlying trouble was simply that this army lacked the one
great ingredient for success: grim, ferocious, driving force
at the top." Sheridan was cruel to Warren, but had someone
of Sheridan's stamp been in command earlier in the war,
a man who dealt ruthlessly with delays, mistakes, genteel
efforts, and general incompetence, thousands of lives that
Chamberlain saw sacrificed on so many bloody fields might
have been saved and the war brought to an end in 1863.

That night of April 1, after Chamberlain had walked over
to Fifth Corps headquarters at the Forks and the officers
were sitting down with their backs against tree-trunks or
battered breastworks, Sheridan suddenly emerged from the
shadows. As the officers fell silent and started to their feet,
Sheridan waved them down and said in a voice that had
none of the strident tone of battle, "Gentlemen, I have come

over to see you. I may have spoken harshly to some of you today; but I would not have it hurt you. You know how it is: we had to carry this place, and I was fretted all day till it was done. You must forgive me. I know it is hard for the men, too; but we must push. There is more for us to do together. I appreciate and thank you all."

At this little speech, said Chamberlain, "All the repressed feeling of our hearts sprang out towards him. We were ready to blame ourselves if we had been in any way the cause of his trouble."

A little later another visitor arrived on horseback. This was George Alfred Townsend, a reporter for the New York *World*. As he looked around, bewildered, Chamberlain got up at once and went to him; he had met Townsend the day before. Now he told Townsend briefly about the victory, for which Sheridan was responsible.

"Where is Sheridan?" Townsend asked.

"There he sits, down there," Griffin and the rest replied.

Townsend then went over to where the short but compact cavalryman was sitting before a small fire, leaning against a tree and munching a piece of cheese. Close by lay young General George Custer, trying to sleep, his long yellow hair sprawled over his face. To Townsend's astonishment, Sheridan, who had few good things to say of reporters, answered all Townsend's questions concerning the battle and sketched the contest for him. The account Townsend submitted to the *World* made his reputation. He was fortunate to have caught Sheridan so relaxed—but, then, why not? As Chamberlain said of Five Forks, "It was Sheridan's battle. The glory of it is his." But it had also been a battle to which Chamberlain himself had made a substantial contribution and to whom a little of that glory properly belonged.

For the South the battle of Five Forks was a humiliation and a disaster. It was a humiliation because three of the Confederate generals were not even around until late in the action; Generals Thomas L. Rosser, Fitzhugh Lee, and George E. Pickett had been having a shad-bake deep in the pine forest north of Hatcher's Run and had not even heard the battle until it was nearly over. Five Forks was a disaster because, to save his line of retreat, Lee had to evacuate Petersburg and Richmond, a move underscored by the Sixth Corps' successful assault on the thinly held Petersburg defenses on April 2 after the news of Five Forks reached Grant.

With the two cities presently occupied by Union troops, the war in Virginia settled down into a race between the two armies—Lee to reach Johnston, and Sheridan, who led the pursuit, to cut him off. The days from April 2 to April 9 were for both armies an ordeal of ferocious marching, of fierce little fights which never quite blossomed into the last full-scale action that so many expected, and of savage hunger as the Confederates ran completely out of supplies and forage and the pursuers swept far ahead of their commissariat. The only people who really seemed to enjoy themselves were the cavalrymen of Sheridan and Custer, capturing batches of stragglers and foragers, burning barns, houses, railroad rolling stock—anything that might conceivably be of use to the enemy.

For Joshua Lawrence Chamberlain, still sore from his wounds and his exertions, and emotionally disturbed by Sheridan's attitude toward the Fifth Corps, the pursuit was enjoyable only because of its ultimate success. He always felt that it could have been shortened and lives saved had it been conducted differently. Delays occurred with Grant's passing the Sixth Corps and Ord's Army of the James on to Sheridan. Though an admirer of Grant, he deplored the General's deferring to Sheridan at the expense of Warren at Five Forks and of Meade and the Fifth Corps in the pursuit of Lee.

Chamberlain had an active part in the pursuit. On April 2, he swept across the Southside Railroad and captured the last Confederate train out of Richmond. Then as Confederate resistance developed, Bartlett, who now commanded the division, ordered him to take his own and Gregory's brigade and dislodge the enemy while the rest of the Fifth Corps tore up the railroad tracks and ties. After a sharp skirmish the enemy retired. The 3rd, the day Richmond was evacuated, was a day of marching. On the 4th, Chamberlain marched thirty-five miles and threw up a line across the Danville Railroad at Jetersville, where it looked as if a major battle would occur. On the 5th, the Second Corps came up to form on the Fifth's left and the Sixth on its right. The Army of the Potomac was thus together once again, though ailing George Meade was almost entirely ignored by the team of Grant and Sheridan, who did, however, agree to return the Fifth Corps to him. On the afternoon of the 5th, Chamberlain moved out on the Amelia Court House Road to support some of Sheridan's cavalry bringing in prisoners. The next day as the army pushed toward Amelia Court House, it found that Lee had fled. The Second and Sixth Corps then followed on the Confederates' heels, while the Fifth moved south to cut off a retreat in that direction. It had no part in the Sixth Corps' smashing victory at Saylor's Creek on the 6th. In fact, Chamberlain marched thirty-two miles that day and almost as many on the 7th.

The following day, April 8, Chamberlain considered exasperating. As he said in his official report, "Our march was frequently obstructed and tedious." By this time the Second and Sixth Corps were north of the Appomattox River and the Fifth Corps and Ord's Army of the James south of it, while ahead raced Sheridan's cavalry aiming to get in front of Lee and hold him long enough for the Union infantry to come up. At noon, when almost abreast of Lee, who was ten miles to the north, the Fifth Corps ground to a halt to let Ord's army pass. Ord as senior in rank to Griffin had precedence, but Chamberlain admitted that he wondered if it was for "some reasons other than military" that Ord's command should have been brought around to the extreme left to cooperate with Sheridan especially since, having marched long and hard, Ord's men began to straggle so badly that they slowed the Fifth Corps into a constant accordion-like action of sudden moves and halts. "We had managed hitherto to keep in pretty close touch with the cavalry," Chamberlain said, "but this constant checking up was far worse trial. It fretted our men almost to mutiny. . . . The head of our column seemed more like a mob than our patient well-disciplined soldiers. The headquarters wagons and pack mules which made the bulk of that real rabble ahead got unceremoniously helped along. Whoever blocked the way was served with a writ of ejectment in quite primitive fashion." After twenty-nine miles of this kind of frustration, Chamberlain bivouacked his men along the road at midnight.

He had hardly dropped off to sleep when a cavalryman splashed through the mud with a despatch. A sentry touched Chamberlain's shoulder: "Orders, sir, I think."

Chamberlain rose on his elbow, struck a match, and read with eyes smarting with fatigue a brief, thrilling note from Sheridan to the infantry commanders: "I have cut across the enemy at Appomattox Station, and captured three of his

trains. If you can possibly push your infantry up here
tonight, we will have great results in the morning."

In no time the bugles were screaming, and the tired troops
assembled on the road, almost twenty-four hours without
food. Still, with victory now at last within their grasp, many
of them (not all!) forgot their hunger and weariness. At
sunrise Chamberlain reached Appomattox Station. Already
he could hear the treble of the Union horse artillery and
the bass of the Confederate field guns, the fire-cracker sharp-
ness of the cavalry carbines and the heavier roll of enemy
musketry. Ord was hurrying to support the cavalry across
the Lynchburg Pike a mile beyond the court house. Ayres'
division of the Fifth Corps came next, followed by the 3rd
Brigade of the 1st Division, then Chamberlain's brigade and
Gregory's. Crawford's division brought up the rear, as usual
slow and deliberate in its movements.

Suddenly a cavalry staff officer dashed out of a wood road
to the right and approached Chamberlain. "General, you
command this column?"

"Two brigades of it, sir," Chamberlain replied, drawing
Charlemagne off to the side of the road; "about half the
First Division, Fifth Corps."

"Sir, General Sheridan wishes you to break off from this
column and come to his support. The rebel infantry is pressing him hard. Our men are falling back. Don't wait for
orders through the regular channels, but act on this at once."

Chamberlain reined Charlemagne about, facing the column, and his voice boomed out in a burst of orders. Sending
word to Griffin to have Crawford stay on the road, he took
his two brigades at the double through the woods and out
onto the edge of an open field. He dashed up to Sheridan,
who gave him a dark smile and an impetuous gesture,

and with these as his only orders Chamberlain hurriedly swung his troops into a double line of battle and drove forward. To the rear of the Confederates and pressing close were the Second and Sixth Corps. He could see Ord squarely across the Lynchburg Pike and Ayres and Bartlett forming to Ord's right to block General Gordon's greycoats. The Union cavalry, no longer able to stand off the great Stonewall Brigade pushing for the one escape route it thought it had left, whirled away like a swiftly changing curtain to reveal to the Confederates the blue wall of Chamberlain's infantry on the crest of a great bowl and moving rapidly forward behind a strong skirmish line. As the Confederates swung toward him, Chamberlain dropped a few shells among them which caused them to draw back.

Then Griffin rode up and joshed him for mistaking a peach tree in full bloom for a Confederate flag. Chamberlain grinned and jocularly apologized, saying he was getting a bit near-sighted and was unaccustomed to long-range fighting.

But Griffin was back again in a few minutes. "General," he said grimly, "I want you to go back and bring up Crawford's Division. He is acting in the same old fashion that got Warren into trouble at Five Forks. He should have been up here long ago. We need him desperately. He deserves to be relieved of his command."

The spirit of Sheridan was evidently contagious, and Chamberlain sought to turn Griffin's mood by dryly remarking that surely Griffin did not intend to relieve Chamberlain himself of his command to send him on a staff officer's assignment.

But Griffin remained serious. "I mean to put you in command of that division; I will publish an order to that effect."

"General, pardon me, but you must not do that," said Chamberlain earnestly, alarmed at the possible consequences for his friend which he did not hesitate to point out. "It would make trouble for everybody, and I do not desire the position. It would make great disturbance among Crawford's friends, and if you will pardon the suggestion they may have influence enough at Washington to block your confirmation as Major-General. Besides, I think General Baxter of the Third Division is my senior; that must settle it."

To his relief Crawford at last led his troops into line, forming between Gregory and Bartlett on the left. Chamberlain acknowledged that the incident was singular for such an occasion but that it showed "the variety of commotions that occupied our minds."

Presently he had all eyes for what was happening below him. It was, as he described it, "a mighty scene, fit cadence of the story of tumultuous years. Encompassed by the cordon of steel that crowned the heights about the Court House, on the slopes of the valley formed by the sources of the Appomattox, lay the remnants of . . . the Army of Northern Virginia —Lee's army! . . . It was hilly, broken ground, in effect a vast amphitheater, stretching a mile perhaps from crest to crest. On the several confronting slopes before us dusky masses of infantry suddenly resting in place; blocks of artillery, standing fast in column or mechanically swung into park; clouds of cavalry small and great, slowly moving, in simple restlessness. . . ." All at once the Union cavalry bugles sounded, and Sheridan's squadrons, their sabres glittering in the sun, wheeled into attack formation led by young Custer of the golden locks, with his broad sombrero turned up in front and the ends of his crimson cravat streaming over his shoulders. This was to be the end, a smashing, overpowering charge that would shatter forever the remnant of that once magnificent grey host. Chamberlain hastily moved over to his right flank which had been exposed by the cavalry withdrawal, and readied his infantry for the last great assault.

Suddenly a lone grey horseman bearing a white flag rode out of the Confederate lines and galloped straight toward Chamberlain. As the young staff officer approached, Chamberlain observed that the flag was a towel, and he wondered, whimsically, where in either weary, dirty army one could have found a towel, and a white one at that. Then the officer drew up before him, saluted, and said, "Sir, I am from General Gordon. General Lee desires a cessation of hostilities until he can hear from General Grant as to the proposed surrender."

Surrender! Chamberlain forced himself to be calm. "Sir, that matter exceeds my authority. I will send to my superior. General Lee is right. He can do no more."

While Chamberlain sent word to Griffin, two additional horsemen rode up. One was another Confederate officer from Longstreet's corps; the other, Colonel Whitaker from Custer's staff. Whitaker shouted, "This is unconditional surrender! This is the end!" Then after introducing his companion, he said, "I am just from Gordon and Longstreet. Gordon says 'For God's sake, stop this infantry, or hell will be to pay!' I'll go to Sheridan."

But the men were so excited at this point that Chamberlain had trouble halting them and not before a cannon shot killed a young lieutenant in the 185th New York, the last man to fall in the Army of the Potomac. Finally the order arrived to cease firing. Some of the soldiers simply stared at one another, disbelieving, and, when convinced, felt only relief that it was all over and a sympathy for their defeated enemies. Others, more exuberant, burst into cheers, threw their hats in the air, pummeled one another, and wept. Many

climbed up on fences, haystacks, even on the roofs of farm
buildings to see what was going on.

At this point General Gregory galloped up to Chamberlain
to find out what this weird departure from discipline meant.
" 'Only that Lee wants time to surrender,' I answer with stage
solemnity. 'Glory to God!' roars the grave and brave old
General, dashing upon me with an impetuosity that nearly
unhorsed us both, to grasp and wring my hand, which had
not yet had time to lower the sword. 'Yes, and on earth peace,
good will toward men,' I answered. . . ."

A truce was agreed upon until one o'clock with officers
from each side meeting between the lines and waiting for
Lee's answer to Grant's summons to surrender. Sheridan
alone, said Chamberlain, disliked the truce. He was all for
slamming into the Confederates and settling all questions
without asking them. On the other hand, "His natural disposition was not sweetened by the circumstance that he was
fired on by some of the Confederates as he was coming up
to the meeting under the truce." Three hours later, with the
expiration of the time, Griffin said to Chamberlain, "Prepare
to make, or receive an attack in ten minutes."

Obediently but reluctantly Chamberlain strode over to
Charlemagne, and rode to where his troops were waiting.
It seemed to him not like war but murder to reopen hostilities, but he got his troops into formation, his advanced
line across the road.

All at once he felt a strange sense of a powerful presence.
"Disquieted, I turned about, and there behind me, riding
in between my two lines, appeared a commanding form,
superbly mounted, richly accoutred, of imposing bearing,
noble countenance, with expression of deep sadness over-
mastered by deeper strength. It is no other than Robert E.

Lee! And seen by me for the first time within my own lines. I sat immovable, with a certain awe and admiration.

"Not long after, by another inleading road, appeared another form, plain, unassuming, simple, and familiar to our eyes, but to the thought as much inspiring awe as Lee in his splendor and his sadness. It is Grant! . . . Slouched hat without cord; common soldier's blouse, unbuttoned, on which, however, the four stars; high boots, mud-splashed to the top; trousers tucked inside; no sword, but the sword-hand deep in the pocket; sitting his saddle with the ease of a born master, taking no notice of anything, all his faculties gathered into intense thought and mighty calm. He seemed greater than I had ever seen him. . . . I forgot altogether to salute him."

About four o'clock the quiet but momentous conference in Wilmer McLean's house in Appomattox village ended, and the two principals departed. As he watched them leave, Chamberlain found himself again admiring both, but impressed with their differences. With the news of the surrender many of his men cheered. Throughout the army the rejoicing spread, regimental bands began to play, and someone started a cannon salute which Grant ordered to cease. But even authority could not suppress the glow in so many hearts, a glow kindled not so much by exultation—though that, too, was present—as by a soul-shaking relief that the killing was over at last. The day—warm, sunny, the blue sky broken only by an occasional white, puffy cloud—was filled with the promise of the awakening season. Peace had now come to the Virginia countryside, and this spring the dogwood would bloom as never before, enriched by the sacrifice of so many thousands of men the previous year. It was, somehow appropriately, Palm Sunday.

☞ ☞ ☞ VIII ☞ ☞ ☞

APPOMATTOX SURRENDER
TO GRAND REVIEW

THAT Palm Sunday night, April 9, 1865, General Griffin summoned Chamberlain to his headquarters. Griffin, General John Gibbon of the Twenty-Fourth Corps in Ord's Army of the James, and General Wesley Merritt of Sheridan's cavalry had been appointed as commissioners to work out with Confederate Generals Longstreet, Gordon, and Pendleton the details of the troop surrender. Though generous in his terms, Grant had insisted on a formal surrender of the Confederate arms and colors before a representative portion of the Union army. Chamberlain, said Griffin, was to have the honor of receiving the infantry surrender.

Chamberlain was deeply touched. At the same time he could not account for the honor except for his never having indulged in loose talk, for having minded his own business, for never having tried to curry favor with superior officers or newspaper reporters, and for having disciplined himself in self-control and patience—a virtue he acknowledged was not one of his prominent endowments. He was further mystified since he believed himself to be "socially unpopular among the 'high boys'"—he was never one to hang around higher headquarters and, of course, he was not Regular Army. Griffin, however, while undoubtedly having Chamberlain's minor virtues in mind, deeply appreciated the extraordinary

185

service that Chamberlain had rendered at great personal cost
and without, as yet, the recognition he merited. To give him
the honor of receiving the surrender would be both just and
proper. Grant, who liked Chamberlain, evidently felt the
same way himself. But Chamberlain always believed, and
rightly so, that Griffin had much to do with "General Grant's
kind remembrance."

Chamberlain was never truer to himself than in the modest
manner in which he accepted the command. The honor he
regarded as falling more to the Fifth Corps and the Army
of the Potomac, long-suffering and at last triumphant, than
to himself. In this spirit he requested that he be transferred
from the 1st Brigade, of which he was immensely proud,
to the 3rd Brigade, the real veterans of the 1st Division and
the Fifth Corps, the one with which he had been associated
in the early battles and which he had commanded after
Gettysburg.

Two days of rain followed the surrender conference, and
Tom Chamberlain, now division provost marshal, wrote home,
"How queer it seems—no artillery firing—no musketry firing—
all is quiet." He said Union and Confederate officers were
shaking hands and riding around together, the enlisted men
talking and chatting pleasantly together. On the 11th, the
Confederates had surrendered their artillery and cavalry,
with the Southerners grateful to Grant for allowing the men
who owned the animals to keep them for the spring plough-
ing. All this seemed strange when only days before the two
armies were at each other's throat.

But the prospect of the infantry surrender cut deep. It was
a humiliation for the Confederates that was almost intoler-
able. Few of them knew Chamberlain except as a terrific
fighter; he might be like Sheridan and Custer, who had taken

few pains to conceal their satisfaction. Gordon would lead
the grey remnant onto the field, and he was deeply distressed.
The morning of April 12 was chill and grey. It was the
anniversary of that day four years ago when a mortar shell
had burst over Fort Sumter in Charleston harbor. But this
was not 1861; it was another age. Chamberlain had his troops
up early. He had bade farewell to his gallant little 1st Brigade
and released the 2nd from his command. But he could not
forget them, for he considered that they, too, deserved to
share in the honors of this day of days. Accordingly he placed
the 1st Brigade in a line slightly to the rear of the 3rd, and
the 2nd across the street facing the 3rd and 1st. The left
of the 3rd Brigade rested near the fence enclosing the
McLean house. He thus had the whole 1st Division on parade,
and he thought this troubled the Division's real commander,
General Bartlett. But Bartlett made no comment; accompanied by his staff, he rode around and talked with groups
of Confederate officers. Chamberlain himself, mounted on
Charlemagne and in company of his own staff, took position
at the right of the 3rd Brigade line beneath the Stars and
Stripes and the flag of the 1st Division, a red Maltese cross
on a field of white.

It was now nine o'clock. The Confederates were falling in,
the Stars and Bars and the regimental battle-flags "crowded
so thick, by thinning out of men," said Chamberlain, "that
the whole column seemed crowned with red." Soon the dusty,
tattered troops moved forward at route step. There was no
band, not even a drum. Some soldiers were dejected; others,
defiant or apathetic; all, depressed. At their head rode General Gordon, who had risen from a captain to a major general
and corps commander. In the last months he had been Lee's
greatest fighter, and Tom Chamberlain thought him the best-

looking soldier he had ever seen. Somehow it was fitting that the commanders of the troops in this solemn ceremony— Chamberlain and Gordon—were both superb soldiers and men of great ability and character.

As Chamberlain watched the remnant of Lee's once-great army, perhaps the most effective fighting instrument of its size ever created by the American people, the significance of the occasion profoundly impressed him. He had earlier resolved to recognize the moment by saluting the Southern troops and had so informed his regimental commanders. He was aware of the responsibility he was assuming, aware, too, that criticisms would follow, as indeed they did. But his chief reason, he said, "was one for which I sought no authority nor asked forgiveness. Before us in proud humiliation stood the embodiment of manhood: men whom neither toils and sufferings, nor the fact of death, nor disaster, nor hopelessness could bend from their resolve; standing before us now, thin, worn, and famished, but erect, and with eyes looking level into ours, waking memories that bound us together as no other bond; was not such manhood to be welcomed back into a Union so tested and assured?" What people often forgot was that Chamberlain had once been a theological student and a professor of religion and that the moral values of a question or situation weighed heavily in his decisions.

Presently Gordon and the head of the leading division column—in this instance, the old Stonewall Brigade—drew almost abreast of the little knot of Union officers under the flags. Chamberlain turned and spoke a word to a man at his side. Instantly a bugle call rang out, and the entire 1st Division of the Fifth Corps, regiment by regiment in succession, brought its muskets from "order arms" to "carry arms," the marching salute.

Gordon was riding erect, but with his chin on his chest and his eyes on the ground. As he heard the call and the machine-like shift of arms, he looked up, startled. Then he caught the significance of the movement, and his whole attitude changed. Wheeling his horse toward Chamberlain, he touched the animal slightly with the spur so that it reared, and as the horse's head came down in a graceful bow, Gordon brought his sword-point down to his boot-toe. Then wheeling back toward his own column, he gave the command to carry arms. The two armies thus accorded each other the final recognition of gallant opponents. But, said Chamberlain, "On our part not a sound of trumpet more, nor roll of drum; not a cheer, nor word nor whisper of vain-glorying, nor motion of man standing again at the order, but an awed stillness rather, and breath-holding, as if it were the passing of the dead!"

He watched as the Confederates of each division halted, faced the Union troops and dressed their ranks. Then they stacked their arms, unslung their cartridge boxes and hung them on the stacks. Finally they folded their tattered colors and laid them down, a number of soldiers rushing from the ranks and pressing the worn banners to their lips, while tears trickled down many a leathern cheek. Presently Union details gathered up the arms and flags. To one such group, a Confederate said, unashamedly weeping as he delivered his flag, "Boys, this is not the first time you have seen that flag. I have borne it in the front of battle on many a victorious field and I had rather die than surrender it to you."

"My brave fellow," said Chamberlain, leaning forward in his saddle, "I admire your noble spirit, and only regret that I have not the authority to bid you keep your flag and carry it home as a precious heirloom."

Small wonder that an incident like this should have been repeated all over the South and that Gordon, who became a remarkably effective and popular public speaker in the post-war years, should time and again allude in the highest terms to Chamberlain, whom he called, "One of the knightliest soldiers of the Federal army."

In the course of that trying day a number of Confederate officers of general rank came up to speak to Chamberlain. "General," said one, "this is deeply humiliating; but I console myself with the thought that the whole country will rejoice at this day's business." Another said, "You astonish us by your honorable and generous conduct. I fear we should not have done the same by you had the case been reversed." A third went even further: "I went into that cause and I meant it. We had our choice of weapons and of ground, and we have lost. Now"—pointing to the Stars and Stripes—"that is my flag, and I will prove myself as worthy as any of you."

Most of the Confederates, however, were too deeply humiliated to reverse themselves so quickly, though they were rarely as outspoken as the brother-in-law of General Meade's wife, a former governor of Virginia, a caustic, aggressive lawyer, and an able military leader if not very popular. Toward the Confederate officers and men, the Union troops had been uniformly sympathetic and respectful, but when they saw this smartly attired officer, a small, thin man with a red face, a sharp shrill voice, and tobacco juice trickling from his mouth start abusing his brigade for not dressing its line quickly enough, they grew angry. One of his own men called out, "Look at him! he is brave enough now, but he never was so near the Yankees before in his life." "Who is he? Who is he?" a private in the 118th Pennsylvania asked. "Oh, he's General Henry A. Wise!" a Confederate replied.

This was too much for veterans like those in the 118th Pennsylvania and the 20th Maine. They thought of brave, crazy old John Brown and Governor Henry A. Wise who had ordered his execution. Instantly the bluecoats started to jeer: "Who hung John Brown?" "Where did you steal your coat?" "Hang him to a sour apple tree!" "Shoot him!"

Chamberlain saw Wise looking sour and disgusted and tried to cheer him up by saying he thought the conduct of both sides this day augured well for the future. "You're mistaken, sir," Wise said. "You may forgive us but we won't be forgiven. There is a rancor in our hearts which you little dream of. We hate you, Sir."

A moment later, noticing two rips in the breast of Chamberlain's coat and a torn sleeve as well, he said in a milder tone, "Those were ugly shots, General. Where did you get these?"

When Chamberlain said that he had received them on the Quaker Road fighting Wise's own brigade, Wise exclaimed, "I suppose you think you did great things there. I was ordered to attack you and check your advance; and I did it too with a vim, till I found I was fighting three army corps, when I thought it prudent to retire."

At Chamberlain's informing him that it was three regiments rather than corps, he switched the subject to the way the paroles had been made out, which he denounced angrily as most un-lawyerlike. As Chamberlain finally turned away in disgust, Wise said, "You go home, you take these fellows home. That's what will end the war."

"Don't worry about the end of the war," Chamberlain answered. "We are going home pretty soon, but not till we see you home."

The long, momentous day finally ended, a never-to-be-forgotten experience in the life of Joshua Lawrence Chamberlain.

The next day, April 13, General Griffin strongly recommended his promotion to major general. Mentioning specifically Chamberlain's work on the Quaker Road, at Five Forks, during the subsequent marches, and at Appomattox, Griffin said, "General Chamberlain's bravery and efficiency were such as to entitle him to the highest commendation." Griffin followed this up with a reminder on April 29. In the summer the brevet of major general finally came through, given "for conspicuous gallantry and meritorious service in action on the Quaker Road, March 29, 1865," and ranked from that date.

Meanwhile he received formal command of the 1st Division, and one of his first duties was to keep his men in hand when news of Lincoln's assassination arrived. The Fifth Corps had left Appomattox on Saturday, April 15, and on Sunday afternoon reached the vicinity of Farmville. About four o'clock the headquarters officers of the 1st Division were listening to their fine German band when a mud-splashed cavalryman handed Chamberlain a telegram. He read that Lincoln was dead, Secretary of State Seward was dangerously wounded, and the rest of the Cabinet, Grant, and other high government officials had been marked out for destruction.

His sense of responsibility overbore his shock, and his first thought was for the effect of this news on the soldiers. He quietly thanked the members of the German band, then dismissed them and summoned his regimental commanders. He wanted a double guard thrown around the camp; they should get all their men in and allow none to leave. He felt that the soldiers could be trusted to bear any blow but this, so great was their love for Lincoln. They might take this town apart in their anger and grief.

Afterward, the lady of the mansion, in the yard of which the headquarters tents were pitched, asked what had disturbed him.

"It is bad news for the South," Chamberlain said.

"Is it Lee or Davis?" she asked anxiously.

"I must tell you, Madam, with a warning," he said. "I have put your house under a strict guard. It is Lincoln."

To his regret he saw relief on her face. "The South has lost its best friend, Madam," he said stiffly.

He went at once to Griffin, and the two hunted up Meade. The result of the conference was that, with the assassins evidently intending to destroy the government, the army should move on to Washington at once and make Grant dictator until confidence was restored in constitutional government. Chamberlain admitted subsequently that, when the crisis had passed, the plan seemed ridiculous but that, at the time, there was little to laugh at.

Fortunately the troops kept their poise, though tents, colors, sword-hilts and left arms were presently draped with mourning rosettes of crape and the army halted its march, on orders from the War Department, for the period that Lincoln's funeral cortege was expected to be passing the Capitol. The division was formed in a hollow square facing inward, with Griffin as corps commander, and Ayres and Gregory on hand. In the center of the square was a platform of ammunition boxes from which Father Egan, the senior chaplain of the division, was to speak. Egan had a passionate love for the Union and was overwrought by Lincoln's murder. Chamberlain, who sat on the platform with him, cautioned him against stirring the men beyond control.

But, with his Irish warmth and oratorical power in full flight, Egan forgot the admonition. Using as his text, "And she, being instructed of her mother, said 'Give me here the head of John Baptist in a charger,'" he explained how the spirit of rebellion had led its advocates to murder the innocent and the just. He reminded the soldiers that Lincoln had loved them, and they, him. His death had been a sacrilege, and he asked them, rhetorically, if they intended to put up with it—here he paused dramatically.

At this point, observing the soldiers flushed and ready to reach for their stacked muskets, Chamberlain seized Egan's arm. "Father Egan, you must not stop. Turn this excitement to some good."

"I will," Egan whispered. His arm moved up and down in a sweeping gesture as he said to the troops, "Better so. Better to die glorious, than to live infamous. Better to be buried beneath a nation's tears, than to walk the earth guilty of a nation's blood. Better, thousand fold, forever better, Lincoln dead, than Davis living." Now he quickly turned the passion he had roused into a spirit of consecration to the cause of freedom and right. To Chamberlain's relief—and gratitude, Father Egan "gave us back to ourselves, better soldiers, and better men. Who that heard those burning words can ever forget them? And who that saw, can ever forget that congregation in the field?"

The next day the Fifth Corps resumed its march. From April 21 for over a week Chamberlain put the division to guarding a portion of the Southside Railroad for twenty-five miles outside Petersburg and restoring order in the area. Citizens were being subjected to a great deal of marauding by bands of Negroes, many of whom Chamberlain found very unruly and whose numbers gave them a kind of frenzy.

In their ignorance many of them turned their freedom into license, and Chamberlain issued stringent orders to his regimental commanders to suppress and punish such lawlessness.

Then, on May 3, the Fifth Corps marched toward Petersburg, moving past the recent battlefields and the long lines of entrenchments—"All forsaken now, the thundering salients and flaming crests." In Petersburg, General Warren reviewed the Corps from the balcony of the Bolingbroke Hotel. The drums ruffled, bands played, and the men cheered their old commander as he stood, his wife at his side, and took the final salute of the soldiers who had loved and trusted him. Yet of the Corps he had led over the Rapidan in that beautiful spring a year ago, one half had gone forever. "Warren, too," mused Chamberlain, "had gone in spirit, never to rise, with deeper wound than any who had gone before."

The Corps now moved rapidly through Richmond and on to Washington for a grand review of the Army of the Potomac and of Sherman's army. Across the Chickahominy and over the Totopotomoy the Corps went, much too swiftly for the men, who growled at the pace. One night on this march, when all was still in a bivouac under some straggling pines in the vicinity of Hanover Court House and heavy clouds moved across the sky, a nervous sentry woke Chamberlain to tell him that his horse was acting strangely. Chamberlain got up and went to the tethered Charlemagne, who was pawing the ground in a restless fashion. Suddenly Chamberlain's foot crunched on something that broke with the sound of dried twigs. He drew back and saw to his horror that he had put his foot through the rib cage of a skeleton. He noticed, too, that Charlemagne had pawed up two skulls. It was a disquieting scene in this brooding light, which disclosed other bones shining whitely amid the forest debris. The next

morning the soldiers also discovered the bones, and a few
veterans remembered that the 1st Division had fought a
battle on this spot back in 1862. They recognized the remains
of old comrades by breast-plates and other tokens—the 2nd
Maine had fought here. Mournfully they gathered up the
bones, packed them in empty cracker boxes, and loaded them
on the supply wagons for burial in the North.

Across the Pamunkey and the Mattapony the division
moved and, on the night of May 9th, bivouacked near
Fredericksburg. Soldiers visited the battlefield. Private Gerrish of the 20th Maine walked past a little church once filled
with screaming, groaning wounded; now he heard only the
strains of a familiar hymn: "Jesus, lover of my soul." He
found the breastworks on Marye's Heights leveled, the green
grass covering all. The air was soft and balmy. He heard the
tinkle of a cowbell in a distant field and the voices of children
playing in a yard below him. As he thought of the war now
over, of the comrades who had perished on these very slopes
in the roar of battle, he found the place and the silence
oppressive and hurried back to the bivouac. Chamberlain
likewise recalled with sadness those slopes once so heavily
flecked with blue that dreadful day of the army's life two
and one-half years ago—"what years and with what changes
of men!" As if to place the seal of tragedy on this field, the
next morning a wagoner about twenty rods away from the
tent of Lieutenant George H. Wood of the 20th Maine
carelessly fired a carbine. The bullet seriously wounded
Wood, who died the next day. The tragic irony of his having
fought from the beginning of the war and now to be killed
on the eve of his departure for home was not lost on either
his regiment or Chamberlain. The event cast a deep gloom
over the 20th Maine, while Chamberlain, though acknowl-

edging it as an accident, said that he did not treat it as such.

On the 10th the division passed near the old camping ground of 1862 where Chamberlain had learned from Ames what it meant to be an officer in command of troops. He recalled "Fighting Joe" Hooker and his famous reviews, the cavalry tournaments, the lively "Ladies Days" so dear to Dan Sickles—"days so bright and nights so silver toned." He also remembered Burnside's "Mud March," the failure at Chancellorsville, the return to Stoneman's Switch and the dreary smallpox hospital. How long ago it all seemed. Soldiers from his command visited the old camping ground, but, seeing the tall weeds, rank grass, and undergrowth overrunning everything, even the cemetery where they had buried comrades that first winter, they—like Gerrish at Fredericksburg—hastily rejoined the column "with heavy hearts." It was all part of a brave but melancholy past.

The next day was the hardest of the march. The roads were rough and ragged, the hills steep. A thunderstorm broke out, and the first bolt of lightning nearly stunned Chamberlain as he rode along the crest of a high hill. He saw the entire corps below him illuminated by an unearthly glare. Above the long, straggling black column of troops lightning leaped in a writhing river of flame along the muskets, spurting from the barrels so intensely that it looked as if the men were marching with bayonets fixed instead of sheathed. It was a wonder that hundreds were not killed instead of the driver and horses of a lone ambulance. On the column marched until well into the evening—and to a sodden bivouac, the water standing in pools where the men must lay their blankets. Chamberlain could not understand, any more than could his troops, why Army Headquarters had placed the bivouac areas so far apart that each day was almost like a forced march: "It seemed as if somebody was as anxious now to be rid of us as ever before to get us to the front."

The last morning, May 12, dawned bright but intensely cold after a night of high wind. The column took the road at nine o'clock half-frozen but with light hearts. Briskly now the men swept past Fairfax Court House, along the Columbia Pike, past Falls Church Station, and up to Arlington Heights. Presently Washington came into view, at first dimly because of a fog bank, then clearly as the fog blew away. To a Pennsylvania soldier the sight of the white dome of the Capitol against the blue sky was something incredibly beautiful, and his heart filled with gratitude. Private Gerrish of the 20th Maine felt like a crusader who, after weary marches and bloody battles, finally stood upon one of the hills encircling Jerusalem. Many soldiers cheered, but Chamberlain was silent as he considered what all this meant. At frightful cost the nation was delivered, and he and those in his beloved 20th Maine had come full circle. Arlington Heights was the place to which they had marched—or tried to march—on first arriving in Washington. It was from here that they had left for Antietam when they and the war were young. Not since those early days had he been on this ground, and neither he nor those in the regiment who had survived were quite the same men. He gazed earnestly at Lee's old home, lost forever to its owner. "Poor, great-hearted Lee," he mused. He wondered what Lee's place would be in the new country, wondered, too, if only in poetry it was true

> "That men may rise on stepping-stones
> Of their dead selves to higher things."

Not until May 23 did the grand review of the armies begin—the march had been, after all, part of the old army technique of "hurry up and wait." But there were many administrative details to attend to, old associations to renew and new ones to cement before the troops went home, and extra guards to post as Sherman's "Bummers" and Meade's "Bowery Boys" quarreled bitterly over the merits of their respective armies. Chamberlain, however, was grateful for the rest, though nothing but surgery would ease the sharp, persistent agony of his Petersburg wound. It was during this period of comparative inactivity that, in behalf of the officers of the 1st Division, he presented General Griffin with a jeweled battleflag in miniature. Griffin, who was to die of yellow fever in Texas within two years, accepted with a graceful speech in which he said to Chamberlain, "You yourself, General, a youthful subordinate when I first took command of this division, now through so many deep experiences risen to be its tested, trusted, and beloved commander, —you are an example of what experiences of loyalty and fortitude, of change and constancy, have marked the career of this honored division."

The grand review, in which the Army of the Potomac passed in review the first day and Sherman's army the second, was a great emotional experience for Chamberlain. The color of the spectacle was immensely stirring: the battleflags; the bands; the sidewalks, windows, balconies, even the house-tops crowded with gaily clad onlookers; the garlands, ribbons, and flowers bedecking the avenues; the never-ceasing but wave-like roar of welcome beating like surf on mighty rocks; the prancing cavalry; the rumbling gun-carriages; the seem-ingly endless blue column of infantry marching in company fronts equalized to twenty files each. After passing the re-

viewing stand on Charlemagne, with Tom Chamberlain and
Ellis Spear on his staff, Chamberlain was invited by the new
President to join the other notables and watch the troops.
Thereafter, for Chamberlain, the review was like a series of
pictures in which was written the history of the war as he
had seen it—the victories, the defeats, the gruelling marches,
the heroism, the suffering, the many thousands who had died.
So very many had perished whom he had known: Vincent
and O'Rorke, Weed and Hazlett, who went down on Little
Round Top; General Fred Winthrop of Ayres' division who
shared a homely lunch with him on a log at Five Forks a
half-hour before he was shot dead; "Crazy" James Rice of
the old 44th New York who caught it at Spottsylvania and
died gasping, "Turn my face toward the enemy!"; young
Major Charles MacEuen killed on the Quaker Road, brave
Glenn at the White Oak Road; thirteen officers, good friends,
shot at the head of their commands; innumerable acquaintances among the officers; and infinitely greater numbers of
his own enlisted men. All of these, the dead as well as the
living, were passing in review, for they shared a partnership
in the deliverance of the Union.

Nor had Joshua Lawrence Chamberlain done so badly
himself in any roll call of valor. He had engaged in almost
innumerable reconnaissances and skirmishes, and in twenty-
four battles large and small, capturing 2,700 prisoners and
eight battle flags. He had fought skillfully and heroically
almost beyond imagination, winning (eventually) the Congressional Medal of Honor for his gallantry and distinguished
service at Gettysburg, a promotion to brigadier general for
his effort at Rives' Salient before Petersburg, and (presently)
promotion to major general for his courage and efficiency
on the Quaker Road. At least five times horses were shot

from under him (counting Charlemagne thrice), and six times he was seriously or slightly wounded, twice by the same bullet at the Quaker Road, which would have finished him but for the field order book and brass mirror in his breast pocket, while the Minié ball at Rives' Salient nearly killed him in any event and was to cause him untold agony as long as he lived. Nor need one more than mention his bouts with malaria and pneumonia. This former theological student and professor of religion and modern languages at Bowdoin College was indeed one of the most remarkable soldiers in the Union army, combining to an extraordinary degree ability and valor.

As he reflected on the Civil War long afterward, Chamberlain, though still miserable from his wound, could find war not so dreadful, could, indeed, discern in it solid human values. While disposed to think that war, as a test of character, makes good men better and bad men worse, he said, ". . . we cannot accept General Sherman's synonym as a complete connotation or definition of war. Fighting and destruction are terrible; but are sometimes agencies of heavenly rather than hellish powers. In the privations and sufferings endured as well as in the strenuous action of battle, some of the highest qualities of manhood are called forth—courage, self-command, sacrifice of self for the sake of something held higher—wherein we take it chivalry finds its value; and on another side fortitude, patience, warmth of comradeship, and in the darkest hours tenderness of caring for the wounded and stricken—exhausting and unceasing as that of gentlest womanhood which allies us to the highest personality." In the last analysis Chamberlain was a romantic who could cheerfully defy war's terrors. He did not regard war as glamorous, but neither did he regard it as necessarily sordid and mean. For him it was still something of a contest between gentlemen, which was a long way indeed from Sherman's expressed view of later years and unrealistic even for the entire period of the Civil War, certainly from the time Grant entered the Wilderness. But Chamberlain was an individualist. Though his view of war was an anachronism, he never relinquished it nor fundamentally modified it.

At last the great pageantry of review was over. The muster rolls were checked, the payrolls tallied. Chamberlain saw the 20th Maine leave Washington in early June in the rush of men to their homes that follows every war in which Americans engage—some back to the farms, others to the factories, still others to the lands opening up in the Great West where the buffalo still roamed and where the Sioux were eventually to do to Custer what the outnumbered Confederates could not. What Chamberlain himself should do was not entirely clear to him but was becoming so. Yet, come what might, he was convinced that what he and so many like and unlike him had accomplished these past years would not disappear as the Army of the Potomac, that great organization, was now disappearing. For there was the overwhelming consciousness that "what we had lost and what we had won had passed into the nation's peace; our service into her mastery, our worth into her well-being, our life into her life."

⚔ ⚔ ⚔ **IX** ⚔ ⚔ ⚔

GOVERNOR OF MAINE

IN the summer of 1865 Chamberlain applied for relief from duty in order that he might have surgical treatment. As a consequence, instead of being simply relieved from active duty, he was mustered out of service with the first batch of generals, specifically on August 24, 1865. This was a mistake, injurious to his pride and embarrassing since the surgery was to have been at government expense. He therefore requested temporary reinstatement. Senators Fessenden and Morrill of Maine and U. S. Grant himself, who had come to Bowdoin College with Chamberlain for Commencement exercises and received a Doctor of Laws degree, were among those who petitioned that the order in Chamberlain's case be revoked and he be mustered out in mid-January, 1866. Grant's intervention was evidently the decisive factor. Chamberlain was accordingly reinstated and then released on January 16.

He now returned to Bowdoin and the college life which he had sworn he would not again endure. Three years of hard campaigning, however, had made a career of college teaching seem less undesirable, while his physical condition made a permanent army career impossible. He therefore resumed his teaching post for the remainder of the academic year, 1865-1866, reconciled, so he thought, to the quieter existence. But he was no longer professor of modern lan-

guages; instead, he was back in the capacity he had filled
from 1856 to 1861, namely, professor of rhetoric and oratory.

It was a restless term for him. A professor's life in a little
college in a little town in a peripheral state was pretty tame
after the tremendous events of the recent past. Teaching
classes of boys young in both age and experience and enter-
taining a group of them one evening a week hardly satisfied
his ambition or released his energy. Before long his attention
was drawn almost inevitably to the political stage where
action was stirring over the problem of readmitting the
Southern states to the Union. The "erring sisters," as Horace
Greeley had once called them, were returning under the
plans drawn by Lincoln or his successor, but the Black Codes
which a number of the Southern states adopted to restrict
the freedom of the Negro, their rejection of the Fourteenth
Amendment on the advice of President Johnson, and the
aggressive and jaunty manner displayed by many of their
new representatives in Congress antagonized beyond endurance the radical Republicans, who began to push hard
their own plans for a more gradual re-admittance. Chamberlain stated his position as early as April 12, 1866, when he
declared that "Secession must be repudiated with its debts
and claims, its spirit and principle. We must have guarantees
good and sufficient against any future attempt to destroy this
government whether in the exercise of a pretended right
by open war, or by the more artful and insidious assaults
against the principles on which this Nation is founded." Until
the Southern states complied with these points, said Chamberlain, "it is wise to hold them in strict probation." Though
no radical Republican, certainly no intransigent Thaddeus
Stephens, Chamberlain had, in sober language, made a point
with which no radical Republican could disagree.

In the course of the spring, leaders of the Republican party in Maine discussed with him the possibility of his becoming their gubernatorial candidate. Chamberlain, more modest in politics than forward in battle, was interested but hardly eager at first. Whatever his feeling about his college work, he was in large measure his own master, whereas in politics he might well have less freedom of movement. At the same time he saw a great work that needed to be done in Maine and felt that only someone with reasonably liberal ideas could carry it through. Hence he finally permitted his name to be entered as a candidate in the Republican convention.

Samuel Cony of Augusta had been governor, but since he no longer cared to run, the Republicans looked to Chamberlain. The leading Old Guardsman was Samuel E. Spring of Portland, a rich merchant whose supporters insisted not only that Chamberlain's liberalism was suspect but also that military men make poor politicians. In the convention that June, however, Chamberlain was given on the very first ballot 599 votes to 438 for Spring.

Before closing out his career at Bowdoin at this time, Chamberlain received a number of honors. Bowdoin asked him to serve for a short while as executive officer, really acting president, a position he was proud to accept. His resignation actually did not mean that his ties with Bowdoin were severed; on the contrary, even when his temporary service as executive officer was over, he continued to see a great deal of the faculty and the alumni, and he kept his door ever open to students. A second honor was his being awarded an honorary degree of Doctor of Laws from Pennsylvania College* in testimony of his worth as a scholar and

* Now Gettysburg College.

a soldier. A final honor arrived when General Warren, who was participating in the reorganization of the army, wrote that he wanted to name Chamberlain as one of six Volunteer officers to Grant for positions as field officers in the new regiments and that he intended to put Chamberlain at the head of the list. But, grateful though Chamberlain was, the prospect of a Regular Army colonelcy in a regiment on the Mexican border, as it turned out, was simply out of the question because of his health. Besides, he was now deeply involved in politics and, once committed to the political arena, was happier than he had been for months.

The campaign was interesting for the candidates, the issues, and the popular attitude. Chamberlain, the college professor and soldier, was pitted against Democrat Eben F. Pillsbury, an Augusta newspaperman. Pillsbury had been a bitter critic of the war and of Lincoln. Yet Chamberlain never became personal in his remarks during the campaign, which saw a lot of mudslinging on both sides. The Republicans urged the adoption of the Fourteenth Amendment and strong support for Congress in its struggle with President Johnson. Chamberlain himself was so doubtful of the complete justice in the position of Congress that until he came out with a statement endorsing the Republican majority, though only in very temperate terms, at least one influential newspaper, the Bangor *Whig*, refused to support him. The Portland *Press*, normally Republican, was skeptical of him throughout the campaign. Not so the voters. When election day arrived, Chamberlain was voted in 69,637 to 41,917 for Pillsbury, the largest majority ever polled by a gubernatorial candidate up to that time. Truly this was popular confirmation of the opinion of General Warren, who said that he would be glad to write in behalf of Chamberlain "as an acknowledgment of my appreciation of your great worth and character as a man and a soldier."

If, in his elation, Chamberlain was likely to become over-confident, he had little opportunity. It would have been a bright feather in his cap if General Grant could have attended his inauguration, but, to his keen disappointment, Grant was unable to accept. Furthermore, there was always someone to give him sound advice. Alfred C. Godfrey, a former chaplain in the 20th Maine whom he had commended for bravery, pulled no punches. "Well, Gen.," wrote Godfrey, "honors have come down upon you gloriously and I am glad of it. The way the world reckons it is a great thing to march up the hill of honor as fast as you have. It was decidedly a double quick movement. You have reached the top of the highest hill in the State of Maine. Great place to see, and be seen.... Don't get dizzy-headed. Be as true in Me. as you were in Va. and no man can take you down."

His inaugural address in the first week in January, 1867, naturally dealt with problems of the day. But Chamberlain recognized that a number of them might continue into the future unless some real solutions could be found. He spoke of Maine's sacrifices during the war. In men alone, the State contributed, according to the Adjutant General, 72,945, of whom 8,792 died and 11,309 were wounded or discharged because of illness. This was quite a contribution for a state whose population totaled about 600,000. Chamberlain proposed to settle the claims of the State against the Federal government for raising and equipping troops during the war and appointed Samuel Cony to head the claims commission. In view of the war's result, Chamberlain had sharp words for the Southerners of 1867 "who with scorn and contumely spurned the Constitution, and defied the Government, and sought with violence, without an apology for the past, without a guaranty for the future, the unconditional restoration of their rights under the Constitution, their places in the Union and their prestige in the Government. This is so little in the spirit of surrender as to seem like mockery of triumph." If steps were taken to curb them, they had only themselves to blame. "War is not a game where there is everything to win and nothing to lose. Those who appeal to the law of force should not complain if its decision is final." He asked the Legislature to pass the Fourteenth Amendment.

Internal improvements claimed much of his attention. He was keenly interested in the new agricultural college at Orono which he hoped would emphasize "practical science and mechanic arts." Such an institution, one which later became the University of Maine, would offer splendid opportunities to the youth of Maine. Speaking from a background of solid accomplishment based on a combination of brains and hard work, Chamberlain said bluntly, "We need something in this State which will educate our young men not out of their proper sphere, but into it; so that when they are educated they will not disdain to work." In the line with his educational interests, he pressed for strong support of the *Documentary History of Maine.*

Other internal problems distressed him. He emphasized the need for additional facilities for caring for the insane and the separation of the harmless from the violent. He wanted a reform school where the young and comparatively innocent could be separated from the incorrigible. The State prison should be enlarged. Capital punishment, under heavy fire, should be accepted or rejected. As Chamberlain said, "Either abolish capital punishment altogether, or fix upon a day after the year of grace on which the sentence shall be executed." The law should be made to conform with practice, and practice with the law.

What disturbed him more than any factor was the economic condition of the State and the annual departure of thousands of Maine's young people to more promising opportunities elsewhere, and here the politicians of the twentieth century have merely been bringing his concern up-to-date. Lumbering was on the skids with the development of the western forests and the decline of shipbuilding. With both lumbering and shipbuilding diminishing in Maine, and the industrial cities and the western lands drawing people from the little farms, means must be found to deliver the State from the "lethargy and timidity under which she has buried her talents. We have been too long content with the doubtful compliment that 'Maine is a good State to go from.' She must be made a good State to come to, and stay in."

Chamberlain had an interesting program for grappling with the problems of his day. He urged that serious efforts be made to bring Scandinavian immigrants to Maine as farmers. He proposed a hydrographic survey, particularly of the lower sections of the principal rivers, which might result in attracting capital and developing the natural advantages. He urged the extension of the system of railroads, "One of the chief means of modern civilization." He thought the State should face openly the question of public loans as an encouragement to industry: "I trust it will not be deemed an undue boldness if I venture to put the question whether it would not be advisable for the State to open her hand just wide enough to give a limited guaranty by her endorsement to such of her public enterprises as she might select, with such restrictions and securities as should ensure her against any reasonable likelihood of loss, or the necessity of asking a single dollar of the people in the way of taxation." Cautious advice in the later twentieth century, it was bold indeed for 1867 and in Maine, at that.

People liked the address, which lasted for one and one-half hours. "What it lacks in brevity," said the Bangor *Daily Times*, "it makes up in perspicacity—the only valid excuse that can be adduced for length in State essays." The Lewiston *Evening Journal* commented that the message "will be read not only with interest but with pride." The Portland *Transcript*, while lauding the Governor's view of public affairs as "broad, liberal and comprehensive," criticized him for characterizing the proposed Canadian Federation as an unfriendly scheme. James G. Blaine wrote Chamberlain from Washington that the address "does you great honor. It is able, bold, clear, comprehensive and statesmanlike—in every respect just what an Inaugural address *should* be." The *Democrat and Free Press* of Rockland capped the eulogies by observing how "very fitting it seems ... that the brave, dauntless ... soldier, Gen. Chamberlain, should have been selected by the loyal people of this State for the highest office in our gift."

Chamberlain quickly fitted into his new job with a minimum of strain, though the Legislature, overwhelmingly Republican in both Senate and House, did not always see eye-to-eye with him. The Legislature supported him by ratifying the Fourteenth Amendment but regarded it as rather weak. An issue on which the Legislature was less in agreement with the Governor was the Liquor Law and its enforcement. If ever a man drank in moderation, it was Chamberlain; furthermore, he deplored excessive drinking and its effects on a man and his family. At the same time he thought the

strong temperance group in Maine was applying pressure
on politicians beyond the realm of common sense and democratic government. The Legislature showed in its action the
effects of this pressure. It passed one law imposing a penalty
of imprisonment for the sale of liquor, and had the better
than three-to-one results of a special referendum as endorsement of its action. It also passed another law establishing a
State Constabulary to enforce the first law. Chamberlain
strongly opposed a State Constabulary as a violation of the
rights and security guaranteed citizens by the Federal Constitution. As a consequence of his position, a clamorous
criticism fell upon him from church groups, temperance
societies, and many individual reformers.

Notwithstanding the tides of emotion over the liquor
issue, Chamberlain refused to become excessively disturbed
and addressed himself conscientiously to the less contentious
problems facing him. Two of these were of special interest
to the citizens of Maine. One was the report on the hydrographic facilities, and, on May 9, Chamberlain wrote the
commissioners of the survey that since the object of the
venture was to call to the attention of business men the
opportunities in the State for manufacture and the invest-
ment of capital, the final report should be a well organized
digest of the water resources, yet something more than a
mere collection of bald statistics. The other problem concerned a group of one hundred and fifty-six American colonists from Maine who, under the inspiration of leaders of the
Church of the Messiah, had sailed to Jaffa in the Holy Land
in the summer of 1866. Once there, they found farming, the
climate, and their neighbors extraordinarily difficult and the
Turkish authorities perhaps more so. Within a year, seventeen were dead, sixty-three had come back, and the re-

mainder were in desperate straits. These last appealed to Chamberlain and the Federal authorities for aid in returning to America. Chamberlain wrote in their behalf, as indeed —most vividly—did Victor Beauboucher, Consul at Jerusalem. Although negotiations dragged, ultimately the colonists succeeded in returning, disillusioned and poorer in pocket and health.

At the political conventions during late June, 1867, the candidates of the previous year were renominated. Eben F. Pillsbury and the Democrats stood on a platform which strongly denounced the Constabulary Law as an arbitrary and offensive innovation in the system of government. The Republicans defended the law and advocated the full restoration of the Southern states. Chamberlain, however, felt somewhat inhibited since he did not like the Constabulary Law himself. Despite his hesitancies, he won the September election by a substantial margin, 57,332 to 45,590 for Pillsbury.

His inaugural address in January, 1868, while similar in many respects to his first, differed significantly at certain points and further illuminated his stand on prominent issues. He called for a State militia of limited size, a reform school for girls, an enlargement of the Hospital for the Insane, and support for the "College of Agriculture and Mechanic Arts" at Orono. Then, with a year of gubernatorial experience behind him, he turned to the economy and took off his gloves. Shipbuilding, one of the mainstays of coastal Maine for many years, had continued to fall off alarmingly. We now know the causes more clearly than did Chamberlain: the disappearance of the Maine forests; the accelerating transition from wooden to iron ships; the mounting cost of construction; the fact that so many ships which had transferred to British registry during the war because of Confederate commerce raiders remained under British registry, and, when worn out, were replaced from British shipyards; the slackening off of national interest in foreign trade as the West and the great internal market opened up. Chamberlain saw the only salvation for Maine shipbuilding as lying in assistance from the Federal government. As for agriculture, Maine farmers should investigate the market with great care; Chamberlain urged them to plant more wheat. He still saw a real future for Maine agricultural expansion in the encouragement of Scandinavian immigration. "Maine," he said, "is surely as good a State to migrate to as Minnesota."

Turning to industry and railroads, Chamberlain said, in effect, that unless the State changed its attitude, the future looked dim. Both industry and railroads had to be assisted. The Portland and Ogdensburg Railroad running through New Hampshire and Vermont to Ogdensburg, New York, was a link with the West, while the European and North American, then under construction, would link Halifax and Boston. With railroads, industries, and port facilities, Portland could become the largest port east of New York. But, notwithstanding the potentialities of Maine, the State persisted in withholding its approval and aid to great public enterprises. This, with the resulting lack of economic opportunity, was the principal reason in his opinion why young people were leaving Maine and immigrants avoided it. He denounced "This snug policy of letting well-enough alone, of being content to fill the places of others." The constitutional restriction on State aid, amended in 1841 to prevent the Legislature from lending State funds or increasing the State debt above $300,000 except for war purposes, should be removed.

Generally approved by the press as showing "nerve" and "a clearness of insight," as well as "sound judgment in the discussion of practical questions," the speech touched off a surprising degree of legislative support. Among other provisions, the Legislature voted to contribute to the towns $100.00 for each soldier who had served three years in the war and repealed both the Constabulary Law and that part of the Liquor Law requiring a jail sentence for the first offence. It appeared to feel that public opinion would not long sustain the prohibitionists, and evidently took its cue from Chamberlain himself. Notwithstanding a drumfire of criticism from religious and temperance groups, Chamberlain, as Governor, had refused to act as chairman of a temperance convention in Augusta. Even if, as has been suggested, he knew that most of the people of Maine were not in favor of prohibition, his own position had been consistent throughout. The Legislature's action against the Constabulary and the Liquor Law was now, in a sense, an endorsement of that position.

The base of criticism of the Governor was broadened by his stand on the proposed impeachment of President Andrew Johnson. Attacking Johnson's character and his liberal views on Reconstruction, the radical Republicans in Congress found a real weapon against the former Tennessee tailor and Democrat when he removed from office the "hard" Reconstructionist, Secretary of War Stanton, in defiance of the Tenure of Office Act of 1867, which declared that the President could not dismiss an officeholder without the consent of the Senate. Indicted by the House of Representatives on eleven charges, nine of them pertaining to violations of the Tenure of Office Act, which the Supreme Court declared unconstitutional in 1926, Johnson was tried by the

Senate from March 5 to May 26, 1868, with Chief Justice Salmon P. Chase in the chair and with the fanatical Thaddeus Stevens of Pennsylvania and the ineffable Benjamin F. Butler of Massachusetts heading the prosecution. The prosecution argued Johnson's unfitness for office; the defense, the legality of the President's challenge of the Act. Had it not been for twelve Democrats and seven Republicans, the impeachers would have won. As it was, the vote was 35 to 19, one short of the necessary majority.

One of the seven Republican Senators was William Pitt Fessenden of Maine. The hue and cry to persuade him to vote against Johnson was nation-wide and particularly strong in Maine. Mass meetings were held in the principal Maine cities demanding that he vote Johnson guilty, while letters poured into his Washington office accusing him of being at least as bad as Benedict Arnold and about as dishonorable as John Wilkes Booth. General Neal Dow, proponent of prohibition in Maine, a vehement radical Republican, and the former commander of the 13th Maine Infantry, which saw service in the bayous of the Gulf, wrote Fessenden, insisting that the Senate "Hang Johnson by the heels like a dead crow in a corn field, to frighten all his tribe. . . . In saying this, I am sure I express the unanimous opinion and feeling of every loyal heart and head in this State."

Not quite—not Chamberlain's heart and head, at any rate. What has been called "The Great American Farce" disgusted him. He supported Fessenden warmly despite his awareness of what this might mean to his own political future. In this, as in so many other acts of his political career, he placed principle ahead of party, and the criticism that now poured upon his head was so vitriolic that friends feared not simply for his career but for his life as well. Notwithstanding the offense he gave to the party leaders in the State, as well as to many of the rank and file, he was still the obvious candidate for Governor at the Republican convention in June and continued to possess enough favor with the people at large to win the September election from that hardy Democratic perennial, Eben Pillsbury, 72,523 to 56,207. In fact, there was a delightful irony in the situation: the Republican failure to get rid of President Johnson made the party in Maine work harder than ever to elect a Republican governor, who happened to be a man who had strongly opposed the action against the President! The result in terms of the Chamberlain victory was actually the largest Republican vote ever cast in Maine up to that time and the origin of the expression that was to have currency and considerable truth for ninety years, "As Maine goes, so goes the nation."

Chamberlain's address in January, 1869, brief beside his two previous inaugurals, further illuminates his concern for the welfare of the State of Maine. He urged biennial rather than annual elections, reiterated the need for removing restrictions on State assistance to industry, and insisted again that the Liquor Law should either be executed or repealed. While deploring drunkenness and recognizing the need of restraining men, he frankly acknowledged that legislating what a man should eat or drink was a pretty strong assertion of a state's authority over an individual. He stressed the importance of equipping a few volunteer companies of militia, again endorsed Scandinavian immigration, and announced the successful completion of the hydrographic survey.

The most interesting and courageous statement in the address was that concerned with capital punishment, the opponents of which were animated by a fervor equalled only by that of the prohibitionists. The specific issue focussed on a convicted Negro, Clifton Harris, a rapist who murdered his victims. There had been a great deal of sympathy for Harris, despite his atrocious offenses, not only because of his background and race but also because he had "turned State's evidence." To the Attorney General, William Frye, this appeared reason for mitigating the sentence of death, and the anti-capital punishment adherents and a number of the Legislature agreed with him. Chamberlain differed profoundly:

... if a person can be convicted of capital crime by evidence given under the pressure of this consummate hope of reward, then the altar of justice is no longer the asylum of innocence, and life and liberty must seek some other defence. But if this was so, let those who made the promise keep it—let them see that their witness had his reward while the case is still in their hands. But did the Attorney General avail himself of his privilege and withdraw any portion of the indictment in token of the service rendered? Did the jury in their verdict, or the judge after sentence, recommend to the mercy of the Executive? Nothing of the kind.

But Chamberlain was not finished. He was, after all, the Governor and saw his duty to enforce the law in terms of the welfare of the whole state. The disbelievers in capital punishment were eventually to win in Maine, they continue active in the United States in our own day, and they have achieved their most recent notable (though by no means complete) victory in England. Chamberlain put his opinion squarely on the line, and it is a fine expression of a group that sees value in capital punishment:

However the experience of suffering may have affected my personal sympathies, the consideration of the public safety convinces

me that this is not the time to soften penalties. Too much crime
is abroad, and emboldened by the mildness and uncertainty of
punishment . . . Mercy is indeed a heavenly grace, but it should
not be shown to crime. It is the crime and not the man, at which
the law strikes. It is not to prevent that man alone from repeating
his offense, but to prevent others from so doing. If the wretch
who meditates crime sees the sure and sharp penalty before him,
he may take better counsels. This is merciful to him, to his
intended victim, to his possible imitators, and to the community.

Some might think Chamberlain lacking in compassion, hard-
ened by the war, but "I deem it not wise," he said with
old-fashioned directness, "when weakness usurps the name of
mercy and pleads for the impunity of crime." Nor did he
budge from his position. He presently ordered that the
sentence of hanging be executed.

In general the press was favorable to the address, although even traditionally Republican papers were critical
that Chamberlain, as one writer put it, a little extremely,
"advocates capital punishment as a reformatory measure."
There was criticism also that Chamberlain's position on the
liquor question was something less than clear or firm. The
Legislature, however, was disposed to praise rather than
carp, and the House voted that thanks be tendered him
for his "able and eloquent" address.

There was little tension between the Governor and the
Legislature during this session. The Legislature's most important act was to ratify the Fifteenth Amendment giving
the Negro the right to vote. Perhaps remembering the ignorance and belligerence of the Negroes in Virginia after Appomattox in the area which the 1st Division of the Fifth Corps
policed, Chamberlain himself had doubts about the wisdom
of conferring on the newly liberated slaves so responsible a

right; he felt that such a move would only make more difficult an already complicated problem in the South. Ultimately, in his opinion, the South would have to solve its own
problems.

But if harmony prevailed between Chamberlain and the
Legislature, the same good feeling could not be said to exist
within the Republican party. The prohibitionists within and
without the party vehemently reiterated their demand for
a more rigorous enforcement of the existing Liquor Law
and the establishment of a State Constabulary that would
put teeth into the law. They promised that if neither political
party produced a candidate who would take a strong anti-
liquor stand, they would form a party of their own and
nominate a candidate about whose opinions there would be
no doubt.

The problem of securing strong candidates troubled the
party leaders that spring. Chamberlain had served the three
terms beyond which Governors were reluctant to commit
themselves, and he had no desire to spend an additional
year in Augusta. On the other hand, no suitable Republican
candidate was available to succeed him. Former Governors
Morrill and Cony declined a fourth term; former Governor
Washburn, a third term. The party chiefs then turned back
to Chamberlain and persuaded him, out of loyalty to the
party in time of need, to agree to a fourth term. He was
nominated by the Republican convention, which met in June,
1869, at Bangor, as "one of our most eminent citizens, distinguished for his scholarship, his patriotism, and his undy-
ing military record." For substantially the same reasons he
also received that spring another honorary Doctor of Laws
degree, this time from his own college, Bowdoin.

He faced two political antagonists this summer. True to

their word, the prohibitionists formed a Temperance Party; those who were Republicans were particularly angry at Chamberlain for his refusal in the winter of 1868 to preside at the great temperance convention in Augusta. The prohibitionists nominated a former State treasurer, N. G. Hichborn of Stockton. The Democrats, meanwhile, turned from the perennial Pillsbury to a new candidate, Franklin Smith of Waterville. In the elections the combination of Republican strength and Chamberlain popularity was still potent. Although Chamberlain's vote was not large, it was enough: he received 51,314; Smith, 39,033; and Hichborn, only 4,735.

In his inaugural address in January, 1870 Chamberlain hammered away on familiar themes. Money was a sore want: "What this State needs is capital—money in motion, whether gold or currency. Our material is stagnant, our industry crippled, our enterprise staggered for want of money, which is power." It was therefore necessary to perfect and make practicable the free banking law and to legalize higher rates of interest. The State had great opportunities, but to realize them and provide incentives for the youth of Maine to remain, the State should make effective use of its water power, grow wheat, conserve its forests, and promote immigration— particularly from Scandinavia, manufactures, and railroads. Should the railroads insist on consolidation, the State could permit it but make the railroads responsible to the State.

Chamberlain had some pertinent remarks about the Hospital for the Insane. His remarks, indeed, are as applicable in most states today as in the Maine of 1870. Already the development of an industrial society and the tensions which appear to be a concomitant, too often resulting in derangement, were reaping their toll. Facilities were inadequate. Two years earlier the Director of the Hospital had written

Chamberlain that conditions had never been so crowded. Each year saw more people admitted than in any previous year, and Chamberlain begged for funds for expansion. "Cells and corridors and stone walls," he said with force and insight, "are dreary confines for minds broken under the weight of real or fancied wrongs ... A brief treatment of a sane man in these crowded corridors would very soon give him a title to stay there."

He had courageous if not very tactful words to say to the Temperance Party. Though no enemy of temperance as principle or practice, he deplored the lack of moderation which characterized the movement and which had impelled the prohibitionists to form a third party. He urged calmness and boldness in attacking the evils of liquor, but not rashness. Something should be done about the State Liquor Law, to be sure, but there were limits to the extent to which any law could restrain or intimidate. In the long run, only the spiritual element in man could be effective in diverting him from an evil course. It was not inappropriate that Chamberlain, the former theological student, should see the ultimate answer in the efficacy of the Gospel of Jesus Christ.

The press was moderately receptive to his address, though the Portland *Transcript* remarked that in trying to vindicate himself of the charge of being an enemy to temperance, Chamberlain adopted "a censorious tone toward those citizens who saw fit to support a temperance candidate." The *Transcript,* however, was now frankly suspicious of Chamberlain whose opposition to the Johnson impeachment and to giving the vote to the former slaves had stirred up Democratic interest to the point that the Portland *Eastern Argus,* a Democratic organ, defended the address. Indignantly the *Transcript* observed, "The *Argus* has constituted itself the special champion of Gov. Chamberlain, and is very sensitive to any criticism of his message, however slight. What's in the wind?"

His last term as Governor saw a movement in the Legislature which tended to undermine his position. An anticapital punishment bill went down, but only by a vote of 69 to 56; and in 1872 Maine abolished capital punishment for the first time, thus making the fourth state in the Union to put aside the death penalty. Although the Legislature refused to endorse the proposal by the annual temperance convention that a State Constabulary be established, it greatly strengthened the Liquor Law. Chamberlain gave the comparative absence of opposition as his reason for signing the bill. Otherwise, his final term saw little of real significance occur.

Of especial interest to him, however, were two arrivals in Maine. One was the January appearance in Portland harbor of the then great British battleship *Monarch* bearing the body of the American philanthropist, George Peabody, for burial in his homeland. An American squadron under Admiral David Farragut escorted the man-of-war into Portland harbor where the *Monarch* anchored in the lower harbor off Fort Gorges. Chamberlain went aboard, and thoroughly enjoyed meeting the British commander and his staff. Military display always appealed to him, even on a solemn occasion like this. Although the city was still struggling back after a disastrous fire in 1866, it pleased Chamberlain to see the citizens, many of whom had lost ships and cargoes at the hands of the British-built-and-equipped *Alabama* and her sisters, take the *Monarch*'s crew to their hearts with a warmth that won the gratitude of the British Foreign Office.

The second arrival was that of the first contingent of Swedish immigrants in July. Sailing from Gothenburg, they landed in Halifax, traveled across Nova Scotia and the Bay of Fundy and up the St. John River, reaching their new homes in New Sweden on July 23. Speeches, salutes from cannon, and brass bands met them in Fort Fairfield and Caribou. Hundreds of townsfolk in the latter place turned out to feast them and shake their hands. Although there were only fifty-one, including children, in this initial contingent, they made a fine appearance. The Commissioners' *Report* said of the men, "All are tall and stalwart, with blue eyes, light hair, and cheerful, honest faces. There is not a physical defect or blemish among them." Soon hundreds more arrived to Chamberlain's deep pleasure. It has been aptly observed that he had fostered this enterprise with "truly parental care."

His gubernatorial career was coming swiftly to an end. At the Republican convention in June 1870 he was not mentioned as a candidate. While the Democrats were inclined to consider him, Chamberlain remained loyal to his party despite the enemies he had made, whether over national issues like the President's powers and Reconstruction policies or State of Maine issues like prohibition and a State Constabulary, the former of which he considered an invasion of personal rights, the latter an infringement of municipal rights. President William DeWitt Hyde of Bowdoin College said of Chamberlain, years later, "As statesman he was in advance of his time. Called to solve the problems entailed by the Civil War, his administration as Governor was marked by patience and fairness; he refused to use the power that people gave him for ends other than the people's good: and when the leaders of his party advocated the impeachment of the President; the protracted agitation of sectional differences; and immediate suffrage for the emancipated Negroes; he stood firmly, sagaciously and self-sacrificingly for more moderate and pacific measures—measures which subsequent history has shown to be far more beneficent than those which in the flush of military victory, the heat of party strife, and the fire of personal ambition, unfortunately prevailed." Chamberlain had therefore clearly refused to slip into the pattern of a regular party man, and this objective attitude is always a cause of perplexity and despair to party chiefs, who prefer compliance or at least some degree of flexibility in their politicians and who find it extraordinarily difficult to work with a man whose motivation, like Chamberlain's, is often deeply rooted in moral principles. They were not sorry to see him leave Augusta, nor was he sorry to go.

But even his most rigorous critics could not deny that his years as Governor had been fruitful. The hydrographic survey had been an important accomplishment, likewise the reorganization of the State militia. War claims against the Federal government for the Civil War and even the War of 1812 were settled. The State took fresh interest, thanks to his insistence, in what was to become the University of Maine and in the Normal School at Farmington and the proposed one at Castine, the latter now the site of the Maine Maritime Academy. He fostered the successful establishment of Scandinavian immigrants in northern Maine. Although he was unsuccessful in getting State aid to industry, no real modification in the law occurring until 1912, he encouraged industry as well as he could, seeing at least to the establishment of commissioners of banking and insurance. While he was also unable to assist railroads materially, he gave them his moral support, and in late 1871, he saw the opening of the European and North American Railroad between Bangor and St. John, New Brunswick; it became part of the Maine Central system in 1882.

He had been an active, progressive Governor generally in advance of his party chiefs, the Legislature, and the voters, which is where a chief executive should be even if part of the cost be in popularity. A number of people, though not the party leaders, talked of sending him to Congress. It is doubtful, however, if, in his relief at being free for the moment from the barbs of critics and the importunings of office-seekers, Chamberlain looked beyond the confines of his comfortable home in Brunswick just off the Bowdoin campus. Besides, he had duties of another nature that demanded his attention.

PRESIDENT OF BOWDOIN COLLEGE

WHILE he was at Augusta, Chamberlain had a brief falling-out with Fanny. The causes are somewhat obscure, and one is reduced in part to speculation, but it is possible to reconstruct the situation in terms that are probably very close to the truth. Fanny was an excitable woman, lovable but "flighty," as her foster father had observed years before. Demonstrative, she craved attention, and when this was not forthcoming, she became moody, suspicious, and depressed, and likely to do things which she later regretted. During the war she saw little of her husband save when she visited him or when he was home on sick leave. Her ties to Brunswick by family and environment were very strong, and she loved her contacts with Bowdoin, especially her role as a professor's wife. Chamberlain's decision to enter politics was not one to which she took kindly, particularly if it meant uprooting herself. This she refused to do and remained in Brunswick. At the same time, she resented his absence in Augusta, perhaps his political friends as well, and began not only to think he no longer cared for her but also to talk to some back-door gossips about a divorce.

It was this last propensity of hers, namely, to confide in people unworthy of her confidence, that cut Chamberlain to the quick. In late November, 1868, he wrote her a frank letter in which he said that he was shocked to learn from a mutual friend who had come to him in great distress that at least one of her confidants was telling of how he abused her physically, even to striking her and pulling her hair! He said that he would make quick work of such calumniation if he were the only one involved. Unfortunately what touched him also touched her, so he begged her to act with wisdom and discretion and stop confiding in such people. If, however, there was any basis to the rumor that she was seeking legal action, she need not go to such trouble since surely both of them had sufficient intelligence to work out terms of a separation without making their families wretched. Again he warned her that, although she never took his advice, she should cease talking with such low people about her grievances and plans; otherwise, she would make a hell of both their lives.

Chamberlain was beset at the time by the temperance people and the supporters of the rapist-murderer, Harris, and these and his opponents within and without his party would have leaped to a juicy morsel of scandal involving a high-principled public hero, an ex-college professor and divinity student besides! That he was aware of the opportunity the situation afforded his enemies is clear enough; that this was as nothing to him compared with the possible wreck of his and Fanny's marriage is even clearer. His is not a holier-than-thou letter. It reflects bewilderment, anger, even reproof, but not recrimination; and implicit throughout is an acute concern for Fanny, who did not seem to realize the implications of a legal action. The lot of a divorcée in that era in a conservative part of the country was not likely to be a happy one.

On the other hand, the responsibility for the threat to their marriage was undoubtedly shared by Chamberlain. He was enormously restless after the war, and possibly less patient with Fanny's impulsiveness and willfulness than before. The habit of command he had acquired during the war may have led him to speak sharply to her when they differed. Furthermore, his wound gave him frequent bouts of inflammation and fever, which certainly did not make for peace of mind, and there is a possibility that his condition inhibited to some extent the physical aspect of marriage. As he turned to politics as a channel for his energies, a thoroughly alien field to her, it is not difficult to understand Fanny's thinking that he was neglecting her and had lost his affection for her. She reacted in a reckless, unwise manner but one not out of keeping with her natural impulsiveness.

The storm blew over, and the two came together again in a firmer bond of understanding than ever before. Furthermore, with his gubernatorial career at an end, Chamberlain began to look more kindly on the prospect of returning to academic life, a change of mind that immensely pleased Fanny. He did not choose to return to academic life simply to gratify her, but he could not have been unaware that, in doing so, he would remove at least one basis of disagreement; and he was determined that their marriage should not again be placed in such jeopardy.

In early 1871 he was informed that, with the impending departure of President Samuel Harris of Bowdoin to accept the chair of systematic theology at Yale, the Board of Trustees, of which Chamberlain was a member, was interested in him as Harris' successor. The more Chamberlain thought about the presidency of his alma mater, the better he liked the prospect. Not only was it a high honor, it was also an opportunity to put into effect a number of educational ideas long fermenting in his mind. Unless, however, he were permitted to institutionalize these ideas, he was not interested in the position regardless of its prestige and honor, and said as much. Since the Trustees themselves were in substantial agreement that reforms were indicated at least partially in the direction in which Chamberlain was interested, they assured him he would be given the necessary latitude; he then accepted. The Trustees elected him unanimously, the Overseers ratified the choice, and a committee publicly announced the election while Chamberlain was addressing a meeting of the Alumni Association, which broke into applause when it was given the news.

Chamberlain had in mind three areas of reform: a loosening of discipline with a view to treating the students henceforth as adults, a revision of the curriculum with a greater emphasis on science and modern languages as well as the inception of a graduate program leading to the Master of Arts degree, and the introduction of military drill. In the faculty meetings starting early in September these proposed changes were discussed. It would be interesting to learn how the faculty regarded these reforms; unfortunately, the faculty minutes are sparse and non-committal. That Chamberlain had his way is evident, but there must have been some anxious hearts among the older professors at the drastic revision of traditional procedures.

Reforms in the first area were probably not too difficult for anyone to take. The old custom of holding formal morning prayers before breakfast was eliminated. Henceforth prayers were held after breakfast at 8:30 with all classes for the day to follow at hour-intervals. Evening prayers, with the exception of Sunday, were abolished altogether, as were Saturday classes and the long vacation in the winter. Commencement was to occur in June. Library hours were extended for the benefit of students. By way of further concession to students, scholarship alone was now to determine the award of college honors; hitherto, irregularities in conduct or in attendance at college exercises had figured in the awards. At the same time, Chamberlain raised the tuition from $60 to $75 for the year and, instead of continuing the room rate of $10 for each student, he authorized that students be charged according to the desirability of the rooms.

The revision and enlargement of the curriculum were more serious matters. The student newspaper, the Bowdoin *Orient*, liked the new emphasis on "thinking and the formation of independent judgment" as well as the "larger and needed infusion of the living and available truths which belong to the present age." "It is a matter of fact," the *Orient* continued, "that the college course in the past has been shaped too much in the interests of a particular class, the education of clergymen, and on their account the classical element has largely predominated." For the students, therefore, the changes were desirable, including Chamberlain's decision to hold Thursday evening receptions for students during term time. Said the *Orient*, ". . . he proposes to root out the erroneous idea that a student is not to be considered a companion of professors until he can affix A. B. to his name." It was an old custom for Chamberlain but a new one for the presidents of Bowdoin.

In addition to shaking up the general curriculum with courses in science and modern languages and reading of the classics in translation, Chamberlain set up a scientific department and a course in engineering. In the scientific department, which was really a college of science, a Freshman took French, English, ancient history, and mathematics;

a Sophomore: logic, mathematics, chemistry, botany, and mineralogy; a Junior: German, zoology, physiology, astronomy, and physics; a Senior: geology, mental and moral philosophy, political economy, constitutional and international law. The engineering curriculum consisted of a course in civil and mechanical engineering in addition to the science department curriculum except that drawing took the place of ancient history for Freshmen and of logic for Sophomores, while Juniors and Seniors were excused from other science department courses with the exception of physics, political economy, and German. Such innovations were indeed radical, but, in the decade that the science department lasted, thirty per cent of the students entering Bowdoin signed up for it and twenty-five per cent of Bowdoin graduates received a Bachelor of Science degree. Among these graduates were a future engineering adviser to the Chinese government, a dean of the Massachusetts Institute of Technology, and the discoverer of the North Pole.

Chamberlain also instituted his graduate plans. In 1871, the same year in which he established the science department, he announced that Bowdoin would offer a Master of Arts degree, to be awarded at the termination of a two-year course in science, letters, and philosophy. Six years later he started a summer school of science in chemistry, mineralogy, and zoology for teachers, college graduates, and others —women as well as men. Twenty-seven people attended, including eleven women, and the college offered the same course the following summer. After that, the course was dropped, the college explaining that the arrangement had been intended only as an experiment.

Chamberlain's inaugural address, not delivered until July, 1872, is valuable for explaining his changes and setting forth his educational philosophy. Speaking to the Boards of Trustees and Overseers, the alumni, and the students, he deplored the fact that many young men had passed the college by since they demanded a kind of education Bowdoin could not give. Bowdoin should therefore concentrate on strengthening its existing offerings or "accept at once the challenge of the times." He preferred the latter. He did not wish to cut away completely from the past with "its treasured acquisition and wisdom" but, rather, to apply these garnerings "to the conditions of the present." He deplored the cloister spirit of the monastery with its "tendency away from life; the natural affection rebuked; the social instincts chilled; the body despised and so dishonored; woman banished and hence degraded, so that to admit her to a place in higher education is thought to degrade a college. The inmates separate, secluded, grown abnormal and provincial, came out into the world strangers to it. . . . Now that is not what the college wants to make of men."

Nineteenth-century science was having a massive impact on the popular mind. The old way of life was fast breaking up and with it old traditions, old values, and revered religious conceptions. Many thoughtful men took alarm, while others looked at science and virtually deified it. Chamberlain's was a calm voice in a rising cacophony of fear, protest, and adoration. "This is a peculiar age but I do not fear these men of science," he told his audience. "Sooner or later . . . they will see and confess that these laws along whose line they are following, are not forces, are not principles. They are only methods. . . . Laws cannot rightly be comprehended except in the light of principles . . . Laws show how only *certain* ends are to be reached; it is by insight into Principles that we discover the great, the integral ends . . . Now the *knowledge of these Laws* I would call *Science,* and the *apprehension of Principles* I would call *Philosophy,* and our men of science may be quite right in their science and altogether wrong in their philosophy." Fear over the advance of science and what might happen to theories or men did not disturb him. "I know," he said confidently, "that all true working and real discovery must lie directly in those lines which lead surely to principles, and can rest in no other theory than truth, and no other goal than God." For those who called the age materialistic and evil he had a shake of the head. "I say this is a good age, and we need not quarrel with it," he said stoutly. "We must understand it, if we can."

In Chamberlain's view, the way to understanding was not to lose oneself in the past but to address oneself to the present. He therefore believed that Greek and Latin should be replaced for most students by French and German, though he wished it were possible (while recognizing it was not) for everyone to learn both the ancient and modern tongues. He would have students learn the ancient classics through translation. He would have science. He would have Bowdoin cherish "true religion" but "not the church of sect and dogma," not the church with a stake in its creed; not the church of the Pharisee or the fanatic; but the church of brotherly love, the church of the Redeemed on earth, the church Universal!

Changes had to come, and in the new liberal arts college that was Bowdoin he saw not only "a lofty seeker after truth, but more than all a lifter up of men." There was no need to fear the new age with all its "hot haste." He welcomed it. "Let it be a new Elizabethan age," he said: "dazzling discoveries, broadening science, swift-following invention, arts multiplying, civilization advancing, new fields of thought and labor, new prizes of courage, new rewards of toil, new aspects and fashions of all things!"

Altogether it was a remarkable address, particularly for its era. Certainly Bowdoin was never the same after Chamberlain's arrival; the modern college dates from him.

The third area of change involved the introduction of military drill. The Federal government was concerned lest it ever enter another war with the dearth of men trained as soldiers and officers with which it was confronted in 1861. It therefore encouraged the creation of military units in the colleges and universities, and Chamberlain wanted a unit at Bowdoin. His experience in the Civil War strongly influenced his recommendation. The establishment of required gymnasium work for all students in January, 1872, while desirable, did not go far enough, for he saw in the drill not merely a means of acquiring military knowledge and cultivating the body, but of developing character as well. Hence, his recommendation approved by the Boards, he selected Major Joseph P. Sanger from the list of officers submitted by the War Department, and Sanger arrived in January, 1872, to organize the unit.

Sanger, a diminutive officer but intelligent and firm, made an excellent commander, and the students liked him. Seniors were excused from the drill because the year was already well along. Juniors, however, were taken in hand in March and the Sophomores and Freshmen in May. Organized in June into an infantry battalion of four companies, the students made a fine appearance in their new uniform, patterned on that of West Point. Most of them accepted the drill with enthusiasm, although some Seniors wondered if too much academic time was not being sacrificed to the drill manual.

Chamberlain was delighted with the results Sanger achieved, and informed the Boards that the drill was "The kind of exercise particularly recommended by Plato, even in opposition to strictly athletic training as most suitable for young men."

Unfortunately for Chamberlain's peace of mind, opposition began to raise its head against the innovations he considered most significant. What he seems to have desired for Bowdoin was that it become a distinguished university, facing outward rather than inward, rooted in tradition but oriented toward the present and the future, and possessing an abundance of intellectual facilities which should be made available to the youth of Maine. In his first report to the Board he said, "It is a great pity that today we see four colleges [Bowdoin, Bates, Colby and the Orono institution that became the University of Maine] standing back to back and working away from each other, quadruplication of the men, appliances, forces and means which united would make a college of the first rank and a glory to Maine." To carry out an enlargement of the curriculum, he increased the faculty from sixteen to twenty-six by 1874. Such an expansion, even with an increase in the student body, cost a great deal of money. The Trustees had turned to Chamberlain as a college president who might be "not only a ripe scholar but a successful beggar." During Chamberlain's administration, a sum of two hundred thousand dollars was raised from outside sources, an enormous contribution in that day; largely because of Chamberlain's own efforts, the alumni contributed one half the sum.

Before long, owing to the expense and the comparatively radical nature of the new scientific and military programs, as well as to the lightening of the accent on religion, factions among the Trustees, the faculty, the alumni body in general, and the townspeople, not to mention the students, became highly critical of Chamberlain. Accordingly as early as July, 1873, he submitted a letter of resignation to the Board of Trustees and the Board of Overseers:

When I assumed the duties to which you honored me by your election, I was aware that they involved difficulties and trials from which older and abler men than I had retired in despair. I have exerted myself beyond any previous experience to be equal to this place and to meet your wishes. I hoped to succeed, but I have not met my own expectation. A spirit seems to possess the College with which I cannot harmonize, and under which I cannot advantageously work. I owe the world some better service, and it is my duty to seek it.

The Boards, however, refused to accept his resignation and called on all friends of the college to support the more liberal course in college instruction until such time as the Boards terminated the experiment. The decision did not mean that opposition ceased; on the contrary, it increased. But the decision served official notice that Chamberlain was to be given further opportunity to develop his plans without interference from any source.

The next academic year brought new difficulties that tested severely the good sense and resolution of Chamberlain, his faculty, and the Trustees. These difficulties rose as a result of student opposition to Chamberlain's military program. For the students the glamor of soldiering, even on the Bowdoin campus, passed very suddenly when the faculty voted in its meeting of September 15, 1873 that "each student not exempted from drill be required to purchase either a uniform or a fatigue dress—the latter consisting of blouse, cap, belt and gloves at an expense not exceeding six dollars." Said the student newspaper, "The last, worst, and most unpopular act of our military government, so fast becoming a military despotism, has been enacted and carried into effect. Henceforth every student must provide himself with a uniform, whatever may be his means, whatever his individual choice." The *Orient* looked upon the alternative of expulsion as "Glorious martyrdom!"

The students resolved to bypass Chamberlain and the faculty and approach the Boards directly. A committee of three addressed a letter in November to the Boards, presenting a petition for the abolition of military training that was signed by 126 students, or all but seven of the three upper classes. Reasons listed included such factors as the injury to Bowdoin from loss of students, the facilities for "more popular and profitable exercises," the expense incurred, loss of time that could otherwise be given to study, and the growing unpopularity of the training. A committee from the Board of Trustees met twice with the student committee. The meetings were friendly, but the Trustees were critical of the students' having neglected to act through the faculty, and took no action. Rebuffed, the students brooded over their future course.

With spring, Chamberlain was confronted with a major college revolt, a situation incredible and shocking to conservative sensibilities in 1874. On May 19, the Junior class expressed its feelings so luridly about the artillery drill from which it was dispersing that, on the 20th, Major Sanger sternly warned against further demonstrations. Immediately on breaking ranks a number of the class began to groan, while one bolder than the rest declared that "Whoever does not keep his mouth shut about the drill now, must understand that he is sitting on his coffin." At once the class broke into cheers.

Chamberlain called his faculty into session. As a result of an investigation, the unwise if daring spokesman was dismissed from college on May 21, and five other Juniors were suspended until the next term. Far from intimidated, the Juniors at once voted never to drill again. On that afternoon, Friday, the Sophomores and Freshmen took a similar action. Again Chamberlain summoned his faculty, which met until midnight, having appointed committees to meet with the students and try to divert them from "the folly and wrong of their intended course of action." All weekend professors labored with students, but to no avail; youth would be served but not by a continuance of the drill manual. On Tuesday the Sophomores signed a pledge, "We refuse ever again to drill in this college." Their example was quickly followed by both the Junior and Freshman classes. When the Juniors failed to report for drill that afternoon, they were sent home. Soon practically all members of the Freshman and Sophomore classes likewise found themselves en route to their homes, where a letter from Chamberlain arrived, informing their parents that the students must agree within ten days to comply with the laws of the college, including the requirements concerning drill, or be expelled. If, however, the students who submitted should continue to object to the drill, they would receive an honorable dismissal at the end of the term.

To Chamberlain and his exasperated faculty came an unsettling rumor that Dartmouth College might open its doors to the recalcitrant students. Chamberlain at once wrote President Asa D. Smith of Dartmouth, anxiously inquiring if there was any truth to the rumor. Back from the hills of

Hanover came the reassuring reply that for the sake of Bowdoin, all colleges, and the young men themselves, law, order, and legitimate authority must prevail; of course, Dartmouth would not admit the rebels! A relieved Bowdoin faculty ordered three hundred copies of Smith's letter struck off for public distribution. But it was no doubt with an even greater relief that Chamberlain and his professors observed all the students except three return to college by the stipulated time. Even the three holdouts ultimately came back to the fold.

If the situation had its amusing aspects, the serious aspects were dominant. The "revolt" excited interest throughout the country. Even papers critical of military training insisted that college authority must be maintained and respected. Chamberlain personally received support and criticism. From H. W. Benham at the U. S. Engineer's Office in Boston whose pontoon bridges Chamberlain had guarded one dark night in the Chancellorsville campaign came warm praise for now making "a *far more important struggle for the national strength and well being,* than any made as yet." Against this lavish laudation should be placed the censorious newspaper comment that Chamberlain's "craze for epaulets and gold lace has at length borne fruit. The same sickly longing for the exercise of autocratic power that once sent a thrill of disgust and horror through the State by needlessly and obstinately insisting on a legal homicide [the Negro, Harris] which was demanded neither by the laws nor by public sentiment, has made the halls of Bowdoin tenantless." The Boards themselves hinted at a reproof when they declared, "The President of a college must deal both with Faculty and Students face to face with unswerving directness of statement, and in the manner of one doing the duties of his station, because they are duties and not because his station is superior." The habit of command was not an easy one for Chamberlain to shake off, and it is possible that in the emergency the general had taken over the position of the president.

The "Drill Revolt" doomed his military program. The Boards voted in June that it become optional, although they continued to support it in principle and practice even when the number of students electing it was small. Chamberlain hated to see it die. He saw it as a preparation for the great crises which came in about every generation. "Our educated young men," he said, "should be so instructed as to be able to assume command of men, and to direct the defense of society against its foes." In 1879, the faculty expressed itself in favor of having the drill abolished. Chamberlain himself admitted, "The experiment has not been so successful as I could wish, and perhaps it is impracticable to bring such exercises into a regular college with traditions like ours." Three years later the Boards discontinued the entire military training program. As Christopher H. Wells of the Class of 1875 said long after the "Drill Revolt," "Of course we were wrong, and we all went back and submitted to the rules of the College, but the backbone of the drill was broken, and it died a speedy and unregretted death as a Bowdoin institution." Unregretted, that is, except by Chamberlain.

With the breakdown of the military program and fiercely renewed attacks from many quarters on the science program, Chamberlain was having difficulty maintaining his poise. Furthermore, not only was he assailed by those who opposed his de-emphasis of religion but also by those who thought he had not gone far enough. One alumnus wrote him, expressing fears that another alumnus, a wealthy Minneapolis manufacturer, "will back out after all in his donation to Bowdoin. He takes the ground that Bowdoin is too sectarian, that she is not out of the hands of *old fogies* and that you, Sir, are too strong a sectarian to manage its concerns."

Being a college president confers a good deal of prestige on a man. Nor can it be denied that the position carries a considerable degree of dignity, power, and potential value in education. But any college president worth his salt has ideas that he wishes to try out, and these ideas have to be presented in a convincing manner to the numerous groups interested in the college. Unfortunately for his intentions (and what college president is not certain of the educational rectitude of his intentions?), the moment he opens his mouth to speak, he is likely to find himself in difficulties—and this regardless of whether his ideas are good or bad, his plans precisely delineated or amorphous, his language a model of lucidity or hopelessly obscure.

His predicament is often painful. Unless he prefers to carry on the tradition already established without significant adjustments to meet the changing times, he becomes a target for those people who are convinced that the college is good enough as it is, people who often confuse needed reform with an irresponsible desire for change. On the other hand, unless he moves away from the traditional pattern, which, because it is traditional, may be properly suspect, he is vigorously assailed as a stand-patter. This criticism usually emanates from an intense, highly articulate group of reformers who—whether motivated by a love of novelty or a sincere desire to bring about the educational Millennium— may well wish to revise not only the entire curriculum in substance and principle but the basic social plan of the college as well, without sufficient regard to the values adhering to the established tradition. If, as sometimes happens, the president himself is such a reformer, he is likely to find himself in deep trouble indeed.

But however firmly persuaded of the virtues of his program —whether it be conservative or radical in nature—he cannot completely ignore any single group: his faculty, the students, the trustees, the alumni, even outside opinion from which contributions often come. In a sense, therefore, a college president has to be a good juggler, for if he drops one of the balls, it may ruin his entire performance. Chamberlain was finding this out, and, in 1876, he thought he had reached the limit of his endurance. Hence, in June, he again submitted his resignation to the Boards. He was nothing if not candid:

Some difficulties I have met with were unexpected and, I think, unnecessary, and some doubtless the result of my own too sanguine and self-reliant spirit. However that may be I am willing to leave to time the justification not only of what I have done, but of what I have attempted and not been able to carry through.

There was no disposition in the Boards, however, to see a president leave whom they respected and liked, notwithstanding the reservations some members shared as to the wisdom of his program.

That the scientific course was having difficulties does not admit of doubt. Criticism simply would not cease and continued to grow. Notwithstanding the criticism, the Boards would, presumably, have persisted in their support had not the program encountered financial difficulties. In those days a college was still largely dependent on tuition from its students to meet expenses. Consequently building expansion was limited, facilities were often inadequate, and salaries were low—Chamberlain, for example, received an annual salary of only $2600 with a rental allowance of $300 which he applied to the maintenance of his own home. Apart from the medical school, which consisted of about 125 students, the majority of the undergraduate body, which totaled less than 200, continued to choose the liberal arts rather than the scientific or engineering programs. Although this was to have been expected, it had been hoped that a higher percentage of students than 25 or 30 per cent would have chosen the scientific program. It appeared, however, that many students thought the B. S. a less distinguished and less reputable degree than the B. A. Furthermore, in its drawing power, the scientific program encountered competition from the State Agricultural College at Orono and the Massachusetts Institute of Technology. The program was not paying its own way. Moreover, Chamberlain's refusal to heed its expense distracted and infuriated some of those charged with handling the college's funds. As the college treasurer wrote a friend, "The philosophy of dreams is not fully understood, but I have often thought that those of some persons had more sense in them than in their waking thoughts. The *Prest.* is certainly very adroit in avoiding an issue he does not wish to meet."

Finally, in 1878, even Chamberlain admitted the failure. But he added, "We may console ourselves with having made an earnest effort to meet what was a demand of the times, with having done good work and earned a good fame...." In 1880 and 1881, the Boards discontinued the scientific and engineering programs respectively.

Chamberlain left his mark on the college curriculum. Ever after, the Bowdoin of Longfellow and Hawthorne emphasized the principle of election, and, in particular, it made available more courses in science and modern languages. Chamberlain was, indeed, ahead of his time. As his distinguished successor, President Hyde, observed so acutely, in 1914, Chamberlain had ". . . advocated the very reforms, using often the very phrases, that are now the commonplaces of progressive educational discussion. Modern Languages, Science, Classics in translation, political and social science, research and individual instruction. . . ." But, as Hyde also remarked, Chamberlain "had the misfortune, or rather the glory, to advocate these expensive reforms before the college had the funds to make them completely effective; yet with the most meagre resources he established . . . that remarkable course in Civil Engineering which gave us a splendid body of scientific men; and as its crown and consummation the fame and glory of Peary and the Pole." Despite Chamberlain's success in raising money, therefore, the lack of sufficient funds to maintain his program, rather than the widespread and sharp criticism of its nature, had defeated him.

During these years at Bowdoin, Chamberlain's children reached maturity and left the shelter of home. Grace was the first to go. Chamberlain, enormously fond of both his children, had a special place in his heart for his daughter. Once, in 1876, returning home late at night from a faculty meeting, he wrote her a note in which he expressed a father's love for her but at the same time regarded her in a different dimension. He was fond of her, he said, not simply because she was his daughter but "because you are a splendid soul and belong to eternity." His love and admiration were reciprocated, too. In view of his feeling for her, it must have been with mixed emotions that he gave her in marriage to the lawyer son of a Boston business man. For on April 28, 1881, at eight o'clock in the evening, Grace married Horace Gwynne Allen in the First Parish Church of Brunswick before the very altar where Chamberlain had married Fanny a little more than twenty-five years before.

Wyllys likewise left the family fold. In 1877 he entered Bowdoin and graduated in 1881; he was therefore present during the days when his father's scientific program was expiring. Though Wyllys revealed a real interest in science and a remarkable aptitude for invention, he went to law school at Boston University and presently settled in Florida not far from where his father had recently purchased land in Ocala on the Gulf coast.

Throughout Chamberlain's career at Bowdoin, ill health, caused by his wound, continually dogged him. No doubt the strenuous schedule he kept did little to ease him—and strenuous it was, for besides his college duties he gave frequent addresses at town festivals, meetings of the Loyal Legion and the G. A. R., and gatherings of civic groups; delivered the State oration at the nation's centennial in Philadelphia in 1876; served as United States Commissioner at the Paris Exposition in 1878; testified at the hearings concerning General Warren; and, as the commander of the State's militia, prevented civil war in Augusta in 1880 over an election crisis. A lover of the sea and the Maine coast in particular, he authorized his friend, A. Dalton of Cumberland, to buy for him a quarter share in a trim, little ten-ton schooner yacht, *Pinafore*. When Dalton purchased the share in 1879, Chamberlain was delighted; and the Chamberlains often explored the island-studded Casco Bay with the Daltons, whose two young daughters, Mary and Edith, wrote him hero-worshipping letters from their home, St. Stephen's

Rectory in Cumberland. But even cruises in the *Pinafore* were but a temporary anodyne to constant physical pain. To what extent his discomfort was aggravated by disappointment and depression over the collapse of his educational plans for the college it is impossible to be sure. All one can be certain of is that in the early 1880's he became increasingly restless and eager to play a role where he might be more effective than at Bowdoin and that his health deteriorated alarmingly. Even the salubrious effects of a trip to Florida in 1881, a place he found enormously interesting, did not last long.

Finally, on March 12, 1883, after a winter of acute pain for Chamberlain, the secretary of the faculty wrote the following minute of the regular meeting:

The President announced that the condition of his health made it imperative for him to be absent for the remainder of the term. . . .

This announcement followed by only ten days a letter from Dr. J. H. Warren of Boston, to whom he had gone for an examination. Warren told him that he must stop working temporarily and submit to surgery for his wounds, which had been neglected too long. The physician also strongly urged a change of surroundings, and recommended Florida. Chamberlain submitted to an operation, came very close to dying, but, constitutionally very strong, recuperated rapidly.

News of his illness brought expressions of concern from all over the country. One letter that Chamberlain cherished in particular was from the Reverend John Pike, Bowdoin '33, who regretted that Chamberlain would not be at the Commencement dinner, which, in Rowley's opinion, the General always made "so bright, interesting and happy." Chamberlain likewise preserved a letter from his old friend and comrade of the 20th Maine, Ellis Spear, who expressed gratification at learning of Chamberlain's improvement.

Notwithstanding his swift recovery from surgery, Chamberlain remained physically weak for months and resigned the presidency, holding his last meeting of the faculty on September 10, 1883. The reforms which he regarded as most significant had failed, he had made enemies whose opposition to him he regarded as dangerous to Bowdoin's development so long as he was president, his precarious physical condition would continue to impair his function as president, and he was becoming increasingly interested in the world of business. The Boards graciously accepted his resignation but earnestly entreated him to remain at Bowdoin. Accordingly, at their request, he agreed to lecture for the time being in political economy and in constitutional and international law. Then, in 1885, his health again deteriorating, he resigned even his professorial position. As President Hyde said of him, "... at one time or another between 1855 and 1885 he taught every subject in the college curriculum with the exception of Mathematics and Physical Science." It was a remarkable display of versatility, and, as professor and president, his was a remarkable record of service to the little Maine college he never ceased to love.

☞ ☞ ☞ XI ☞ ☞ ☞

PHILADELPHIA, FRANCE, AND
THE TWELVE DAYS

WHILE Chamberlain was president of Bowdoin, he made
three notable contributions outside his college duties. He
delivered a remarkable address on the State of Maine to the
great Centennial Exhibition at Philadelphia in 1876. He
served as United States Commissioner to the Paris Exposition in 1878 and wrote a long and searching report on
education in France and other countries for the Federal
government. Finally, called out as a major general of militia
during the great election crisis of 1880 in Maine, he saved the
State from the horror and shame of an armed revolt. For
this last service in particular many citizens thought him entitled to serious consideration for United States Senator.

The Centennial Exhibition was one of the gala events in
the post-Civil War era. More than any other single event,
it revealed to the world the coming-of-age of American
industry. Marking the nation's centennial, it also stood as
a symbol of the healing of the wounds of the Civil War;
now the nation enjoyed a firmer bond of union than ever
before, it seemed to proclaim. Socially, it was an enormous
success, as people flocked to it from all over the world. Like
the other states, Maine was given its place and time for
glorifying itself, and, in response to a number of suggestions,
Governor Selden Connor wrote Chamberlain in February,

1876, inviting him to deliver "an historical and descriptive address upon the State of Maine."

Connor knew his man well, for Chamberlain loved Maine with a passion and keenly enjoyed sharing his feeling with others. The year was not an easy one for him at Bowdoin, being, in fact, the time when he composed his second resignation. But he let no sense of frustration interfere with the preparation of his address, which he entitled, "Maine: Her Place in History."

He gave the address on November 4, to a large and enthusiastic audience as the climax of "Maine Day." It was long and idealistic, yet permeated by the sharp realism that had characterized his gubernatorial addresses. He spoke of Maine as being "conservative, self-reliant, calm; slow, even, to wrath or novelty. She will lead in a noble cause when convinced; but she is not fanatical, narrow nor self-seeking." At the same time her conservatism had led her to resist corporations, to afford no assistance to large-capital enterprises. Consequently her young people were leaving in droves. If she would but develop her water power and encourage business and industry, a wonderful future was possible. He wanted her to emphasize skilled rather than hard labor: "Hard labor is a prison sentence; skilled labor is the enfranchisement of man." Striking a romantically idealistic note, he envisaged a time, still not realized in large part, "When in the revolutions and evolutions of history the shore of this Gulf of Maine will be the seat of industrial, social and political empire, even beyond the early dreams; for it will be an empire where no despot either of politics or traffic, shall make merchandize of souls, but where MAN, in making himself master, makes all men free!"

There were people present who considered his address the

most interesting and significant of all those delivered. The applause was tremendous, and press comments were almost unqualifiedly complimentary. The address made such a stir in Maine that Chamberlain was invited to present it again to a convention of the Legislature at Augusta on February 6, 1877. It so impressed its auditors that they authorized its publication as a state document.

Chamberlain's stature as an educator, his ability to mix well with people, and his knowledge of languages prompted President Rutherford B. Hayes to consider him as a United States Commissioner to the Universal Exposition at Paris in 1878. Learning of the likelihood of appointment, Chamberlain consulted Judge John Appleton of Bangor, chairman of the Board of Trustees. Appleton urged Chamberlain to make the trip since it would be beneficial to his health and he would see Paris under exceptionally agreeable circumstances. "I should not excuse your refusal," said Appleton. Reassured, Chamberlain was delighted to accept the appointment which was conveyed to him in March by William M. Evarts, Secretary of State. In May a special passport arrived, and in the summer he sailed on the *England*. Since Grace and Wyllys were still at home, Fanny evidently chose not to accompany her husband.

Chamberlain thoroughly enjoyed his European trip. He was a happy combination of introvert and extrovert tendencies; hence, while, at times, a lover of solitude and contemplation, at other times he relished meeting people, and his sage and sometimes witty comments, his appreciative sense of humor, and his dignified affability won him many friends. Certainly he made a most favorable impression on his fellow travelers and the French authorities. He attended numerous social events, and long preserved the invitation from Minister of Foreign Affairs Waddington and his wife to spend the evening at their home on October 24 for dinner and dancing. But Chamberlain was not one to neglect the serious side of his duties. Not only did he seek and receive permission to explore the public libraries and archives of France for the purpose of procuring historical information relative to the French occupation of Maine in colonial days, he also appraised for the United States government the educational systems as evidenced in the education exhibits at the Exposition submitted by nations all over the globe; the report, however, was to have particular reference to France. In his inspection, which extended from nurseries to scientific museums, Chamberlain had his eye on six specific points: administration, organization, support, methods and appliances, buildings and furniture, recent improvements and current tendencies.

His report, embodying 165 closely printed pages in a volume published by the government, contains some interesting observations. He saw the European progressives in education as trying to make education "obligatory, gratuitous, and neutral in religion," and he thought that so far as primary education was concerned the United States had achieved the last two to a higher degree than France but that certain of our states lagged behind in making a sufficient degree of education obligatory. He noted that in Europe primary education remained largely in the hands of men, while in America women had taken over, and that on both continents a reaction to the prevailing extreme had set in. "There is a just mean somewhere," said Chamberlain. "But," he added, "it will probably remain true that the reserved force and the power to command and to deal with masses, which is a characteristic of manhood, will be deemed an

essential factor in the proper discipline of youthful character, and the successful administration of schools on any considerable scale." He saw the United States as ahead in the
education of girls but behind "in the education of the senses,
of the power of observation, and manipulation." He thought
the schools and colleges of the United States "far behind"
in the study of social and political science. "Nor," he added
in a comment as pertinent in the later twentieth century
as in 1878, "can there be any branch of the 'humanities' more
important or more urgently demanded by the times than the
knowledge of the facts, the forces, and the laws by which
civilization advances, and man emerges from the brute." He
noted approvingly that "It has never been the custom in
France to regard education as unfitting men for practical
affairs and for high political responsibilities." He liked, too,
the attention given to adult education in Europe. "More of
this sort could be done in our higher schools of learning,"
he said. "The college should not only be a place where a
student can get an education; it should be a light set on a
hill, to shine into the dark places below it."

The report is comprehensive and perceptive, and Chamberlain received a bronze medal from the French government and the compliments of the director of the Education
Exhibit of the United States, John D. Philbrick. The latter
considered the report "A very excellent piece of work,"
soundly conceived, well executed, complete and remarkably
accurate. He was especially impressed with "the judicious
selection and arrangement of the matter, from the great mass
to be digested. The work must have cost you much labor
in its preparation,—to say nothing of your industry and success in collecting the material." The report was "quite the

best original production on public schools abroad which has been printed in America."

Chamberlain was back at Bowdoin only a little over a year when he was again called away from Brunswick, but this time for something more pressing and important than an oration on his state or a report on European education. This was the great election crisis in Maine in January, 1880, caused by the rise of the Greenback party. The familiar Greenbacks, or paper money, of Civil War days had persisted after the war despite the efforts of the business men in the Northeast to drive them out of existence. These men represented the deflationary, hard-money interests and were identified with the Republican party, although many Democrats were included in their number. As against this body were the agrarian groups of the West and South who thought that only by opposing resumption of specie payments by the Federal government and securing an expansion of the currency through a larger issue of Greenbacks could they hope to pay off their mortgages. These were the inflationary, soft-money interests, usually identified with the Democratic party but containing many Republicans. Since neither party put its shoulder behind a movement for soft money, a number of the soft-money people in both parties formed a third party, the Greenback party, in 1874. Two years later it ran the engineer and philanthropist, Peter Cooper, for President of the United States, but Cooper received fewer than 100,000 votes. In 1878, reorganized as the Greenback-Labor party, it cast a million votes in the elections to Congress, and, in 1880, James B. Weaver ran as the party candidate for President. He received only about 300,000 votes. Thereafter, with the return of prosperity following the acute depression of

1873-76 and the rise of the controversy over silver, the Greenback movement declined in the country at large.

As happens not infrequently, states on the periphery become excited over national issues after they are no longer national; certainly this was true of Maine, which received the full tide of Greenbackism in 1879. The year before, the Greenback party cast over 41,000 votes for its gubernatorial candidate, Joseph L. Smith, an Old Town lumberman; this was 13,000 more votes than the Democratic candidate, Dr. Alonzo Garcelon of Lewiston, received, but 15,000 short of the Republican incumbent, General Selden Connor, Lieutenant Colonel of the 7th Maine and former collector of internal revenue for the Augusta district. Since Connor did not win a majority of the popular votes, the election went to the Legislature, where the Republicans joined with Democrats in voting for Garcelon rather than tolerate Smith. In 1879, the situation was similar. The Republican candidate, Daniel F. Davis, an ambitious young lawyer, received 68,967 of the popular votes; the Greenbacker, Smith, 47,643; the Democrat, Garcelon, 21,851, and a maverick Democrat, Bion Bradbury, 264. Again, with no majority of the total vote attained by any candidate, the election went to the Legislature, which, with a clear Republican majority in both houses, appeared certain to vote for Davis as Governor. The Republicans had made an extra effort to get out the vote in view of the likelihood that, despite their putting forward separate gubernatorial candidates, the Democrats and Greenbackers would cooperate closely in the new Legislature.

All did not turn out as expected. There were cries from the newspapers, particularly the Democratic organs, of corruption in the election, and the Governor and his Council conducted an investigation of the official returns from the localities. They found a number of real or alleged irregularities which shifted the Republican majority of seven in the Senate and twenty-nine in the House to a total Democrat-Greenbacker majority (the Fusionists) of seventeen with twelve vacancies—changes largely the result of technicalities in reporting the returns but with Garcelon and his advisers exploiting every imaginable technicality. The shift meant that a Fusionist majority in the Legislature would elect a Fusionist Governor, Smith, and assure a Fusionist Council and Fusionists in other executive positions.

The announcement by the Governor and his Council on December 17 touched off a roar of exultation from the Fusionists and one of protest from the Republicans. There is little doubt that so far as a rigorous interpretation of the voting laws was concerned, the Governor and his Council had a pretty strong case, and they were convinced that many of the Republican seats had been won by bribery and fraud. On the other hand, the men whose elections were summarily cancelled in the famous "count out" insisted that their constitutional rights had been infringed. They contended that the local returns, which had been in the keeping of selectmen and town clerks from election day until thirty days before the meeting of the new Legislature on the first Wednesday in January, had been tampered with in favor of Fusionist candidates, and in a number of instances it turned out that they were right. The "counted out" Republican candidates were supported by many Republicans throughout the State who felt that Garcelon's action not only was fraudulent in itself but also was a move to establish a dictatorship. This they would not tolerate whether the law was on their side or not.

Republican action against Garcelon's move took three

forms: recommendation of moderate measures, the holding
of indignation meetings, and a march of armed men on
Augusta. Lot M. Morrill, former Governor and United States
Senator who resigned the latter post to become President
Grant's Secretary of the Treasury, counseled patience and
urged Garcelon to let the Supreme Court of the State decide
on the legality of the conflicting claims. On Christmas Day
Chamberlain supported Morrill's suggestion in a telegram
to Garcelon, considering Morrill's advice "eminently wise."
Dr. Garcelon was a Bowdoin man whom Chamberlain knew
well and liked, except for his politics, though he had more
respect for him as a Democrat than for the disgruntled Republicans who comprised the bulk of the Greenbackers.

It is possible that the situation might have been more or
less quietly resolved but for James G. Blaine; his intervention was crucial in raising the political temperature. Blaine
had been in Washington busy with plans to defeat New
York Senator Roscoe Conkling's attempt to promote Grant
for a third-term President. The smooth-talking, supple-
minded Blaine and the huge, rough, but able Conkling—
neither the quintessence of circumspect behavior!—had been
political adversaries for years. The blond Conkling, who was
something of a "lady killer," had a vanity so enormous that
it was said he was the only man in the country who could
strut sitting down. Blaine's vanity was no less towering but
more carefully contained and decorously expressed. Unlike
Conkling's "Ice-cream trousers" and "moon-on-the-water
vests," Blaine wore a black, almost clerical garb, which, with
his dark eyes and olive skin, gave him a deadly, hooded-
hawk appearance. And indeed, although Conkling was a
personality and a speaker of great force and sarcastic wit,
Blaine, in the opinion of the Washington press gallery, was

the ablest debater of his time, a master of language who toyed with Conkling on the floor of the Senate as a cat would toy with a mouse—a rather large mouse. Blaine prided himself on his political skill and on the personal magnetism which he exerted over many people, and the role he envisaged for himself in the future was nothing less than that of President. Conkling must therefore not be permitted to run Grant, the ailing, formerly idolized hero, for a third term.

In the midst of Blaine's planning came the news of the Maine election on September 8, 1879. Republicans from all over the country entreated him not to let the State wander from the party fold; the fear of "a greenback Governor" or "a copperhead United States Senator" from Maine, the latter favorable to the South, was still great. Blaine, however, was less worried than most about the election results. Although there was no majority in the popular vote for Governor, the slim but certain Republican majority in the new Legislature was a guarantee of a Republican Governor. Then word arrived of the action by Governor Garcelon and his Council and the reverse prospect of a Greenback Senate, a Democratic House, and a Greenback or Democratic Governor—a thumping victory for the Fusionists and a humiliating defeat for the Republicans. Blaine, who was in Boston at the time, could hardly believe the possibility; after all, he had been the chairman of the Maine Republican Committee for over twenty years. But entreated by Republicans in and out of Maine to come to the rescue of the party, and convinced that if he could not control the State, his own political career might be jeopardized, he spent all night walking the floor of his room planning his next moves. First he went to Augusta and set up headquarters in his spacious home next to the Capitol. Through his door streamed many followers, a number of whom were not averse to regarding the Capitol as a hostile stronghold to be taken literally by armed assault. Blaine, cleverer than such rash ones, preferred other means. Though he was willing to see the issue settled in the courts if need be, he had no intention of letting the Fusionists remain in power unchallenged until the next election. He urged the holding of indignation meetings throughout the State to intimidate the Fusionists into giving ground.

Chamberlain viewed Blaine's procedure with great distaste. "As to the indignation meeting proposed here," he wrote Blaine from Brunswick on December 29, "it was my opinion that the demonstrations of that sort had already been sufficient to impress upon the Governor the state of public feeling; and that what we now need to do is not to add to popular excitement which is likely to result in disorder and violence, but to aid in keeping the peace by inducing our friends to speak and act as sober and law-abiding citizens . . . I deprecate all suggestion of bloodshed in the settlement of the question . . . I hope you will do all you can to stop the incendiary talk which proposes violent measures, and is doing great harm to our people." That the action of ill-advised and ambitious men should endanger his beloved Maine distressed and angered him: "I cannot bear to think of our fair and orderly State plunged into the horrors of a civil war." The issue should be left to the Court.

Actually the normally "fair and orderly" State of Maine was moving more swiftly toward civil war than even Chamberlain was aware. With men pouring into Augusta from all over the State eager for action, many reporting at Blaine's headquarters, others at Fusionist headquarters in Eben Pillsbury's rooms at one of the hotels downtown, anxious moderates begged Governor Garcelon to call out the militia.

Though strongly tempted, he realized that this would be an overt recognition of the emergency which might precipitate bloodshed. While declining to take such a step, he made a decision which was possibly worse. He enlisted a body of about one hundred men, armed them, and placed them in and around the Capitol. Short of sufficient rifles and ammunition, he sent to Bangor for additional supplies, but the people in that Republican stronghold at first prevented the supplies from leaving. Eventually, at the Governor's insistence, 120 rifles and 20,000 rounds of ammunition arrived from Bangor on December 30 under heavy guard. The Capitol "army" then loaded their weapons, while Blaine's riflemen swarming at his house across the street needed only some minor irresponsible act or word to send them dashing up the slope of the lawn opposite in a headlong assault on "Fort Garcelon" as the Portland *Daily Press* alluded to the Capitol. With trains bringing additional men daily, reckless, angry and determined, with newspapers throughout the State taking sides in furious partisanship, an explosion seemed imminent.

Recognizing on January 5, 1880 that the situation was practically out of control, Garcelon ordered Chamberlain, as Major General of the Maine militia, to take command of the first division of the militia, and directed him to repair to Augusta to protect the public property and institutions of the State until the Governor's successor was properly qualified. Chamberlain at once made an important decision. Although he effected arrangements with militia commanders for the mobilization of their units on order and with the railroads for the dispatch of those units to the capital and for the priority of his telegrams, he resolved not to let a single soldier appear in Augusta unless, in his opinion, the situation was beyond redemption. His was the only military uniform in evidence, and in a city swarming with riflemen he refused to wear any arms.

Chamberlain had to move with extreme delicacy, but he did not hesitate. He conferred at once with Charles E. Nash, the able Mayor of Augusta, who pledged him the full police facilities of the city. He persuaded Governor Garcelon to withdraw the armed men in and around the State House, locked up the Governor's chamber and the Council rooms, deposited important papers in the Treasury vaults, and stationed police before all executive chambers. Although there were rumors that leaders of both the Republicans and the Fusionists had attempted to persuade militia command-ers not to obey his orders, pledges of loyalty jammed the wires and the mails, expressing, in the words of one battalion commander, "full confidence in your integrity as a man, and your loyalty and devotion to the best interests of our noble though disgraced Commonwealth."

From a little office in the Capitol Chamberlain directed the campaign of maintaining order. He insisted throughout on the primacy of civil authority, relying heavily on Mayor Nash and his police force. He was, of course, the target of violent attention, as each faction sought to catch his ear; but although a Republican, he tried to preserve a strict neutrality. Whether Chamberlain regarded himself as "the right man in the right place," as one of his supporters con-sidered him, is difficult to say, but there is no doubt that he made up his mind not to be "bulldozed." He insisted that only the Legislature could determine the Governor and that, given the circumstances, only the Supreme Court could re-solve the dispute over the elections to the Legislature.

Notwithstanding his announced position, pressure in-creased to induce him to recognize a Governor. This was especially strong in behalf of the elderly James D. Lamson, a Democrat of Freedom, elected president of the Senate by a combination of Democrats and Republicans. Lamson was a man of principle who conferred with Chamberlain before making a formal demand for recognition. Chamberlain told him he considered him a Senator-elect but hardly a properly qualified president of the Senate who might serve as Governor since the Court had still to pass on the qualifications of a number of the very Senators-elect who had voted for him. When Lamson, pressed by his supporters, subsequently made a formal demand that Chamberlain recognize him, several leading Republicans advised Chamberlain to consult Judge Libby of the Supreme Court. The Judge told Chamberlain, "Lamson is *de facto* Governor and you have no other course but to recognize and obey him." Chamberlain replied, "That is equivalent to saying that I have been a usurper all this week and very nearly a traitor." "I do not say that," retorted the Judge, "but your only safe course is to recognize him." "This is to beg the question and surrender the position," said Chamberlain. He stood his ground even when, as he explained to Judge Appleton, "I was informed . . . by a gentleman of the highest standing [Nelson Dingley, former Governor and future Congressman] who professed to speak by permission and authority from three judges of the Supreme Court, that the Court were ready and desirous to have *me* put certain questions which they would answer in a certain way." Chamberlain disliked "that way of doing such business" and doubted "the binding force of, and general acquiescence in answers made to questions put by a military officer to whom the constitution gave no such right." Chamberlain stood firmly on the ground that the questions concerning who should be recognized as Governor must be placed before the Court by those properly entitled by the Constitution to ask such questions, not by himself as a military officer. Once the judges sitting as the Court had given their opinion, all should accept their decision; he would recognize the new Governor and resign his authority as defined by Governor Garcelon.

It was difficult enough to deal with the claims of Lamson, whom Chamberlain considered a reasonable, honorable man, but Chamberlain soon found himself confronted by the claims of another. This was Joseph A. Locke of Portland, whom the Republicans elected as their president of the Senate and who therefore became a candidate for Governor. Locke and the Republicans had previously supported Lamson, but Chamberlain told Locke as he had told Lamson, in effect, "Submit your case to the Court and abide by its decision."

The situation grew increasingly tense and bitter. Lot M. Morrill called on Chamberlain, sent by the Blaine people to find out more concerning the General's views and his plans in the event of an outbreak of violence. Chamberlain replied that his position in the crisis was announced at the start but that he did not purpose to reveal his military plans. Actually he and Morrill were agreed on the basic policy of submitting the question to the Court, and Morrill was trying hard to persuade Blaine to do so.

Meanwhile, on January 10, an Augusta lawyer and former United States Senator, who was also a Bowdoin Trustee, James W. Bradbury, visited Chamberlain in Lamson's behalf. Bradbury, by reputation a moderate-minded Democrat, told Chamberlain there was "not the shadow of a doubt" that Lamson was Governor. Chamberlain replied that more than half the members-elect of both Houses protested the organization that had been effected on the ground that the men who had elected Lamson president of the Senate had not as yet had their own election as Senators validated. When Bradbury insisted that Chamberlain's own party leaders had assented to the organization, Chamberlain said that in his present capacity he had no party leaders and that the claimants should appeal to the State Supreme Court. "I would advise you to escape serious trouble," Bradbury warned him. "I shall not surrender my trust till I know what I am right in doing by all the tests our civil order affords," was the proud reply.

Actually, Chamberlain hoped Lamson would be entitled to be recognized as Governor, and in a rare display of indiscretion he wrote as much to Chief Justice Appleton. Lamson's validation would afford a way out of the difficulty; besides, "Mr. Lamson has borne himself so honorably and has aided so much in trying to bring about a peaceful solution, that I have come to entertain a high respect for him." Chances of a peaceful solution, however, appeared slim on January 12. "The excitement is now terrific in bitterness," wrote Chamberlain. "The fusionists swear they will resist with blood and fire if the Court sustains the Republican programme."

But the Republicans were breathing hotly, too. Members of the Republican committee favored using force to oust the Fusionists, and Blaine was especially exasperated that Chamberlain had not done so in the beginning. He sent the future founder of the Bath Iron Works, Thomas W. Hyde, to the General in his Capitol headquarters with word that the party chiefs were ready "to pitch the Fusionists out of the window." Chamberlain, who knew Hyde well, shook his head. "Tom," he said firmly, "you are as dear to me as my own son. But I will permit you to do nothing of the kind. I am going to preserve the peace. I want you and Mr. Blaine and the others to keep away from this building."

Violence was now very near. Discovering a plot to kill Chamberlain, Mayor Nash sent a squad of policemen with the General whenever he left the Capitol. There was also a design on foot to kidnap Chamberlain and keep him hidden in some remote village until the rival factions had fought the issue out. Chamberlain is said to have foiled the would-be kidnappers by never staying twice at the same night lodgings. At about this time, too, a member of his staff ran into his office from the rotunda of the Capitol crying out that a gang of men was waiting outside to kill him. Buttoning up his coat, Chamberlain strode out to meet them. "Men, you wish to kill me, I hear," he is reported to have said. "Killing is no new thing to me. I have offered myself to be killed many times, when I no more deserved it than I do now. Some of you, I think, have been with me in those days. You understand what you want, do you? I am here to preserve the peace and honor of this State, until the rightful government is seated—whichever it may be, it is not for me to say. But it is for me to see that the laws of this State are put into effect, without fraud, without force, but with calm thought and purpose. I am here for that, and I shall do it. If anybody wants to kill me for it, here I am. Let him kill!" When he tore open his coat and waited, the group remained uneasily silent. Then, evidently stirred by memories of a more honorable day, one war veteran thrust his way through the group and shouted, "By God, General, the first man that dares to lay a hand on you, I'll kill him on the spot!" The group broke up, muttering and still resentful, but left Chamberlain alone. Although the General had resorted to melodrama, it had paid off.

Presently Chamberlain and Nash learned of a plot to assassinate Blaine and burn his mansion, while rumors grew that Republican gunmen brought into the city were about ready to attack the Fusionists. Chamberlain at once notified Blaine of the plot against his life, and Nash's police arrested the conspirators.

The result of the sudden action by Chamberlain and Nash had a number of interesting repercussions. Blaine now thought the candidates should submit the question to the Court, a move Lamson had been convinced was the only wise procedure after his meeting with Chamberlain. Likewise Eugene Hale, a future United States Senator, persuaded the Republican supporters of Locke to rely on the Court's decision. Chamberlain could now issue a public statement to the people of Maine giving assurance that "up to this moment calm counsels have prevailed" and that there was "no present occasion for public alarm," but expressing regret "that messages should be sent from any quarter which bring crowds of men into this city."

Those "crowds of men," most of them armed, troubled Chamberlain as he contemplated how reckless leaders might use them. He felt especially perturbed as a body of Fusionists, furious with Lamson for agreeing to submit his case to the Court, rejected him and elected as Governor one of the original popular candidates for that office, Joseph S. Smith. Although not so extreme as his lieutenants, Smith carried matters with a high hand. He announced his election and, in a letter from the Adjutant General's office on January 16, revoked Governor Garcelon's famous Special Order Number

45 ordering Chamberlain to duty. Smith also forbade anyone to obey Chamberlain's orders.

The streets at once became turbulent again as men shifted sides, most—but by no means all—Republicans closing ranks against Smith, to whom Blaine preferred either Lamson or Locke. Chamberlain, however, stood as firmly against Smith as against Lamson or Locke, though the situation was peculiarly annoying. When Chamberlain refused to surrender his authority, Smith sent an officer to arrest him. With Chamberlain adamant and Charles Nash's policemen still on duty, the officer retired in confusion.

At last, on this day of glory and embarrassment to Smith, the Supreme Court reached a decision. It validated a Republican Legislature. News of this action touched off an uproar throughout the city as Fusionists swore they would not accept the decision. But Chamberlain and Nash proved equal to the occasion, and no violence of consequence took place during that anxious night.

The following day, Saturday, January 17, the Legislature elected Daniel F. Davis Governor of Maine. Davis informed Chamberlain of his election and furnished him with a copy of the Supreme Court opinion sustaining the legality of the Legislature that had elected him. Davis also wrote, "In common with all the citizens of this State I have watched with great anxiety the events of the past few days, and rejoice with them in the good results of the wise and efficient measures adopted by you for the preservation of the peace and protection of the property and institutions of the State; and more especially that those results have been accomplished without resorting to military force, or permitting violence to be used." Chamberlain at once recognized Davis as Governor and said, "I consider my trust, under Special Order No. 45, as at an end."

The Twelve Days had been a mortifying experience for the State of Maine and an extraordinarily trying experience for Chamberlain. Not only had he literally been in peril of his life but he had also been the object of contumely, misconstruction of motives, and misunderstanding. Newspapers had denounced him as "The Republican Renegade," "The Fusionist Sympathizer," "Chamberlain the Most Dangerous Man in Maine," "The Lawless Usurper," "Traitor to His Trust," "The Serpent of Brunswick," "The Tool of Blaine." A personal friend in Thomaston thought he had made grave mistakes in his attitude toward Lamson. Political friends, grossly misunderstanding him, sought unsuccessfully to have him officially commit himself to a Republican or, in the case of Lamson, to a man with whom the Republicans felt they could work. But Chamberlain's sense of honor would not permit him to deviate from the course he considered his duty to maintain. His only departure was in the indiscreet disclosure to Appleton of his preference for Lamson, which was publicized a year later.

However nettled by some of the criticisms, Chamberlain could not but feel upheld by the loyal support and expressions of gratitude from citizens in and out of the State. Commendations came crowding in for his "prudence and valor" and for his "standing as a barrier between despotism and liberty," for showing "the highest qualities," for taking a position as "wise" as it was "noble." Old comrades had offered their services, old personal friends had stood fast. He could return to Brunswick and his duties at Bowdoin with the satisfaction of having discharged a difficult duty with consummate tact and ability. Truly, as has been ob-

served, he had been the "Champion of Civil Liberty in
Maine," and it was the good fortune of the State of Maine
that "The General's moral power . . . was . . . in the ascend-
ant."

Charles D. Gilmore, Chamberlain's second-in-command of
the 20th Maine, had expressed the hope that the General's
role during the crisis would lead to "higher honors." Unfortunately the Twelve Days from January 5 to 17, 1880
not only made him a host of political enemies whose ani-
mosity he considered harmful to Bowdoin so long as he remained its president but also indubitably ruined his chances
ever to hold a major political office. He was altogether too
independent to suit the political chiefs of his party, yet this
very quality was appealing to many individuals throughout
Maine. As early as June, 1879, opinion had been expressed
that he should become the next United States Senator, and
one of his correspondents was eager to see his name again
put up for Governor if another term in that office would help
his election to the Senate. A year later, so favorable an impression had he made by his handling of the election crisis,
people from all over the State were urging him to accept
support for the Senate. Intrigued at last, Chamberlain wrote
to a number of friends, soliciting their opinions and their
appraisal of his possibilities with their representatives in
the Legislature. Almost whimsically he asked one friend,
". . . do you see anything preposterous in my being a candidate before the people of Maine or the Republican party?"

Had he been a shrewder person, politically speaking, he
might have realized that his candidacy, if not preposterous,
was at least unlikely. Back in 1869, when Senator Fessenden
had died, Chamberlain, as Governor, was urged to appoint
John B. Brown to fill out Fessenden's term; Brown would

then be expected to step aside when the term expired and let Chamberlain become a candidate. But Brown, though capable, was less so, in Chamberlain's opinion, than Lot M. Morrill, former Governor and Senator, whom he proposed, much to the anger of Chamberlain's coat-tail holders and the dismay of his friends. When Morrill subsequently resigned to become Grant's Secretary of the Treasury, he said he understood that Chamberlain was to be appointed to the Senate in his place. Political pressure in behalf of Blaine, however, was too strong for Governor Connor. Still, hope was not lost. Hannibal Hamlin, Vice President under Lincoln and Senator since 1867 when he had defeated Morrill by one vote, was retiring at last. Furthermore there were strong indications that Blaine might be designated by Garfield to become Secretary of State, in which case he would resign from the Senate, thus leaving another place open.

But the hopes of Chamberlain and his friends that he had a chance for either of these seats were not to be realized. Not all his friends, to be sure, were sanguine of his possibilities, certainly not Charles Nash, who had served so well with Chamberlain as mayor of Augusta during the Twelve Days. Writing early in January, 1881, he told the General, "The ingratitude—yes, indecency—of men from whom a year ago I fondly hoped better things has disheartened me somewhat. I will be on hand and do everything possible in my humble way." But in the Republican convention, a strong tide rolled in behalf of Eugene Hale, who was elected Senator by the Legislature to succeed Hamlin, the father of Hale's law partner. Hale, first elected to the House in 1868, and now beginning his thirty years of service in the Senate, was a strong Blaine man, having led Blaine's supporters in the Republican National Convention in 1876 and 1880. As for the seat Blaine vacated to become Secretary of State, this was taken by William P. Frye, who graduated from Bowdoin two years before Chamberlain and who was elected a Bowdoin Trustee in 1880. Frye, who had previously been mayor of Lewiston and six times a Congressman and who was to serve in the Senate until 1911, was also a Blaine man and active as a delegate to the Republican National Convention in 1872, 1876, and 1880. It paid to be a Blaine supporter in the days of that singular individual's power and glory. Actually both Hale and Frye were capable men devoted to Maine's interests and active in the Senate. Hale was extraordinarily effective in committee work, particularly in matters pertaining to the Navy and finance, while Frye, more articulate on the Senate floor, chaired the commerce committee and served on the foreign relations committee. Neither Hale nor Frye, however, possessed Chamberlain's power of intellect, range of interests, breadth of view, or facility of expression. His rejection as a Senatorial candidate was a serious loss to the State of Maine and the nation.

In the winter of 1884, with Chamberlain in retirement as president of Bowdoin but still active as a lecturer in political science and public law, Dexter A. Hawkins, of the law firm of Hawkins and Gedney in New York, wrote to President Chester A. Arthur recommending Chamberlain as minister to Russia. Hawkins spoke of Chamberlain's qualifications as soldier, scholar, statesman, gentleman, and loyal American. Hawkins likewise wrote Chamberlain advising him to see that his friends became active in his behalf. Chamberlain was interested. At once he reminded the President that the latter had told him two years earlier that if any post should open in the administration which would be agreeable to him, he should notify the White House. Unfortunately Arthur had another candidate, so the St. Petersburg post—like two even more remote possibilities for which he had been suggested: in 1876, the embassy in London, and in 1877, that in Paris, which he really wanted—vanished so far as Chamberlain was concerned. It is likely that with his background and personal qualifications, including his facility for languages, he would have made an excellent representative of this country abroad.

Though out of politics, Chamberlain did not lose his interest in them nor did politicians entirely lose their interest in his opinions. On April 26, 1884, the Republicans in Brunswick elected him a delegate to the State convention which was to meet at Bangor. He took his political obligations seriously and, notwithstanding his party's treatment, retained a remarkable degree of party loyalty. The year, however, must have sorely tried that loyalty, for the Republicans nominated Blaine for President. Blaine might be the "Plumed Knight," as Robert Ingersoll called him in 1876, but he was also the shameful "Tattooed Man" of *Puck's* famous cartoon who had trafficked with dishonest financiers and, while in Congress, had assisted the Little Rock and Fort Smith Railroad to obtain land by selling stock to Congressmen on a commission basis. Against him the Democrats put up Grover Cleveland, a Buffalo lawyer, who, as sheriff of Erie County, had hanged men; furthermore, he had an illegitimate child by a dipsomaniacal widow, Maria Halpin. The public and private lives of both men were thoroughly aired during the campaign. Until the Halpin story burst upon the country in late July, sentiment was running in favor of Cleveland, but, after that, it was a tight race as the press and the voters weighed and compared, now with facetiousness, now with anger, the relative iniquity of financial irregularity and sexual immorality.

To Chamberlain the campaign had become nauseating. Certainly he owed nothing to Blaine, and he hardly knew Cleveland, but he had little doubt concerning the ability of both men, and he deplored the campaign's having become so scurrilous. At the same time, while disliking the possibility of the Democrats winning the election, he was now as disturbed by the dominance of the worst elements in the Republican Party as he had been when Hayes had taken office and he had entreated Hayes "not [to] yield to their assaults or their artifices." Stung by his criticism, Republicans accused him of deserting the party. To this he replied, "There is no authority for the statement that I shall vote for Cleveland. It probably grew out of the feeling on the part of some of the 'ring men' in the Republican Party that they had abused me so much that it would be more than human (or less) to expect me to support a party they expected to manage. But I am a Republican and deem it the best course for me to stand by my party, in hopes that before long the best elements in it will be able to prevail. I do not rebuke others with whom I sympathize on general grounds for taking a different course from mine; but for me to abide quietly within the lines of the party seems the consistent and manly course."

As it turned out, the loyalty of men like Chamberlain was not enough. The Reverend Samuel Burchard, a Presbyterian clergyman, made a political speech in New York City in the closing days of the campaign in which he identified the Democratic party with "rum, Romanism, and rebellion." A number of Irish Catholic voters who had supported Blaine now swung to Cleveland, who won the State of New York and all its electoral votes by the narrowest of popular margins, 1040. In fact, though the nation's electoral vote was 219 to 182 for Cleveland, the Cleveland plurality in the popular vote was but 23,000. Successful in controlling his own state, Maine, and in winning the votes even of high-principled men like Chamberlain, with his conception of party loyalty, Blaine had lost his last great chance for the White House. But it had been a near miss.

The Twelve Days, as well as his party's rejection of him as a candidate for national office, help further to explain Chamberlain's reluctance to continue at Bowdoin. He had made political enemies who were also Bowdoin men and other political enemies who, if not Bowdoin men, might be in a position to injure the college. Frustrated in his educational program, utterly blocked in any political aspirations, Chamberlain could not but think the time had about come to consider a new career. The age was that of Business, of Big Business that was getting bigger. Might not he, too, succeed in such a world? After all, business was like a war, and Chamberlain loved action with its intense drama. At any rate, business drew him strongly, and in 1885 he made the plunge.

⚓ ⚓ ⚓ XII ⚓ ⚓ ⚓

BUSINESS, EDUCATIONAL ACTIVITY, AND ADDRESSES

WHEN, in early 1882, Chamberlain returned from his first visit to Florida, a publication on that state appeared in the book stalls rhapsodizing about its attractions for "Tourists; Invalids, and Settlers," but adding that "even Florida is not the garden of Eden, and a man can not live even here like the lilies of the field, 'which toil not, neither do they spin'." Chamberlain had seen Florida in at least two capacities, tourist and invalid, and he was profoundly impressed by the potentialities in the third capacity. "There are great opportunities to get health and wealth," he wrote his sister "Sadie," "and also to do good, and help other people."

He explained at greater length what he meant: "I ... had many invitations to take positions of responsibility which naturally suit my temperament and aspirations. I always wanted to be at the head of some enterprise to transform the wilderness into a garden both materially and spiritually —to be a missionary of civilization and of Christianity at once. Here is a great chance to do it, and in my own country, which is peculiarly dear to me. It would be a delight to me now to give my energies to bringing forward the true results of all our struggle and sacrifice for the country, and to secure the blessings of so great a victory for the right." Then, in a paean of praise rarely surpassed by any chamber of com-

274

merce brochure, he added, "Health surely could be found and kept in that wonderful clime where the sea sands and corals have made a land of strange contrasts of soil, and the days and nights are glorious above, and the airs sweeping from the Atlantic and the Gulf keep a constant and delicious evenness of temperature. I mean to take Fanny there next winter, and think it would cure her of all her ills." He ended on a prophetic note, "It may be I shall have more to say and do about Florida by and by."

Actually his interest in Florida had already become substantial, for he had purchased land even before he visited the state and as early as May, 1881, a Rockland acquaintance had recommended a reliable man in Ocala who would order lumber to be sawed and prepared for Chamberlain's construction plans in late 1881. Chamberlain was preparing to join a number of investors in organizing a land development company. He went to Florida in early 1884, again as much for his health as for business, and his son Wyllys wrote Fanny from Ocala, expressing his gratitude that the General was not on the steamer *City of Columbia*, which was wrecked. Finally, on April 14, 1885, the company organized as the Homosassa Company.

The working headquarters of the company was at Ocala, while Homosassa lay along the Gulf coast about forty miles southwest of Ocala and an equal distance by water southeast of Cedar Keys, a convenient port for blockade runners until 1862. The Homosassa region is described in a Florida handbook, published several years after the company was formed, as low and level land "covered with a remarkably dense hammock growth of palms, wild orange, live oak, magnolia, and the ordinary hard woods, in unusual profusion and luxuriance. The river, fed by numerous fine springs,

is an arm of the sea rather than a fresh-water stream, and
is justly famed for its fine fishing, while the adjacent islands
and the mainland are among the best hunting grounds in
Florida." Obviously alluding to Chamberlain's company, the
book adds, "Large tracts of land have been acquired in this
vicinity by a company of capitalists, surveys have been made,
avenues cut through the hammock, and every effort made
to attract permanent settlers as well as transient visitors.
Probably there is no better or richer soil in the State for
most of the semi-tropical crops." In a notice of sale of a
vast orangery, part of the company's real estate, Chamberlain's own property was described as "extensive" and
"Crowned with a magnificent park of oaks, and with two
or three small orange groves in various stages of development."

In his report to the stockholders in March, 1886, Chamberlain pointed out what had been done, and what was needed.
The region had long been celebrated for its attractiveness,
but it had decayed. Since the company had taken over, roads
to the plantation fields and the landing on the Homosassa
River had been repaired. Likewise repaired were the roofs
and floors of the cabins. Stock was sold and the funds pro-
cured went toward the repairs. Further, Chamberlain had
effected an understanding with Albert E. Willard of Cedar
Keys whereby Willard would finish and furnish a hotel as
soon as possible and would then be permitted to occupy
and operate it.

Chamberlain himself was away from Florida much of the
time, especially in New York drumming up business. Despite
his efforts, the firm had slow going and various reorganiza-
tions occurred, in all of which Chamberlain continued as
president, while offices were established in New York City

as well as at Homosassa and Ocala. But the company, with a capital stock of only $200,000, languished. Until a railroad could be pushed to the Gulf linking Homosassa with the north-south route of the Florida Southern Railroad the area would have to wait before its attractions would become fully evident. In a final effort to open up the region, a group of investors, with Chamberlain as president, organized the Ocala and Silver Springs Railroad in 1891 with a capital of $1,000,000 and offices in the World Building in New York, Philadelphia, Chicago, St. Louis, Boston, Ocala, and Silver Springs. Yet even when successful in driving a spur to the Gulf, a branch later absorbed by the Atlantic Coast Line, the General and his friends were disappointed in the financial returns. In fact, not until the mid-twentieth century did the area really come into its own with good business to be made out of raising oranges and horses and catering to tourists and retired people. Gradually, therefore, Chamberlain withdrew from the Florida companies, although he remained titular president of the Homosassa Company until March 2, 1892.

With Chamberlain withdrawing from Florida his son was not long in doing likewise. A strange ineptitude in making a real financial success seems to have dogged Wyllys. While Chamberlain was in New York, Wyllys tried to make a living as an attorney in Ocala. So sparse was his business that in 1888 he had to write to his father for a loan of $50.00. Almost a year later Chamberlain sent another check for $50.00, and, in acknowledging it, Wyllys explained that the fee which he had won in a railroad case had been collected in his absence by another attorney who was now unable to return it. Significantly Wyllys added that this was what his

mother would have considered "Chamberlain luck." Presently
Wyllys also left for the North.

Although cutting his Florida interests, Chamberlain continued active in business for several years. Railroads especially interested him. As was so often the case in that era
business organizations liked to get hold of a popular Civil
War general and make him president. Even before he relinquished his Florida interests Chamberlain had become
president of the New Jersey Construction Company. This
company proposed in late 1889 to secure control of the
Lebanon Springs Railroad, to buy up or remove claims and
liens against the New York and Albany Railroad and the
New York, Boston, Albany, and Schenectady Railroad, and
to start work on the road in Shaker Valley Pass and on the
line from Brainards to Albany. In his association with this
company Chamberlain was heavily dependent on the advice
and support of a Bowdoin graduate and former faculty
member, H. H. Boody, of Boody, McLellan and Company,
Broadway bankers. A long and discouraging correspondence
exists between Chamberlain and Boody on how to make the
stock of the New Jersey Construction Company more valuable. Chamberlain also became actively interested in the
Troy and New England Railroad which aimed to hook into
the Housatonic system and tap the manufacturing towns
of western Massachusetts. In addition to serving in 1891 as
president of the Mutual Town and Bond Company of New
York, in which Boody was also involved, Chamberlain became president of the Kinetic Power Company. He invested
$5000 in this concern, which was interested in the develop-
ment of motors for street cars, and for elevated and suburban
roads throughout the country.

Executive offices and directorships in textile companies,

real estate companies, bond companies, even the World's Fair Tourist Company, claimed much of Chamberlain's time and energy through the 1890's. Gradually, however, company lawsuits and financial troubles wore him down. Though he continued as a stockholder in a number of these concerns, he began to resign official posts. After one especially trying land-company experience in 1896, he said that he was sick of the constant bickering and wanted to put his strength into good, clean work.

How Chamberlain managed to fulfil his numerous business obligations puzzled many people, whose wonderment was increased by the fact that for a few years he was also president of the Institute for Artists and Artisans. The Institute was founded in 1888 by Professor John Ward Stimson, formerly director of the art department of the Metropolitan Museum of Art, and was described by the New York *Times* as "the most vital American Art-School, and by all odds the best in this country." Plans were drawn up for reorganization and enlargement with a location at 140 and 142 West Twenty-Third Street. Chamberlain agreed to serve as president, Stimson as educational director, Horace J. Fairchild of Claflin Brothers as treasurer, Henry R. Elliot as secretary, while on the board was Chamberlain's old Civil War friend and Meade's former chief of staff, General Alexander S. Webb, president of the College of the City of New York. Chamberlain was active throughout 1892 and 1893 procuring subscriptions, even interesting Andrew Carnegie, though not to the extent that he had hoped.

Chamberlain saw the Institute as occupying independent and advanced ground. "It is conceived and conducted in the spirit of *Vital Art*," he explained, "tending toward a National emancipation from servile imitation and dead literalism, as well as from industrial and commercial dependence on foreign peoples for a supply of a fresh and growing demand in this country for high artistic work, in the common arts." He envisaged the Institute as affording opportunities at moderate cost for a thorough education in the principles and practical expressions of art. Instruction was to be given not only in painting, sculpture, architecture, illustration, and etching but also in those domestic arts that combine beauty with industrial skill, such arts as stained glass, ceramics, carving, metal working, jewelry, and interior decoration in textiles.

The General felt that the Institute should be considered as a training school for teachers as well as a school for developing artistic experts. He wanted instruction to proceed from elementary topics in order to embrace the least mature and cultivated minds. At every step in instruction of progressive difficulty, the instructor should assign appropriate collateral and illustrative reading to stimulate and develop a student's interests. Such reading should be tested by examination or abstracts or essays. Chamberlain saw emerging from the influence of the school's teaching the full development of the student's motivation, the maturing of his purpose, the concretizing of his aim. Proper teaching, therefore, was of the highest importance.

Not content with instruction in New York alone, Chamberlain established a summer school for the Institute in Maine. This was to be at his summer home, Domhegan, on Middle Bay between Mere Point and Harpswell, and about four miles from Brunswick. On a promontory owned by Josiah Simpson, Israel Simpson, his son, had once built a shipyard, while earlier the Indians had liked the point since they could land and launch canoes there whatever the tide. Chamberlain bought the five acres of property after the war, removed the remains of the shipyard, and repaired the house and barn as well as an old wharf. He often rode his horse Charlemagne around the property and sailed the yacht *Pinafore* over the waters of Middle Bay and to Portland, only twenty miles away. He now made this estate—named after one of the Indian chiefs who sold it to the white men— available to the Institute for an eight-week summer course. Thirty persons were to be accommodated, each one to pay a tuition of $25.00 and a weekly board not to exceed six dollars. Instruction was under the direction of Professor Stimson.

Enthusiastic as was Chamberlain over the Institute for Artists and Artisans, and deeply involved though he might be in its work and in his business obligations, he still found time for other pursuits, of which four were of especial interest. One was his becoming president of the *New England Magazine*, an honored periodical which, during the 1890's, enjoyed a period of regeneration. The editors were Edward E. Hale and Edwin D. Mead—the latter an able if irascible man with whom Chamberlain worked satisfactorily. Another pursuit was his assuming the editorship for a time of a massive description and analysis of American colleges and universities, *Universities and Their Sons*. This was a multi-volumed work, of which the first volume was published in 1898 and the last in 1923, nine years after his death. For this publication, which won encomiums for the quality of its editing, he wrote a brief but admirable introduction.

The third pursuit was giving public lectures and addresses. Chamberlain had been a professor of rhetoric, after all, and to his knowledge of the theory of speech he had added a vast amount of practical experience. He possessed a deep, resonant voice, clear in tone, wide in range, flexible in modulation. His addresses were logically constructed, with frequent allusions to God and nature. A contemporary sketch observed, "His writings and addresses show a tendency to reaches of thought somewhat abstruse. They are, however, suffused with a certain poetical idealism, and in religious conceptions with a spirituality almost mystical. But on themes relating to practical life and action he comes to the front with a power that is thrilling." If his speeches contain little that could be considered humorous, there is wit in them, anecdotal incident, substantial matter engagingly expressed, and often moral or patriotic sentiments, particularly in the perorations, that, far from being cant or mere flag-waving, stirred his listeners to intense enthusiasm. There are too many testimonies from contemporary individuals and newspapers for one not to realize that between this man, with his sweeping mustache and hair worn long in the fashion of the day, and his audiences there passed a kind of magnetic sympathy. Normally reserved, though friendly, with individuals, Chamberlain often became impassioned before an audience, yet this fervor never burst the bonds of discipline which he imposed upon himself. Neither language nor manner became extravagant. But the General's intellectual power, his utter sincerity, and his love of God and his fellow men invariably moved people.

A list of Chamberlain's addresses would serve no useful purpose here, but an analysis of a few may illustrate the points mentioned. On October 3, 1889, a ceremony was held at Gettysburg dedicating the monuments erected by the State of Maine on the battlefield. Present were many distinguished people from Maine and Pennsylvania, including the governors or their representatives, Hannibal Hamlin, Selden

Connor, the Reverend Theodore Gerrish of the 20th Maine, and Chamberlain as "President of the day." It was one of those golden days with groups of veterans wandering over the battlefield, reminiscing, and Chamberlain thoroughly enjoyed himself. In the evening a large audience met in the Court House for the dedicatory exercises, and Chamberlain opened the ceremonies.

He saw Maine standing alone here on the battlefield for the first time to commemorate the sacrifice which it had made as one of a great Union of states "in the forward march of man." The assumption that the Union was but a compact of states was false. The Union was a greater unity, its life being "a larger life, aloof from the dominance of self-surroundings," but in it the truest interests of all men, even of those who sought to dismember it, were interwoven. He scarcely more than alludes, explicitly or implicitly, to such causes of the war as slavery, conflicting economies, cultural differences. He takes the conflict into the realm of the States versus the Union, developing, indeed, a *mystique* of the Union, to which every individual is inextricably bound. "Our personality," he asserts, "exists in two identities,—the sphere of self, and the sphere of soul. One is circumscribed; the other moving out on boundless trajectories; one is near, and therefore dear; the other far and high, and therefore great. We live in both, but most in the greatest. Men reach their completest development, not in isolation nor working within narrow bounds, but through membership and participation in life of largest scope and fullness." Gettysburg was not fought in vain; the Union was saved. Yet the monuments erected did not commemorate the dead alone—"Death was but the divine acceptance of life freely offered by every one." Rather, "Service was the central fact. That fact and that truth, these monuments commemorate. They mark the centres round which stood the manhood of Maine, steadfast in noble service."

The address is typical of Chamberlain's interests. Invariably he sought to emphasize the higher values and to involve men in a consideration of their political, social, and moral responsibilities. This was, perhaps, the minister who never had a pulpit but who possessed a minister's concern for man's immortal soul, doubtless also the college professor who taught moral philosophy, political science, and public law. But it was likewise the 'practical' man—the soldier, the governor, the businessman. To him the loftiest conception of man's role in society was also the most practical. Selfishness was natural, but that selfishness which subordinated its peculiar interests to the welfare of the whole was enlightened and to be treasured. Truly the keystone of life was service, and a man should become aware of his potentialities and apply them—wisely.

Earlier on that October day in 1889, Chamberlain spoke briefly at the dedication of the monument to his old regiment on Little Round Top. "We know not of the future and cannot plan for it much," he told his old friends and comrades. "But . . . we may cherish such thought and such ideals, and dream such dreams of lofty purpose, that we can determine and know what manner of men we will be whenever and wherever the hour strikes that calls to noble action. This predestination God has given us in charge." This is not Calvinist predestination, but it is a predestination of a sort, partial but exalted, and an integral part of the belief of a man to whom God, though not anthropomorphic, was more than a mathematical conception, a law of science, or an eloquent-sounding formula invoked on Sunday mornings.

In 1897, Chamberlain spoke more precisely to the question of self in a Memorial Day address at Springfield which the *Springfield Republican* described as "extraordinary" and "remarkable." He conceived of man as having two souls. One acted in the interests of the individual self, being "related to the sphere of our every-day life and work, to the necessities of existence." The other soul lies deeper, "not very manifest unless called out by special occasion; acting in a direction quite contrary to the other, looking not to the good of self, but to some larger satisfaction." This latter soul Chamberlain considered to be "related to the life association with others, in which they belong to us and we to them." He saw room for both these souls, or "forces." Each influences the other, "and these opposing tendencies constitute for us a probation within which we build character." Again this address, like so many others Chamberlain gave, transcended the conventional note of patriotic appeal and underscored the responsibility of man to and for his fellow men.

On January 21, 1900, he sounded again the note of responsibility in an address to the Benevolent Society of Portland, Maine. He examined theories of property as set forth by Locke, Blackstone, Savigny, Maine, and Hegel. He developed also the radical theory of Proudhon, who rejected more conventional views and insisted that "property is theft," yet who repudiated pure communism and could not agree with Karl Marx's program of a sudden and complete overturn of society. Chamberlain's own views were not Proudhon's, but neither were they a wholehearted endorsement of capitalism as it had developed. Property was "man's freedom to use his possessions for his reasonable needs and highest conceived good." It was also the "appointed and necessary means of building up character, and realizing the content of personality, which may be called the 'worth' of it." Although the right to property is necessarily individualistic and it is to the interest of society to encourage individuality, competition may create hazards, even perverting "the instinctive ambition to excel." "We want," said Chamberlain, "a political economy which shall not be the science of wealth, but of well-being—of weal, to which wealth is minister; and whose maxim will not be competition but cooperation, in which each shall contribute according to his ability, and share according to his need." Those who are strong should not forfeit property because they are strong; rather because they possess such strength they have an obligation to assist the weak. Property is "a solemn trust" to be employed for "ever higher ends," and for his stewardship man is accountable to God.

Chamberlain's conception of property, while within the convention of his time, has marked elements at once socialistic and Christian in the stress on the obligation to society as a whole. In reality the emphasis is more Christian, for he sees the Christian religion as possessing the power to regenerate society, providing ideals and motivations not simply available to man but to which man should aspire. Man is his brother's keeper, and should use his property for the welfare of all. In this emphasis on the recognition and assumption of responsibility, there is a consistency in Chamberlain recognizable from his Master's oration in 1855 to the end of his life.

In addition to such pursuits as presiding over a magazine, editing a study of universities, and speaking, Chamberlain became a member of many organizations, particularly during the 1890's. This was not because he was by nature a "joiner" but rather because of his sense of service. The list is long but of interest and value not only for the number and diversity of the organizations but also because they exemplified ways in which he thought he, himself, or the use of his name could assist a worthy cause. He was a vice president of the American Huguenot Society, president of the Alpha Delta Phi Fraternity, and president of the Chamberlain Association of America; president of the Society of the Army of the Potomac, department commander of the Grand Army of the Republic, and department commander of the Military Order of the Loyal Legion, the Maine Commandery of which he founded in 1869 and in which he was more interested than in any other organization. Various learned, educational, religious, and humane societies claimed him. He was an associate member of the Egyptian Exploration Society, the Philosophical Society of Great Britain and the New England Historical and Genealogical Society; a member of the Egyptian Research, the American Political Science Association, the American Historical Association, the Maine Historical Society, the Colonial Society of Massachusetts, the Military Historical Society of Massachusetts, the Webster Historical Society at Boston, the American Geological Society, and the American Geographical Society; senior vice president of the American Bible Society and a life member of the American Board of Commissioners for Foreign Missions; a director of the American National Institute, Paris, France, vice president of the Humane Education Society, a director of the Maine Institute for the Blind, and a member of the National Red Cross. Finally, of course, he continued active, as he had since 1867, on the Bowdoin College Board of Trustees.

A number of these activities normally involve only the payment of an annual fee, but Chamberlain not only paid fees and read periodicals, he also attended meetings and took a lively interest in the organizations. Such activity, added to his business commitments and his work at the Institute, did nothing to improve his health. In December, 1890, he was ill for weeks and confined to his room at 101 West 75th Street. For a time Fanny despaired of his life.

This last illness and the approach of the thirtieth anniversary of the battle of Gettysburg prompted many friends to obtain for him some concrete recognition of his distinguished service at Little Round Top. Accordingly General Thomas H. Hubbard, Bowdoin '57, wrote to the Secretary of War, Daniel S. Lamont, on February 15, applying for a Congressional Medal of Honor. "In Maine," Hubbard said, "we have always thought that General Chamberlain's military service deserved any reward the Government could bestow. I think he never asked for any. When he was prosperous, there were hosts of men to praise him." Governor Henry B. Cleaves of Maine likewise recommended Chamberlain for the medal, while General Alexander Webb wrote twice in behalf of his old comrade. Finally, on August 17, the government belatedly awarded him the Medal of Honor "For distinguished gallantry at the battle of Gettysburg, July 2, 1863."

Unfortunately the bouts of illness, almost all of them caused by his wound, continued. January and February were especially bad months for him. In February, 1895, he was prostrated, and again in February, 1896. Two months later, he suffered another attack, and this time Fanny, whose eyesight was gradually failing, also fell ill. Happily medical attention and the care of a trained nurse brought both patients around, although the death of Tom Chamberlain, his brother, gave him something of a setback.

By 1897, which was brightened by an invitation to attend

President McKinley's dedication of the monument to General Grant on Riverside Drive, Chamberlain decided that his health simply could not withstand the continued strain of business and educational duties. Gradually he withdrew from all formal occupational commitments. He also decided to return to Brunswick for good except for meetings and lectures. The new year, 1898, therefore, found him once again a nearly full-time resident in the comfortable house next to the Bowdoin campus.

But if many people thought, as some did, that the General had come home to his slippers and his fireside to muse and reflect until death tapped him on the shoulder and—as is supposed to happen with old soldiers—he quietly faded away, they were profoundly mistaken. Within a few weeks the explosion of the battleship *Maine* in Havana harbor and the bugles sounding for Cuba brought him to his feet eager for action. Years fell off his shoulders, illness vanished, and he hurried to his writing desk. There was work to be done— now, letters to write; eventually, perhaps, service in the field.

⚓ ⚓ ⚓ XIII ⚓ ⚓ ⚓

SURVEYOR OF PORT OF PORTLAND
AND LAST YEARS

THE Cuban revolt and the likelihood of American intervention stirred Chamberlain deeply. In March, 1898, he started writing a series of articles on the crisis which was published in the *Bangor News* and enjoyed a wide audience throughout New England. Though he acknowledged his uncertainty, he suspected that the destruction of the *Maine* was no accident. He would have the government prepare at once for war, but he would try to avoid it. This attitude was more conservative than that of the country at large. There has never been a more popular conflict in American history than the Spanish-American War, and, after the sinking of the *Maine,* the popular demand for an end to Spanish rule in Cuba was fanned to furious heights, a responsibility shared by numerous sources, including the so-called "yellow" journals of New York—Joseph Pulitzer's *World* and William Randolph Hearst's *Journal,* the sugar interests, many politicians, "Big Navy" men, and a number of prominent clergymen. Chamberlain, who knew war better than most living men, looked upon the use of arms only as a last resort. Cuba, however, must not be abandoned. The United States might buy the island from Spain, though he recognized that the transfer of sovereignty would leave bitter hearts in Cuba. In any event, the United States had no choice but to stand as

290

"sponsor and guardian" of Cuba, and to continue that role, if independence was decided on, until such time as the island was prepared to manage its own affairs. As Chamberlain viewed the dissolution of the Spanish empire throughout the world and the likely development of the American position in the Pacific, he saw also future problems and responsibilities, particularly in relation to the decadent empire of China and the mushrooming Japanese power.

But writing about the crisis was not enough for Chamberlain. He offered his services to Governor Llewellyn Powers, who replied that, in the event of hostilities, "I feel that I shall most certainly avail myself of your counsel and assistance." With war declared and no request as yet from Powers, Chamberlain wrote two important letters. One was to the Secretary of War tendering his services in any military capacity for which he might be considered qualified. The other was to Senator Frye in which he made his own proposal for employment. He suggested that he be authorized to organize a division of New England troops who should be distributed among several camps for training; and he thought that within a few months he would be ready to go to Cuba himself. There is something at once inspiring and pathetic in his statement—from a man nearly seventy years old: "I cannot but think that my day is not yet over for the service of my Country. You gentlemen in Congress and in the offices of the Government are in your right place: I desire to be in mine." Had he been a Congressman like the Confederate cavalryman, Joseph Wheeler, eight years his junior, he might have been able to obtain a real command as Wheeler did. He could not have done worse than Wheeler and, unlike the Alabamian, he would most certainly not have identified the Spaniards as Yankees!

Unfortunately for Chamberlain's aspirations, he was denied a role in this "Splendid Little War," as John Hay called it. The Secretary of War politely acknowledged Chamberlain's "patriotic letter" but turned to younger men. Frye and his colleague from Maine, Senator Hale, then thought of him as one of the peace commissioners, but nothing came of their suggestions. Nor did a proposal from another source bear fruit, namely, that Chamberlain, "an excellent officer" and "a brilliant man," be seriously considered as the head of the new Philippine government.

In 1899, Chamberlain's eagerness to return to some kind of useful public service prompted friends in Maine to try to secure for him, as one of them expressed it in a letter to President McKinley, "some position of trust and profit in the gift of the Federal Government in the State of Maine." People came gradually to center on the post of Collector of Customs for Portland. Three petitions were drawn up in Portland and sent to the President, while two went the rounds in Brunswick—one of them signed by 390 citizens of Brunswick and Harpswell. Letters were written by many prominent men in the First Congressional District and other parts of Maine to the President, Senators Frye and Hale, and the District's representative in the House, Amos L. Allen. Portland's great mayor, James Phinney Baxter, reminded the President that "For ability and high character Gen. Chamberlain stands almost without a peer." F. M. Drew, an attorney in Lewiston, the home of Senator Frye, warmly supported Chamberlain but told the General that while he trusted Senator Hale to work in the General's behalf, he had less confidence in Frye, who, he felt, did not want to see Chamberlain appointed. Actually Frye had committed himself, before the Chamberlain movement began, to recommend to Allen another candidate, General Selden Connor. Chamberlain's friends finally prevailed on him to write in his own behalf to Congressman Allen.

Among the numerous criticisms often made of Chamberlain as a politician was not only that he would not take care of his own supporters but also that he showed a most unpolitical reluctance to speak and work for his own advancement. Such criticisms were often justified. To appoint the man one is convinced can do a job most effectively at the expense of another who, though less competent, worked hard in the campaign, is a political sin of the first magnitude. Likewise to hesitate to stand up in the political arena and announce that one has ideas and ability superior to any other contestant, naturally couching such an expression of superiority in terms neither so pointed nor so extravagant as to offend tender sensibilities, is to reveal an unrealistic grasp of politics. Nor can it be seriously doubted that Chamberlain, for a person who often had political aspirations, suffered from excessive modesty, however true it may have been that the modesty sprang not from a lack of faith in himself but from a profound distaste for self-adulation and a realization that there is no such creature as the indispensable man. The irony in the move to secure the Collectorship is that although he finally did become active in his own behalf, the office was given to another. Allen had had his own candidate in mind, neither Chamberlain nor Connor but Charles M. Moses.

Balked in their quest for the Collectorship, Chamberlain's friends sought for him the position of the Surveyor of the Port of Portland, and to this post Allen was readily amenable to the General's appointment. Concerned with such problems, among others, as the course, anchorage, mooring, and general facilities for ships, the Surveyorship was undoubtedly a less strenuous job. As an old Portland friend observed to Chamberlain, in urging him to accept it, "The position is easier, salary good, and no political work expected, such as attaches to the Collectorship," while Allen himself described the office as "very pleasant" and its duties as "very light." Though disappointed at his loss of the Collectorship, Chamberlain finally agreed to accept the Surveyorship. Allen accordingly sent in his name before Christmas, and on March 20, 1900, President McKinley appointed him Surveyor at the annual salary of $4500.

Amid the flood of congratulations Chamberlain maintained his usual outward composure of graciousness, dignity, and calmness. His calmness, however, was more rigidly disciplined than ever; inside, he was a torrent of distress. To a friend in Augusta, General John T. Richards, he unburdened himself the day after Christmas, 1899, in a letter that is worth quoting at length because of its vigorously expressed revelation of what public service meant at this time to Chamberlain.

After thanking Richards for his letter of congratulations, Chamberlain said that he knew he ought to be grateful since "The surveyorship is a good little office, no doubt . . . It is said to be an easy place—no responsibilities, no duties, no power, no prominence, no part in the governmental representation, and requiring no ability. Whether this description of the place should inflate my vanity when I am told that I am 'entitled to it,' is a question for the meek, who are said to be about to 'inherit the earth.' To me it suggests a free bed in a hospital. It has a good salary for such a place, I confess; and that is something of a silencer. This is a reason why many would be glad to get it, to whom it is the highest thing that ever came into their lives. It is a reason why I do not like to displace others. . . ."

Then Chamberlain really opened his heart. "What I aspired to . . . was the Collectorship. This is a representative office. It is concerned not only with the collection of the customs; but it represents the party in power; it represents the Government in its authority and dignity; it represents the President among the people as the Senators and Members of Congress represent the people in the halls of legislation and government. And this not only in matters of public ceremony and courtesy, but not impossibly in times of public exigency which demand executive ability and experience of great affairs. Hence it has been held not unworthy of the ambition of first-class men. It has been thought promotion even for Governors. I am free to say I thought myself equal to these things."

Turning to the Surveyorship again, Chamberlain became scornful. By comparison, the Surveyorship "has nothing of this character or history about it. It is essentially an obscure office, tending to keep one out of notice, as well as out of responsibility. I am conscious of vital activities which welcome heavier tasks, and demand more scope."

He often resorted to whimsy in stress, as now when he concluded that he supposed he might console himself that he was on "the same retired list with Hawthorne, even if unable out of my own experience to scrape together 'mosses from an old Manse.' "

Though he applied himself energetically to turning the Surveyorship into something more than a sinecure, and soon made good friends of everyone at the Customs House, especially the Collector, he was grateful for the job's lack of strenuous requirements when a violent renewal of inflammation of his wound occurred in 1900. Thinking that a trip to a softer clime would improve his condition, he applied to the Secretary of the Treasury for a leave of absence from November 10 to January 10, 1901, and went to the Mediterranean. He had long wanted to see the classical lands, particularly Italy.

But Chamberlain's tour was not so restorative at first as he had hoped. After he encountered bad weather in central Italy, acquaintances urged him to go to Egypt where the climate would be more favorable. Eagerly Chamberlain accepted their advice and took up lodgings in Cairo. Although prostrated even there for a while, he received the best of care; and, having applied for an extension of his leave, he relaxed, and presently was himself again.

Notwithstanding his ill health for part of the time, he thoroughly enjoyed Egypt and developed a consuming interest in its historic past and exciting present. Interested in the Moslem religion, he started to read the Koran in the original at bed time; then, as if to remind himself that he was, after all, a Christian, he also placed his Bible on his night table and read an equal portion from each book before retiring. He met an important Syrian lawyer, Nicholas Nimr, who hoped to become the leader of all the Syrians who had migrated to the United States. He gained the friendship of the distinguished Moslem leader, Fordure, whose lineal descent from the Prophet entitled him to precede even the Khedive in Moslem festivities. He also made the acquaintance of the great British proconsul in Egypt, Lord Cromer, a man of "great force of character and intense self-control" whom Chamberlain found "exceedingly interesting." "With such friends to help me," Chamberlain said, "my winter on the Nile could not be otherwise than charming and full of historic interest." On the other hand, he soon became restless, also perhaps a little homesick. "Nothing can exceed my anxiety to return to my post of duty and to my country of which I am so proud," he wrote Collector Moses. He begged Moses to give his "best remembrances to our familiar little circle in the customs house which has so much endeared itself to me." He was happy indeed to return to the United States in the early spring.

Back in Maine again he soon found himself faced by the prospect of losing his wife. His impulsive, bewildering Fanny was now blind and seriously ill after falling and breaking her hip in the summer of 1905. She died on October 18 at Brunswick, slightly over 79 years of age. As a friend said, condoling with Chamberlain, "The afflictions of Mrs. Chamberlain in these later years have made her life a burden and doubtless she looked for Death as a welcome deliverer from her sufferings," although when he last saw her, "she talked with her old time vigor of art and literature, and seemed for the moment to quite forget her blindness and helplessness." Whatever differences may once have occasionally existed between Chamberlain and Fanny, the two had been very close for many years. With increasing invalidism, however, Fanny had had to withdraw from much of her husband's active life. Now she was gone altogether, and for a time Chamberlain was overcome by melancholy.

Presently he shook off his depressed mood. His family rallied about him: Grace—his beloved "Daise," her three daughters, Wyllys, his sister "Sadie," and his niece Alice. Visits to and from them—Wyllys, of course, was with him much of the time—cheered him greatly. There was always his work, requests to speak were made of him, publishers were becoming interested in a manuscript he was preparing on the Civil War, and Senator Frye tried, though with no real success, to get his name entered as a brigadier general on the Regular Army retired list. And there were the numerous women who vied for his attention.

All his mature life Chamberlain was attractive to women. He was chivalrous and attentive to them, and respectful of their abilities in an age when, to put it mildly, most men did not unqualifiedly acknowledge their equality. Alert and sensitive, virile and by no means unhandsome, Chamberlain appealed to women regardless of their age or status in the more stratified society of that era. Nor did they hesitate to write him of their regard. Mary and Edith Dalton, daughters of an old friend, hero-worshipped him and frankly acknowledged it, writing him letters that might well have turned a head less steady than Chamberlain's. Elizabeth Kendall Upham was exceedingly solicitous about him when he was in New York, enjoyed having him dine with herself and her husband, used to take him for drives, and admired him as a man and a mind. Sarah S. Sampson was a forthright Maine war widow employed at the Pension Office in Washington whom Chamberlain had helped in many ways, including assistance in obtaining her position. In the early 1900's Chamberlain was her *"glorious* Friend." "I thank the good Father that you still live," she wrote gratefully, "and that occasionally I have an appreciative word from your hand. Since I first knew you, you have given me more encouragement and assistance in my life work than any other person living, or who ever did live... I want you to know that I appreciate all your kindnesses to me in so many ways—ways that you have forgotten but I *never* shall."

Somewhat more romantic were the feelings of Myra E. Porter and Mary P. Clark. The first was a Maine woman whose home was in Bangor but who lived for some time in New York City. Wretchedly poor and ill, she spent a year in a sanatorium in Nyack-on-the-Hudson. Chamberlain sent her gifts of money for years, apparently never much at one time but, cumulatively, considerable. He also occasionally wrote her what she described as "kind letters." Although these do not survive in established collections, several of hers do, letters filled with gratitude ("... you, of all my friends, are the one who has enabled me to keep from *want* ... I thank God for your kindness"). Along with gratitude is a kind of wonder not without pathos ("I am not foolish over it, but no friend has ever come into my life just as you have come.") She became very fond of him, but he was clearly, in his own attitude toward her, but a gentleman assisting an unfortunate woman in her distress and loneliness.

Mary P. Clark, who wintered in Massachusetts and summered in Maine, was a friend of the family and had long admired Chamberlain. A few of her letters survive, written between 1908 and 1911. She was somewhat extravagant in language, was, in fact, a gracious, sentimental woman of years who liked to invest a friendship with feelings more tender and romantic. Occasionally he would write her and call on her. To her he was "My beloved General," and she was deeply grateful for his attentiveness. "Your recent visit," she wrote in 1910 from Milton, "though it gave me only two days of your dear presence, was of rare delight to me— you brought me love and joy and peace, and in parting you left the sweetest and dearest of memories. How trying was the farewell!" She was anxious to remind him of her love and to give him the "undisturbed *rest* which you too often need." In 1911, she entreated him to visit her, if only briefly.

She treasured the rare moments when she saw him and the even rarer moments when he talked about himself—"your dear self," as she expressed it, the subject, of all others, about which "I most wished to know."

Chamberlain enjoyed the company of women, and invariably they responded with admiration and affection. His visits, his generous assistance when needed, his invitations to dine, his gifts of flowers and candy—such manifestations of regard meant a great deal, particularly to older women. Of all those who wrote him, however, Mary Clark was probably the closest in his affections. Not only was she a link with the past, she also helped fill a need of communication, of fellow feeling, of companionship that had been lost with Fanny's death. Reading her letters leaves one in little doubt that Mary truly loved him. It also leaves one in little doubt that she was trying with pathetic earnestness to convince herself, and him as well, that his sentiment for her was much deeper and more exclusive than it really was. Actually there was only one woman who ever completely captivated Chamberlain—his beloved Fanny, to whom he could write in 1852, "I *know* in whom my whole heart can rest—so sweetly and so surely."

Chamberlain's speaking engagements filled a large part of his life at this time. He spoke throughout the East on historic anniversaries and at meetings of the Loyal Legion and the G.A.R. Of all his efforts in this direction, his address on Lincoln's birthday in 1909 was easily the most significant. It was delivered in the Academy of Music in Philadelphia before a large audience, of which the core consisted of members of the Military Order of the Loyal Legion. The Marine Band played; young Hermann Hagedorn read a poem of his own, "Lincoln"; other speakers presented the "Gettysburg

Address" and the "Second Inaugural." The main address was by Chamberlain, who chose the subject, "Abraham Lincoln Seen from the Field."

Chamberlain developed a theme by now familiar with him. "Great crises in human affairs call out the great in men," he declared. "But true greatness is not in nor of the single self; it is of that larger personality, that shared and sharing life with others, in which, each giving of his best for their betterment, we are greater than ourselves; and self-surrender for the sake of that great belonging, is the true nobility." Among the growing body of Lincoln worshippers Chamberlain had early taken a place, and in this speech he made no small contribution to the Emancipator's near-deification. Chamberlain saw him as a truly great man "appointed for great ends." From all the grave political, diplomatic, and military problems of the war he saw Lincoln emerging triumphant, a man of supreme common sense and of wide and deep humanity who stands "like the Christ of the Andes—reconciler of the divided."

He gave an interesting soldier's view of the President, one that has the ring of true coin:

We had often opportunity to see him—for some occasions, too often . . . But always after a great battle, and especially disaster, we were sure to see him, slow-riding through camp, with outward-searching eyes,—questioning and answering heart. His figure was striking; stature and bearing uncommon and commanding. The slight stoop of the shoulders, an attitude of habitual in-wrapped thought . . . Those who thought to smile when that figure,—mounting, with the tall hat, to near seven feet—was to be set on a spirited horse for a ceremonial excursion, were turned to admiration at the easy mastery he showed, and the young-staff game of testing civilians by touching up the horses to headlong speed returning over a course they had mischievously laid, with sudden crossings of old rifle-pit and ditch, proved a *boomerang* for them, when he would come out the only rider square in his saddle, with head level and rightly crowned . . . But always he wished to see the army together. This had a being, a place, a power beyond the aggregate of its individual units. A review was therefore held, in completeness and most careful order. Slowly he rode along front and rear of the opened ranks, that he might see all sides of things as they were. Every horse was scanned: that is one way to know the master. We could see the deep sadness in his face, and feel the burden on his heart, . . . and we took him into our hearts with answering sympathy, and gave him our pity in return.

Small wonder that when Chamberlain finished his address, his voice clear and strong at eighty-one and possessing its old witchery of tone and expression, his audience of veterans sat in momentary silence, almost reverent in nature, then sprang to their feet in tumultuous applause.

The Civil War was more than ever in his thoughts during these years. Accordingly, when the editor of *Cosmopolitan Magazine* asked him to contribute an article, he sent them the valuable "My Story of Fredericksburg," which was published in early 1913. Also appearing in 1913, this time for *Hearst's Magazine,* was the interesting and stirring article bearing the somewhat lurid title, "Through Blood and Fire at Gettysburg." More important than either of these fragments was a book which he was endeavoring to finish. For years he had planned to write a history of the Fifth Corps, and he collected a large amount of data for it. Owing to his many activities, he never got around to writing it, and naturally, after the appearance of William H. Powell's work on that subject in 1896, he dropped it. He realized, however, that, despite the flood of Civil War material, little was being written on the last part of the war. Actually an article of his published in 1897, "Military Operations on the White Oak Road, Virginia, March 31, 1865," was the most satisfactory analysis of the subject that had appeared, while another, published in 1902, "Five Forks," was equally valuable. He therefore wrote a book covering the final campaign of the Army of the Potomac, entitled, *The Passing of the Armies*.

Although his death prevented a final revision, his book still stands as the finest participant's account of those stirring, closing days of the war. He wrote it when he was sufficiently distant from the conflict in time to preserve an admirable objectivity and to have access to material not available to earlier accounts. Such advantages are, of course, even more those of present writers than they were Chamberlain's. But Chamberlain had had an intensely active and important role in the final overthrow of the Southern armies, and his book has a penetration, a sense of immediacy, a quality of vivid, intelligent personalization that makes it lively and authoritative reading. Furthermore, despite the occasional moralizing and patches of "purple" prose, Chamberlain had an extraordinary gift for narration. His soldiers really get entangled in the woods; he encounters, not without trepidation, a furious Sheridan; he sees the humiliation of the gallant Gordon and Lee's drooping veterans at Appomattox and gives them a last pride in themselves as soldiers by bringing his own victorious troops to a chivalric salute at arms. It is exciting reading, one lives through the events, and somehow one knows that this is not simply a brilliant, imaginative reconstruction but a genuinely authentic account of what actually happened.

In 1908, while writing his book, carrying on his Surveyorship, and serving as president of the Maine chapter of the National Red Cross, Chamberlain received a signal honor. A ceremony was held one afternoon, during the weekend of the one hundred and third Bowdoin College Commencement, at which James Phinney Baxter, ex-Mayor of Portland and an honorary graduate of the Class of 1881, presented to the college an oil portrait of the General. After sketching Chamberlain's life as scholar, soldier, statesman, and private citizen, he drew aside an American flag covering the portrait. At once there was a great demonstration from alumni, undergraduates, faculty, and friends. The gift was received by General Thomas H. Hubbard, '57, who spoke glowingly of his old friend. Chamberlain was then introduced, and the applause was again enthusiastic and prolonged. When quiet finally prevailed and he started to speak, he was so overcome by emotion that only by a tremendous exercise of self-control could he keep from breaking down. Turning finally to President Hyde, he said, "I have a trouble with my heart, a rush of blood to my head. Words will not come when I look upon an assemblage like this. Forty years ago I read my obituary in the morning papers, but I was not half so overcome then, as I am today." He then spoke briefly of this famous little college which had meant so much to him through the years. "The fact that one is a Bowdoin man," he said with a burst of loyal pride, "is credential enough to admit one to the highest position in the world."

Five years later, a singular incident occurred in the Bowdoin Chapel. One Sunday afternoon in the late spring during memorial services at Vespers for those who had served in the Civil War, the students by a rising vote expressed their recognition of the courage and other soldierly qualities of Chamberlain, "one of the most noted Alumni of the College," and requested President Hyde to write him to that effect. In his letter, Hyde said, "At this memorial season, and in view of the approaching fiftieth anniversary of the Battle of Gettysburg, the students of Bowdoin College, assembled in the chapel which you left to obey your country's call, and to which you returned after years of heroic and victorious service, by rising vote have requested me to express to you and the brave men who fought with you in the great cause, their gratitude for the privilege of living in a country undivided by secession and unstained by slavery; and to assure you that your noble example will ever be an incentive to lives of patriotic service; in peace so long as honorable peace is possible; in war whenever unavoidable and righteous war shall call."

Graciously Chamberlain replied, "The generous salutation of the students of Bowdoin is gratefully acknowledged in behalf of all the noble young men of my early College companionship who, inspired by the lofty ideal of a nation's mission to man, offered their best for the country's life and honor. I am proud of Bowdoin of the present day, where young manhood is grounded on the high principles so happily expressed in your cherished message." He would have been proud, too, if he could have lived four years longer to see many of the very young men who saluted him through President Hyde's eloquent words answer with generous enthusiasm a call to arms for their own generation.

But time was starting to run out for the General. He attended the reunion of the Blue and the Grey at Gettysburg, where thousands of old veterans from both sides shook hands and roamed about the fateful copse of trees where Pickett was repulsed, through the Peach Orchard where Sickles gambled and lost, and over the rocky slopes of Little Round

Top where Vincent fell and, for a few minutes, the issue of
the struggle on the Union left flank, even of the entire vast
and terrible battle, hung on Chamberlain and the 20th
Maine and the General's marvelous decision to counterattack. But most of these veterans were old, some very old
(Dan Sickles himself was there, ninety-five years old), and
in their reminiscences of their comrades who had passed on,
they could not ignore their own limited mortality. Chamberlain enjoyed the great reunion but returned tired and a little
ill. He was, after all, nearing his eighty-fifth birthday.

Once back, he felt better after a rest in his Brunswick
home and a visit to Monhegan Island where the New York
artist, Robert Sewall, painted his portrait; then he returned
to his Ocean Avenue home in Portland and the duties of
the Surveyorship. Originally commissioned as Surveyor by
President McKinley, he was repeatedly recommissioned by
Roosevelt and Taft. The office he took very seriously, trying
not to miss many days from the Customs House. He was
beloved by the men who worked there, and when he left
his office for the main room, clerks gathered about him.
Always he was affable and kind, inquiring about them and
their families. Even on the coldest of winter days, he was
invariably down on the Grand Trunk docks when the ocean
steamships came in, attended by his Customs House friends.
Closely muffled up, but carrying himself with military erect-
ness, his sweeping white mustache blowing in the wind and
his white hair not quite covered by the black hat, he made a
striking figure. Often a ship's officers would inquire the
identity of the distinguished-looking man on the docks, and
when they learned it, they would touch their hats to him.

He never lost his interest in books or people or his own
family. He had, indeed, a kind of devotion to books, as if

they were alive. He would pick up a book, feel it carefully, comment on its appearance, admire the paper and type, even smell it if it had a leather binding. In his library and study at Brunswick he had more than two thousand books. Naturally many of them were about the Civil War. In fact, the house was filled with mementos of the War: the cap and sword of General Griffin; the bugle of Chamberlain's own 1st Division; the flag of the 1st Division with its red maltese cross; a Confederate battleflag taken by his own troops; a cavalry pistol fired at Chamberlain on Little Round Top by a Confederate officer whom he captured; a tapestry picture of the General's favorite war horse, Charlemagne, buried at Domhegan. There were many other souvenirs of his life, but dominating all were the crowded shelves of books, books which Chamberlain loved to read before the fireplace in his library, over which hung the flag of his old regiment, the 20th Maine.

But people were even more important to him than books. The men at the Customs House, Bowdoin alumni and under-graduates, old friends, the children of the neighborhood—Chamberlain was interested in all of these. Of particular interest, however, were the old war comrades. He was always reaching for his checkbook to help a sick or disabled veteran or war widow. He loyally stood by Colonel H. C. Merriam of the old 20th in the latter's thirty-year struggle to secure a deserved promotion to Brigadier-General—Merriam, who, in 1898, helped set up the military occupation of Hawaii, who invented the infantry pack which, with some modifica-tion, was borne by millions of American soldiers in the twentieth century, whose professional character was finally vindicated only nine years before his death in 1912. Always Chamberlain was interested in the underdog. When, in 1907, his opinion was sought on the policy of prison labor, he insisted that the prison experience must be directed to saving the man for his own sake and the welfare of society and that "In breaking up his propensity to crime, nothing should be done to break down his sense of manhood." Victims not alone of society but of nature invariably found him eager to assist—he was more than an ornament in the Red Cross. The *Titanic* disaster in 1912 moved him profoundly, and he shared the hope that out of the common grief in Britain and America and the need for common action to prevent a recurrence of such a catastrophe people might find a way to solve not maritime difficulties alone but "many of the great troubles of our day." The mounting tensions in Europe, the rise of intransigent nationalism, the developing spirit of militarism evidenced in armaments races on land and sea, the increase generally of racial and social intolerance—these factors filled him with apprehension. He could see only too clearly where it all might end and the horrors and dislocation that would ensue.

He seemed to draw his family more closely about him in these sunset years. It grieved him that Wyllys, torn between law and a natural bent for mechanical invention, particularly in electricity, had never completely realized himself, certainly had never made a financial success. For that matter, the General, notwithstanding his numerous financial engagements and venturesomeness, left an estate which was appraised at only $33,608.11—a respectable estate but hardly evidence of conspicuous financial success. Perhaps for this very reason he was especially anxious that Wyllys capitalize his inventive ability. "Your attention," Chamberlain wrote his son in late 1913, "has been absorbed in the inventions in which your brain is so fertile, so that you have not got into the other stratum, or sphere, of making money of it. That is a 'worldly way' of looking at things: but it has to [be] regarded." Chamberlain may have sensed even then a failing of his powers, and he wanted Wyllys to be able to "stand on his own."

His daughter Grace and his granddaughters, Eleanor, Beatrice, and Rosamond, gave him great joy. The bond between him and Grace had always been very close, while between him and her three daughters a mutual adoration society existed. To them he was "Gennie," the beloved and ever gentle grandfather who loved to eat the popovers their mother made for him, who often suffered but never complained of his wound, who occasionally showed them over the battlefields and reminisced, as is the way with old men, of earlier and braver days, even to "the last cigar I smoked with General Grant." If occasionally they grew restless in following his stories and explanations, they could not but remember his great kindness to them and how appreciative he was of little things. Somehow they could never reconcile his gentleness with his having been an officer in a position where he was forced to give orders to kill.

As 1913 neared its close, Chamberlain's wound again became inflamed, and with the onset of 1914 he was completely prostrated at his Ocean Avenue home. On January 20, he dictated a letter through his faithful housekeeper, Lillian Edmunds, to his sister. "I am passing through deep waters," he said, but "The Doctor thinks I am going to land once more on this shore." He was grateful that she and her daughter Alice offered to come and help, but already "We are gradually discharging Doctors and nurses." As one who had felt the cold breath of final separation so near to him, he added, "I am trying to get a little closer to God and to know him better." Two weeks later he again wrote, "Am gaining strength, but slow work. The bed and bed-side chair are still my habitual place. Have to keep a trained nurse for a while yet."

Then, just as he seemed about recovered, he caught cold and suffered a swift relapse. This time, because his condition was already so weakened, there could be no recovery. Grace rushed down from Boston, and was at his bedside when he died quietly, a little after half-past nine on the morning of February 24, 1914.

His death and funeral received wide attention in Maine. It was as if, through their mourning for Chamberlain, the people of the State were paying their last tribute to the generation that had fought the nation's bloodiest war and had saved the Union. The newspapers were filled with accounts of "The Hero of Little Round Top," of "One of The Noblest Maine has Produced" and like headlines. Three thousand people jammed in and about the City Hall in Portland for the services there on February 27, which were arranged by a committee of the Maine Commandery of the Loyal Legion. Governor Haines issued a proclamation in Chamberlain's honor and attended the services. Also in attendance were representatives of Massachusetts: General Morris Schaaf, Major Henry L. Higginson, and Ex-Governor John C. Bates, to whom Governor David Walsh wrote on the 26th, "The commonwealth [of Massachusetts] will be grateful to you for representing her at the last ceremonies in honor of this great man." Principal officials throughout Maine, and Portland in particular, were present, also a host of Bowdoin men, many old friends and neighbors, and, of course, survivors of the Loyal Legion and the G. A. R. The local National Guard battalion escorted the casket to the

City Hall, where it was placed under a guard of honor. After an address by a prominent clergyman, Regular Army and National Guard troops, members of the Civil War organizations, and many dignitaries again escorted the flag-draped casket to Union Station. The casket was then placed on a train for Brunswick. In all probability, Chamberlain, with his love of military pageantry, would have keenly enjoyed observing his own funeral.

At Brunswick more modest but equally impressive ceremonies awaited the old warrior when his train slowly steamed into the station. The faculty and undergraduates of Bowdoin, the local G. A. R. post, and the Brunswick National Guard escorted the casket to the First Parish Church for services there before the interment. The Reverend Chauncey Goodrich conducted the service, and then President Hyde delivered the eulogy from the place where Chamberlain himself had so often stood as president of Bowdoin and near the spot where he and Fanny had been married so many years before.

Hyde's address was a superb analysis and appraisal of Chamberlain's character and career. Many of the mourners present knew Chamberlain well—these were old friends, old colleagues, old comrades. They did not have to be told of the deficiencies and frailties to which all men are heir and of which Chamberlain possessed his full share. They were interested, rather, in an account and explanation of what had made this man so extraordinary. As Hyde pointed out, Chamberlain had stood in advance of his time in many ways, particularly as a reform-minded president of a college that did not have the money to afford his reforms and as a statesman who courageously opposed the leaders of his party when convinced that to comply with their wishes was to misuse

the power that the people had given him. Similarly his action
at Appomattox in saluting the defeated troops of Lee, whom
he looked upon as no longer enemies but friends and fellow
Americans, was a deed "in which military glory and Christian magnanimity were fused." "Whoever," President Hyde
concluded, "whether as patriot or Christian dares to plant
his standards far in advance of present and sustained achievement, runs the risk of . . . misinterpretation. General Chamberlain never hauled down his flag to the low level of what
he or any man could easily do or habitually be. All he said
and did was bright and burning with an ardor of idealism
which in the home was devotion; in the college was loyalty;
in the State and Nation was patriotism; toward humanity
and God was religion."

The cortege moved to the cemetery among the pines near
his beloved college, the rifles volleyed in final salute, and the
haunting notes of Dan Butterfield's "Taps" echoed through
the cold winter air. For those living who had loved Chamberlain this was a moment of desolation. For the General
himself, it may well have been, as at times he seems to have
believed, only the continuation of a hazardous but exhilara-
ting journey during which he would again meet his vanished
loved ones, his old friends, and his comrades of the war—
those who had gone before him within recent memory and
those he had last seen alive on the rocky slopes of a Pennsylvania hillside or in the lonely woods of Virginia. One
might say of him, as John Bunyan wrote long ago, "So he
passed over, and all the trumpets sounded for him on the
other side."

ACKNOWLEDGMENTS

Writing this book has placed me deeply in debt to numerous individuals and institutions. I wish to express my appreciation to my poet-friend Wilbert Snow, Professor-Emeritus of English at Wesleyan University and former Governor of Connecticut (but as authentic a State-of-Mainer as ever thrust his hand into a lobster pot), for suggesting that I write about Chamberlain; to Bruce Catton, whose work I have long admired and whose endorsement of the suggestion was persuasive; to Gorham Munson of Thomas Nelson and Sons, whose interest in Chamberlain touched off the project and who has been understanding throughout.

Chamberlain's niece, Miss Alice Farrington of Brewer, Maine, and his granddaughters, Miss Rosamond Allen of St. Petersburg, Florida, and Miss Eleanor Allen of Vienna, Austria, have been most sympathetic and accommodating in providing information and letters. President James S. Coles of Bowdoin College generously made available the college archives. Mr. Kenneth Boyer of the Bowdoin College Library was the soul of kindness and helpfulness. Miss Mary Haskell of the Brewer Free Public Library went far beyond the call of duty in assisting my research. The Maine Historical Society was especially cooperative, my indebtedness being markedly great to Miss Marian B. Rowe and Mrs.

314 ACKNOWLEDGMENTS

Marion R. Small. Miss Charlotte W. Hardy of Brewer, Maine very kindly furnished information on the Chamberlain family. Mr. John W. Paton of Middletown, Connecticut made numerous useful suggestions throughout the period of writing.

I wish to make grateful acknowledgment also to Mr. L. Felix Ranlett and the Bangor Public Library; the Maine State Library; the Portland Public Library, particularly Miss Ann Bauer; the Boston Public Library; Mr. Robert W. Hill and the New York Public Library; the Yale University Library in general and Mr. Howard Gotlieb and his staff of the historical manuscripts room in particular; the manuscript division of the Library of Congress; the National Archives; Mr. Watt P. Marchman of the Rutherford B. Hayes Library, Fremont, Ohio, for his extraordinarily generous interest; the Olin Library of Wesleyan University, notably Mr. Wyman Parker, Miss Gertrude McKenna, and Miss Grace Bacon.

Wesleyan University has been most generous in granting me a sabbatical semester and stenographic funds. My colleagues in the History Department at Wesleyan have shown Jobian patience and tolerance and have been helpful with suggestions. Relatives—Mrs. Oscar T. Wallace of South Portland, Maine and the Walter J. Muellers of Washington, D. C. —have been royally hospitable during research trips.

I should be remiss if I neglected to mention my indebtedness to Mr. John J. Pullen for writing *The Twentieth Maine* (New York, 1957), the best regimental history I have ever read, and to Mr. Robert M. Cross, Bowdoin 1945, for a splendid Senior essay about Chamberlain, on file at the Bowdoin College Library.

The Hearst Publications have kindly permitted me to

quote from Chamberlain's articles in *Cosmopolitan Magazine,* vol. LIV, and *Hearst's Magazine,* vol. XXIII.

Mrs. Dorothy Hay of Portland, Connecticut has cheerfully typed innumerable letters on Chamberlain. Mrs. Elizabeth King of Berlin, Connecticut has read hundreds of pages of my scrawling handwriting with never-failing forbearance and has rendered an amazingly accurate typescript.

Finally, my wife has been my good companion in libraries and on battlefields, sharing my enthusiasm for Chamberlain yet never neglecting the role of constructive critic.

My thanks and gratitude to one and all.

WILLARD M. WALLACE

Wesleyan University
Middletown, Connecticut

ABBREVIATIONS

FFC, YU = Frost Family Collection, Yale University, New Haven, Connecticut

LC = Library of Congress (Manuscript Division) Washington, D. C.

MHS = Maine Historical Society, Portland, Maine

MAGR = *Annual Reports of the Adjutant General of the State of Maine* (1862-65), Augusta (Maine), 1863-66

NA = National Archives (Chamberlain File), Washington, D. C.

OR = *War of the Rebellion: A Compilation of the Official Records of the Union and Confederate Armies,* 70 vols. in 128 parts, Washington, D. C., 1881-1902. First Series only.

PA = Joshua Lawrence Chamberlain, *The Passing of the Armies,* New York, 1915

Notes

Chapter I

P. 17, l. 4   William C. Oates, *The War Between the Union and the Confederacy and Its Lost Opportunities* (New York, 1905), 219.

P. 19, l. 14   Joshua Lawrence (b. Sept. 8, 1828), Horace Beriah (b. Nov. 14, 1834), Sarah Brastow (b. Nov. 2, 1836), John Calhoun (b. Aug. 1, 1838), Thomas Davee (b. April 29, 1841).

P. 22, l. 19   Material on Chamberlain's ancestry and boyhood is drawn from George Thomas Little (ed.), *Genealogical and Family History of the State of Maine* (4 vols., New York, 1909), I, 132-33; *Bangor Historical Magazine*, II (1886-87), 123, 136-37, VI (1890-91), 82-83; *Joshua Lawrence Chamberlain, A Sketch*. Prepared for the Report of the Chamberlain Association of America (no author or place and date of publication); *In Memoriam: Joshua Lawrence Chamberlain, Late Major-General, U. S. V.*, Circular No. 5, Series of 1914, Whole Number 328, Military Order of the Loyal Legion of the United States, Commandery of the State of Maine (Portland, 1914); information furnished by Chamberlain's niece, Miss Alice M. Farrington, Brewer, Maine. See also the brief but fine account of Chamberlain in Gorham Munson, *Penobscot, Down East Paradise* (Philadelphia, 1959), 342-44.

P. 23, l. 6   For Chamberlain's Bowdoin achievements, see *Records of the Executive Government of Bowdoin College, Bowdoin Faculty Records, 1831-1875;* Robert M. Cross, *Joshua Lawrence Chamberlain* (unpublished Senior essay, Bowdoin College), 9.

P. 24, l. 31   Material on Harriet Beecher Stowe is drawn from Forrest Wilson, *Crusader in Crinoline* (Philadelphia, 1941); *The First Parish in Brunswick, Maine,* pamphlet (no author or date).

P. 25, l. 14   Chamberlain to Fanny, May 28, 1852 [probably]. *Chamberlain Collection* (hereafter *Cham. Coll.*), MHS.

P. 25, l. 29   George E. Adams to Mrs. H. C. Knight, Aug. 24, 1875. *Chamberlain Papers* (hereafter *Cham. Paps.*), FFC,YU. Fanny's real mother, Amelia, was the daughter of George Wyllys of Hartford, Conn.

P. 26, l. 15   George E. Adams to Fanny, July 9 [no year, but undoubtedly between 1850 and 1855]. *Cham. Coll.*, MHS.

P. 26, l. 28   D. G. Folsom to Fanny, Feb. 17, 1853. *Ibid.*

P. 26, l. 31   D. G. Folsom to Fanny, Dec. 23 [no year, but undoubtedly in the mid-1850's]. *Ibid.*

P. 27, l. 7   Chamberlain to Fanny, June 7, 1852. *Ibid.*

P. 28, l. 22   *Joshua Lawrence Chamberlain, A Sketch,* 9.

P. 28, l. 25   Chamberlain to Fanny [evidently Sept.], 1852. *Cham. Paps.,* FFC,YU.

P. 30, l. 7   Louis C. Hatch, *The History of Bowdoin College* (Portland, 1927), 106-7.

P. 31, l. 10   Quoted by the Reverend William DeWitt Hyde, President of Bowdoin, in an oration at Chamberlain's funeral, Feb. 27, 1914. Brunswick *Record,* March 6, 1914.

P. 31, l. 30   See letter from Joshua Chamberlain, Sr. to Lawrence, Jan. 3, 1858. *Cham. Coll.,* MHS.

P. 32, l. 10   Chamberlain to Fanny, May 20, 1857. *Ibid.*

P. 34, l. 13   Hatch, *Bowdoin College,* 118.

P. 35, l. 13   This particular point was made by one of the older professors, William Smyth, professor of mathematics and a Greek scholar, who introduced the blackboard as a method of teaching at Bowdoin. He was a strong anti-slavery man whose home had been a station on the Underground Railroad (For Smyth, see *ibid.,* 53-58; Nehemiah Cleaveland and Alpheus Spring Packard, *History of Bowdoin College* [Boston, 1882], 90-92, 247). Though a patriot, Smyth was strongly opposed to Chamberlain's leaving Bowdoin for the war (See Chamberlain to Fanny, Oct. 26, 1862. *Chamberlain Letters* [hereafter *Cham. Letters*], in possession of Chamberlain's granddaughter, Miss Rosamond Allen, St. Petersburg, Florida).

P. 35, l. 32   See MAGR for 1862, 7-15.

P. 36, l. 4   *Ibid.,* 17.

P. 36, l. 19   Israel Washburn to Chamberlain, Aug. 8, 1862. *Chamberlain Papers* (hereafter *Cham. Paps.*), LC. Chamberlain accepted the commission "against the most strenuous remonstrance and opposition of his colleagues in the college" (MAGR for 1864-65, I, 330. See also Little, *Genealogical and Family History of the State of Maine,* I, 133-34; *Joshua Lawrence Chamberlain, A Sketch,* 10).

Chapter II

P. 37, l. 13   Unsigned, undated letter in *Cham. Paps.,* LC.

P. 39, l. 19   Material on the 20th Maine and its officers is drawn from the superb regimental history by John L. Pullen, *The Twentieth Maine* (Philadelphia, 1957), 2-6; MAGR for 1861 through 1865; *Cham. Coll.,* MHS.

P. 39, l. 31   Theodore Gerrish, *Army Life, A Private's Reminiscences of the Civil War* (Portland, 1882), 14-17.

P. 41, l. 2   Quoted by Pullen, *Twentieth Maine,* 18.

P. 41, l. 23   Material concerning the 20th Maine's enlistment and travel as far as Antietam has been drawn largely from *ibid.,* 1-27; MAGR for 1862, 113; Gerrish, *Army Life,* 11-40. One of the finest accounts of Antietam is by Bruce Catton, *Mr. Lincoln's Army* (New York, 1951), 269-339.

P. 42, l. 24   William H. Powell, *The Fifth Army Corps* (New York, 1896), 301.

P. 42, l. 30   For action, see *ibid.*, 293-302; Pullen, *Twentieth Maine*, 27-29; MAGR for 1864-65, I, 331; Francis Winthrop Palfrey, *The Antietam and Fredericksburg* (New York, 1893), 128-29.

P. 43, l. 16   OR, XIX, Pt. I, 13-14.

P. 43, l. 29   Joshua L. Chamberlain, "My Story of Fredericksburg," in *Cosmopolitan Magazine*, LIV (December, 1912-May, 1913), 148-49.

P. 44, l. 12   For training, see Pullen, *Twentieth Maine*, 32-37; Chamberlain to Fanny, Oct. 26, 1862. *Cham. Letters*, in possession of Miss Rosamond Allen.

P. 44, l. 19   Chamberlain to Fanny, Oct. 26, 1862. *Cham. Letters*, in possession of Miss Rosamond Allen.

P. 44, l. 22   Information from Miss Alice Farrington, Brewer, Maine.

P. 44, l. 32   Tom Chamberlain to Sarah Chamberlain, Oct. 14, 1862. Pullen, *Twentieth Maine*, 37; Chamberlain to Fanny, Oct. 26, 1862. *Cham. Letters*, in possession of Miss Rosamond Allen.

P. 45, l. 15   Chamberlain to Fanny, Oct. 26, 1862. *Cham. Letters*, in possession of Miss Rosamond Allen.

P. 45, l. 31   Chamberlain to Fanny, Oct. 10, 1862. *Ibid.*

P. 46, l. 10   Chamberlain to Fanny, Oct. 26, 1862. *Ibid.*

P. 47, l. 4   See letters from Chamberlain to Fanny, Oct. 10 and 26, 1862. *Ibid.*

P. 49, l. 7   Chamberlain to Fanny, Nov. 3, 1862. *Ibid.*

P. 49, l. 17   Chamberlain to Fanny, Nov. 4, 1862. *Ibid.*

P. 49, l. 29   See letters from Chamberlain to Fanny, Nov. 3 and 4, 1862. *Ibid.*

P. 50, l. 5   Kenneth P. Williams, *Lincoln Finds A General*, II (New York, 1949), 479.

P. 52, l. 22   Douglas Southall Freeman, *R. E. Lee* (New York, 1935), II, 465.

P. 53, l. 4   Chamberlain, "My Story of Fredericksburg," *Cosmopolitan*, LIV, 152.

P. 53, l. 15   *Ibid.*

P. 53, l. 24   *Ibid.*, 153.

P. 53, l. 31   OR., XXI, 432.

P. 54, l. 3   Chamberlain, "My Story of Fredericksburg," *Cosmopolitan*, LIV, 153-54.

P. 55, l. 12   *Ibid.*, 154.

P. 56, l. 6   *Ibid.*, 146.

P. 56, l. 19   OR, XXI, 555; Burke Davis, *Gray Fox* (New York, 1956), 171-73; Douglas Southall Freeman, *Lee's Lieutenants*, II (New York, 1943), 380-81.

P. 58, l. 8   For incident, see W. C. King and W. P. Derby (editors), *Campfire Sketches and Battlefield Echoes of the Rebellion* (Springfield, Mass., 1887), 133; Chamberlain, "My Story of Fredericksburg," *Cosmopolitan*, LIV, 157-58.

P. 59, l. 24   Chamberlain, "My Story of Frederickburg," *Cosmopolitan*, LIV, 158.

P. 60, l. 10   *Campfire Sketches and Battlefield Echoes*, 127.

P. 60, l. 25 Chamberlain, "My Story of Fredericksburg," *Cosmopolitan*, LIV, 159.

P. 61, l. 9 Incident in *ibid.*, 158.

P. 61, l. 19 Robert Underwood Johnson and Clarence Clough Buel (editors), *Battles and Leaders of the Civil War* (New York, 1884-87), III, 215.

P. 61, l. 23 Quoted by Bruce Catton, *Glory Road* (New York, 1952), 75.

P. 61, l. 32 *Campfire Sketches and Battlefield Echoes*, 135.

P. 62, l. 5 For detailed accounts of Fredericksburg, see Palfrey, *The Antietam and Fredericksburg*, 132-90; Powell, *Fifth Corps*, 363-98; Williams, *Lincoln Finds A General*, II, 480-546; Catton, *Glory Road*, 27-75; Edward J. Stackpole, *Drama on the Rappahannock* (Harrisburg, 1957). For the part of the 20th Maine in particular, see MAGR for 1862, 113-14, Pullen, *Twentieth Maine*, 44-60.

Chapter III

P. 63, l. 6 William Thompson Lusk to his mother. Quoted by Catton, *Glory Road*, 95.

P. 64, l. 13 OR, XXI, 998, 99.

P. 64, l. 15 Williams, *Lincoln Finds A General*, II, 546.

P. 64, l. 22 T. Harry Williams, *Lincoln and His Generals* (New York, 1952), 212-13.

P. 65, l. 18 *Battles and Leaders*, III, 155.

P. 66, l. 32 Pullen, *Twentieth Maine*, 75; MAGR for 1864-65, 331.

P. 67, l. 5 Gerrish, *Army Life*, 86.

P. 67, l. 26 NA.

P. 69, l. 6 Gen. Joshua L. Chamberlain, "Through Blood and Fire at Gettysburg," *Hearst's Magazine*, XXIII (1913), 899-900; MAGR for 1864-65, I, 331-32; Pullen, *Twentieth Maine*, 77-81.

P. 69, l. 29 OR, XXVII, Pt. III, 881-82; Glenn Tucker, *High Tide at Gettysburg* (New York, 1958), 26; Henry Steele Commager, *The Blue and the Gray* (2 vols., New York, 1950), II, 589.

P. 71, l. 6 See letter headed, "Halt at Mannassas Junction, June 15th, 1863," in *Cham. Paps. LC.*

P. 72, l. 7 Williams, *Lincoln Finds A General*, II, 644.

P. 72, l. 15 Williams, *Lincoln and His Generals*, 259.

P. 73, l. 15 Tucker, *High Tide at Gettysburg*, 43.

P. 73, l. 21 *Richmond Examiner*, June 22, 1863. Quoted by *ibid.*, 28-29.

P. 74, l. 25 *Ibid.*, 82-83; Freeman, *Lee's Lieutenants*, III, 48-50.

P. 75, l. 6 Freeman, *R. E. Lee*, III, 58-59.

P. 76, l. 20 For march distances, see Pullen, *Twentieth Maine*, 90; Eugene Arus Nash, *A History of the Forty-Fourth Regiment, New York Volunteer Infantry* (Chicago, 1911), 137-41; Powell, *Fifth Corps*, 513. For march procedure, see Pvt. Geo. W. Carleton to Col. A. B. Farwell, Jan. 8, 1866. *Cham. Coll.*, FFC,YU.

P. 76, l. 29 Chamberlain, "Through Blood and Fire at Gettysburg," *Hearst's Mag.*, XXIII, 894.

P. 77, l. 1 *History of the 118th Pennsylvania Volunteers, Corn Exchange Regiment.* By the Survivors' Association (Philadelphia, 1905), 235.

P. 77, l. 11 Chamberlain, "Through Blood and Fire at Gettysburg," *Hearst's Mag.*, XXIII, 806.

P. 78, l. 18 Edward J. Stackpole, *They Met at Gettysburg* (Harrisburg, 1956), 123-54; Tucker, *High Tide at Gettysburg*, 93-171; Catton, *Glory Road*, 289-305; Freeman, *Lee's Lieutenants*, III, 73-105; *Battles and Leaders*, III, 255-89; Arthur J. L. Freemantle, *Three Months in the Southern States* (New York, 1864), 256.

P. 78, l. 24 Chamberlain, "Through Blood and Fire at Gettysburg," *Hearst's Mag.*, XXIII, 896.

P. 79, l. 2 Gerrish, *Army Life*, 101; *Battles and Leaders*, III, 301.

P. 79, l. 12 Chamberlain, "Through Blood and Fire at Gettysburg," *Hearst's Mag.*, XXIII, 896.

Fifty years after the battle, when asked about the George Washington rumor, Chamberlain said after considerable deliberation, "Yes, that report was circulated through our lines and I have no doubt that it had a tremendous psychological effect in inspiring the men. Doubtless it was a superstition, but yet who among us can say that such a thing was impossible? We have not yet sounded or explored the immortal life that lies out beyond the Bar. We know not what mystic power may be possessed by those who are now bivouacking with the dead. I only know the effect, but I dare not explain or deny the cause. I do believe that we were enveloped by the powers of the other world that day and who shall say that Washington was not among the number of those who aided the country that he founded?" (See Bangor *Daily News*, July 1, 1913).

P. 79, l. 22 Gerrish, *Army Life*, 101.

P. 79, l. 25 Chamberlain, "Through Blood and Fire at Gettysburg," *Hearst's Mag.*, XXIII, 896.

P. 79, l. 31 Oliver Willcox Norton, *Army Letters, 1861-1865* (Chicago, 1903), 322.

P. 80, l. 13 *Corn Exchange Regt.*, 238-39.

P. 82, l. 12 *Battles and Leaders*, III, 245-47, 339-42; Tucker, *High Tide at Gettysburg*, 211-30, 418-19; Stackpole, *They Met at Gettysburg*, 171-81; Freeman, *Lee's Lieutenants*, III, 106-16.

P. 84, l. 32 *Battles and Leaders*, III, 302-3.

P. 86, l. 8 W. A. Swanburg, *Sickles the Incredible* (New York, 1956), 37-56, 206-11; Catton, *Glory Road*, 167-70, 307-11; Tucker, *High Tide at Gettysburg*, 236-45; Williams, *Lincoln Finds A General*, II, 697-700; Frank A. Haskell, *The Battle of Gettysburg*, Harvard Classics (New York, 1910), 367; *Pennsylvania at Gettysburg* (Harrisburg, 1904), II, 622-23; Stackpole, *They Met at Gettysburg*, 190-97.

P. 86, l. 13 George Meade, *The Life and Letters of George Gordon Meade* (2 vols., New York, 1913), II, 72.

P. 86, l. 28 *Battles and Leaders*, III, 303; Jennings Cropper Wise, *The Long Arm of Lee* (2 vols., Lynchburg, 1915), II, 644; *Life and Letters of Meade*, II, 82.

P. 86, l. 32 *Battles and Leaders*, III, 319; Freeman, *Lee's Lieutenants*, III, 115.

P. 87, l. 12 *Battles and Leaders*, III, 359; Tucker, *High Tide at Gettysburg*, 234-36.

P. 87, l. 15 Tucker, *High Tide at Gettysburg*, 235-36.

P. 87, l. 32 Law, in *Battles and Leaders*, III, 321-22; John B. Hood, *Advance and Retreat* (New Orleans, 1880), 57-59; James Longstreet, *From Manassas to Appomattox* (Philadelphia, 1896), 365-68.

P. 89, l. 2 Oates, *The War Between the Union and the Confederacy*, 206-14.

P. 89, l. 17 *Battles and Leaders*, III, 307 n.

P. 89, l. 21 The historian of the Fifth Corps says that Barnes directed Vincent to go (Powell, *Fifth Corps*, 526), but Oliver Norton, who was Vincent's color bearer and bugler, insists that no one had seen Barnes since morning (*Pennsylvania at Gettysburg*, I, 461). Norton, whose book, *The Attack and Defense of Little Round Top* (New York, 1913), is the best work on the subject, always thought poorly of Barnes at Gettysburg. He contended —and evidently with good reason—that the order to occupy Little Round Top with Vincent's brigade came from Sykes, who was notified by Warren of the enemy's approach (Norton to Chamberlain, May 8, 1901. *Cham. Coll.*, MHS). Actually Barnes seems to have been suffering from some kind of ailment, perhaps intestinal. In the battle he was wounded.

P. 90, l. 2 Fairfax Downey, *The Guns at Gettysburg* (New York, 1958), 90-92.

Chapter IV

P. 91, l. 22 Chamberlain, "Through Blood and Fire at Gettysburg," *Hearst's Mag.*, XXIII, 898-99.

P. 92, l. 10 *Ibid.*, 899.

P. 92, l. 16 For approach and assignment of regiments, see *ibid.*, 898-900; Norton, *Little Round Top*, 264-65; A. M. Judson, *History of the 83rd Regiment Pennsylvania Volunteers* (Erie, Pa., no date), 67; *Maine at Gettysburg*. Report of Maine Commissioners (Portland, 1898), 253-54.

P. 92, l. 30 *Battles and Leaders*, III, 315.

P. 93, l. 14 Chamberlain, "Through Blood and Fire at Gettysburg," *Hearst's Mag.*, XXIII, 901; William Swinton, *Campaigns of the Army of the Potomac* (New York, 1866), 347.

P. 93, l. 32 Lieutenant Melcher of the 20th Maine gives to Oates' regiment 42 officers and 644 enlisted men (*Battles and Leaders*, III, 315). Oates had earlier mentioned such a figure but subsequently lowered it (Oates, *The War Between the Union and the Confederacy*, 222).

P. 94, l. 23 Chamberlain describes the procedure in his report of July 6, 1863 in OR, XXVII, pt. I, 623 and in "Through Blood and Fire at Gettysburg," *Hearst's Mag.*, XXIII, 902. See also Gerrish, *Army Life*, 107; Powell, *Fifth Corps*, 527-28; *Maine at Gettysburg*, 255; Pullen, *Twentieth Maine*, 117-18.

P. 95, l. 32 Downey, *The Guns at Gettysburg*, 92-95.

P. 97, l. 14 Norton, *Little Round Top*, 90. See also Judson, *83rd Pennsylvania*, 68.

P. 97, l. 23 Chamberlain, "Through Blood and Fire at Gettysburg," *Hearst's Mag.*, XXIII, 903.

P. 97, l. 30 Gerrish, *Army Life*, 109.

P. 98, l. 2 Oates, *The War Between the Union and the Confederacy*, 218.

P. 98, l. 5 *Ibid.*, 216.

P. 98, l. 6 Oates to Elihu Root, Secretary of War, June 2, 1903. *Cham. Paps.*, LC.

P. 98, l. 28 Chamberlain, "Through Blood and Fire at Gettysburg," *Hearst's Mag.*, XXIII, 904; *Maine at Gettysburg*, 256.

P. 99, l. 16 Chamberlain, "Through Blood and Fire at Gettysburg," *Hearst's Mag.*, XXIII, 905; Gerrish, *Army Life*, 69-71.

P. 99, l. 31 Chamberlain, "Through Blood and Fire at Gettysburg," *Hearst's Mag.*, XXIII, 905.

P. 100, l. 3 *Maine at Gettysburg*, 261.

P. 100, l. 8 Oates, *The War Between the Union and the Confederacy*, 220.

P. 100, l. 18 Chamberlain, "Through Blood and Fire at Gettysburg," *Hearst's Mag.*, XXIII, 904.

P. 100, l. 31 *Ibid.*, 905.

P. 101, l. 13 OR, XXVII, pt. I, 624; Judson, *83rd Pennsylvania*, 68.

P. 101, l. 17 *Maine at Gettysburg*, 261-62.

P. 101, l. 25 Chamberlain, "Through Blood and Fire at Gettysburg," *Hearst's Mag.*, XXIII, 905; OR, XXVII, pt. I, 624.

P. 103, l. 9 Oates, *The War Between the Union and the Confederacy*, 220.

P. 103, l. 18 Chamberlain, "Through Blood and Fire at Gettysburg," *Hearst's Mag.*, XXIII, 908.

P. 103, l. 28 For the charge, see *ibid.*, 905-8; OR, XXVII, Pt. I, 624; *Maine at Gettysburg*, 257-59; MAGR for 1964-65, I, 332; Gerrish, *Army Life*, 109-11; Powell, *Fifth Corps*, 529-30; Norton, *Little Round Top*, 112; Oates, *The War Between the Union and the Confederacy*, 220-21; Pullen, *Twentieth Maine*, 123-26; Judson, *83rd Pennsylvania*, 68.

P. 103, l. 32 OR, XXVII, Pt. I, 617.

P. 104, l. 15 Oates, *The War Between the Union and the Confederacy*, 219.

P. 104, l. 25 Quoted by Tucker, *High Tide at Gettysburg*, 266.

P. 106, l. 12 OR, XXVII, Pt. I, 625.

P. 107, l. 11 For the seizure of Round Top, see Rice and Chamberlain's reports in *ibid.*, 616-20, 622-26 (compare with Fisher's report in *ibid.*, 658-59, and the account in J. R. Sypher, *History of the Pennsylvania Reserve Corps* [Lancaster, 1865], 462); *Maine at Gettysburg*, particularly Chamberlain's field notes, 259-61; Chamberlain to Fanny, July 4 and 17, 1863. *Cham. Letters*, in possession of Miss Rosamond Allen; Oates, *The War Between the Union and the Confederacy*, 225; Tucker, *High Tide at Gettysburg*, 266.

P. 107, l. 31 Chamberlain to Fanny, July 17, 1863. *Cham. Letters*, in possession of Miss Rosamond Allen.

P. 108, l. 2 Chamberlain to Francis Fessenden, March 7, 1899. *Cham. Paps.* LC.

P. 108, l. 14 OR, XXVII, Pt. I, 625.

P. 108, l. 20 Chamberlain to Fanny, July 4 and 17, 1863. *Cham. Letters*, in possession of Miss Rosamond Allen.

P. 108, l. 32　Ames to Chamberlain, July 3, 1863. NA.

P. 109, l. 4　Pullen, *Twentieth Maine*, 131.

P. 110, l. 14　Powell, *Fifth Corps*, 530-31.

P. 111, l. 7　Chamberlain, "Through Blood and Fire at Gettysburg," *Hearst's Mag.*, XXIII, 909.

Chapter V

P. 112, l. 4　Chamberlain to Fanny, July 4, 1863. *Cham. Letters*, in possession of Miss Rosamond Allen.

P. 113, l. 15　OR, XXVII, Pt. I, 626; Gerrish, *Army Life*, 111-12; *Maine at Gettysburg*, 262; Pullen, *Twentieth Maine*, 135, 140-41.

P. 114, l. 7　For Chamberlain's march, see OR, XXVII, Pt. I, 627; Pullen, *Twentieth Maine*, 143-47.

P. 114, l. 17　OR, XXVII, Pt. I, 627; Pullen, *Twentieth Maine*, 147; Swinton, *Army of the Potomac*, 366-68.

P. 114, l. 29　Chamberlain to Fanny, July 17, 1863. *Cham. Letters*, in possession of Miss Rosamond Allen.

P. 115, l. 18　Chamberlain to Fanny, Sept. 12, 1863. *Ibid.*

P. 116, l. 2　NA; MAGR for 1864-65, I, 332; Gerrish, *Army Life*, 122.

P. 116, l. 21　James E. Rice to Wm. Pitt Fessenden, Sept. 8, 1863. NA; *Cham. Paps.*, LC. The NA contain copies of numerous recommendations.

P. 117, l. 16　Chamberlain to Fanny, Aug. 31, 1863. *Cham. Letters*, in possession of Miss Rosamond Allen.

P. 117, l. 24　Chamberlain to Fanny, Sept. 12, 1863. *Ibid.*

P. 118, l. 3　*Ibid.*

P. 118, l. 27　Powell, *Fifth Corps*, 576-78; Francis A. Walker, *History of the Second Army Corps* (New York, 1891), 321-64; *Corn Exchange Regt.*, 320-28.

P. 119, l. 2　Powell, *Fifth Corps*, 578-79.

P. 119, l. 23　Pullen, *Twentieth Maine*, 160-66; Gerrish, *Army Life*, 129-31; *Corn Exchange Regt.*, 335-44; OR, XXIX, Pt. I, 581-82; *Life and Letters of Meade*, II, 155-56.

P. 120, l. 12　Sarah S. Sampson to Chamberlain, June 12, 1903 or 1904. *Cham. Coll.*, MHS.

P. 121, l. 2　Mrs. J. H. Robinson to Chamberlain, May 30 and 31, and July 3, 1888. *Cham. Paps.*, FFC,YU. Grace Edna Fogler told Chamberlain on April 2, 1889 that despite his unsuccessful efforts to secure her father a government job, she was very grateful to him. She had approached Chamberlain with timidity, but "After leaving you I wished that I were a man like you that I might make someone as happy as you made me by a few kind words" (*Miscellaneous Papers* [Chamberlain] Rutherford B. Hayes Library).

P. 121, l. 6　Special Order No. 41, War Department, Adjutant General's Office, Jan. 27, 1864; Chamberlain to Col. E. D. Townsend, May 9, 1864. NA.

P. 121, l. 30　Fanny to "Cousin D," April 14, 1864. *Cham. Coll.*, MHS.

P. 122, l. 14　Chamberlain to Col. E. D. Townsend, May 9, 1864. NA.

P. 125, l. 2   For Pole Cat Creek affair, see OR, XXXVI, Pt. I, 574; 591-92; *Corn Exchange Regt.*, 435-38; Judson, *83rd Pennsylvania*, 99.

P. 125, l. 10   Statement by Private George W. Carleton to Colonel A. B. Farwell, Jan. 8, 1866. *Cham. Paps.*, FFC,YU.

P. 125, l. 27   *Ibid.*

P. 126, l. 1   The Pennsylvania regiments were the 121st, 142nd, 143rd, 149th, 150th, and 187th (newly joined). With the exception of the 187th, the regiments had constituted, until June 6, the 3rd Brigade, 4th Division, Fifth Corps (Powell, *Fifth Corps*, 691).

P. 126, l. 8   See recommendations in NA.

P. 126, l. 15   Private George W. Carleton to Colonel A. B. Farwell, Jan. 8, 1866. *Cham. Paps.*, FFC,YU.

P. 127, l. 5   OR, XXXVI, Pt. 1, 22-25; Swinton, *Army of the Potomac*, 488-508; Andrew A. Humphreys, *The Virginia Campaign of '64 and '65* (New York, 1883), 194-95, 198-202; Bruce Catton, *A Stillness at Appomattox* (New York, 1957), 177-82.

P. 127, l. 22   *Battles and Leaders*, IV, 541; Freeman, *R. E. Lee*, III, 402-441.

P. 128, l. 16   Humphreys, *Virginia Campaign of '64 and '65*, 195-225; Powell, *Fifth Corps*, 696-701; *Battles and Leaders*, IV, 540-44; *Life and Letters of Meade*, II, 206-207; Catton, *A Stillness at Appomattox*, 186-97.

P. 130, l. 21   Copies of Chamberlain's communications are in the *Cham. Paps.*, LC and the *Cham. Coll.*, MHS.

P. 130, l. 31   Emerson Gifford Taylor, *Gouverneur Kemble Warren* (Boston, 1932), 172-76; Powell, *Fifth Corps*, 670-674, 716-17.

P. 131, l. 17   *Lewiston Journal*, Illustrated Magazine Section, Sept. 1-6, 1900.

P. 134, l. 15   For Chamberlain's attack and wound, see OR, XL, Pt. I, 455-57, 481-82, Pt. II, 216; MAGR for 1864-65, I, 333-34; accounts by Capt. R. DeLacy of 143rd Pennsylvania in *Joshua Lawrence Chamberlain, A Sketch*, 31-33 and *Cham. Paps.*, LC, including letter of Jan. 15, 1904 to Chamberlain; West Funk to the Maine Legislature (no date), in *Cham. Paps.*, LC; *In Memoriam, Joshua Lawrence Chamberlain;* Chamberlain's own account in *Lewiston Journal*, Illus. Mag. Sec., Sept. 1-6, 1900; Pullen *Twentieth Maine*, 211-12; *Medical and Surgical History of the War of the Rebellion* (2 vols., each in 3 parts, Washington, 1870-1888), II, Pt. II, 363. The most explicit description of the wound is in the last-named work, and since Chamberlain suffered from his wound the rest of his life, it is worth quoting *in extenso:* "Case 1056. Colonel Joshua L. C——, 20th Maine, was wounded at Petersburg June 17 [18th], 1864, and taken to the hospital of the 1st Division, Fifth Corps. Surgeon W. R. DeWitt, jr., U. S. V., reported that 'a conoidal ball penetrated both hips, and was extracted,' and that Surgeon M. N. Townsend, 44th New York, was detailed to accompany the patient to City Point, when, by direction of Surgeon E. B. Dalton, U. S. V., he was placed on the hospital transport *Connecticut* and conveyed to Annapolis. . . . Surgeon B. A. Vanderkieft, U. S. V., reported that he 'reached the hospital at that place very comfortably on June 20, 1864, with a shot wound involving both buttocks and the urethra.' The progress and treatment does not appear on the hospital case-books, but in a letter to Surgeon J. H. Brinton, U. S. V., September 4, 1864, Dr. Vanderkieft states: 'I send you a catheter used by Brigadier General

J. L. C——, U. S. V. As you will perceive, it is covered by a calculous deposit. This catheter was but five days in the bladder, and was repeatedly covered in the same way. I think it a very important specimen, illustrating the necessity of often renewing catheters when they are to be used *a demeure*. The history you shall get when the patient is discharged'. . . . The patient was furloughed September 20, 1864, and mustered out January 15, 1866, and pensioned. The promised report of the case was not received. From Pension Examiner O. Mitchell's report, September 18, 1873, it appears that 'the ball entered the right hip in front of and a little below the right trochanter major, passed diagonally backward, and made exit above and posteriorly to the left great trochanter. The bladder was involved in the wound at some portion, as the subsequent history of escape of urine from the track of the wound and its extravasation testified. He very often suffers severe pain in the pelvic region. The chief disability resulting indirectly from the wound is the existence of a fistulous opening of the urethra, half an inch or more in length, just anterior to the scrotum; this often becomes inflamed. The greater part of the urine is voided through the fistula, the fistula itself resulting from the too long or too continuous wearing of a catheter. No change has resulted since the last examination; disability total.' This invalid was paid to June 4, 1873, at $30 a month." (*The Medical and Surgical History of the War of the Rebellion*, II [Surgical History], Pt. II 1876, 363).

P. 135, l. 3 *Personal Memoirs of U. S. Grant* (2 vols., New York, 1886), II, 297-98.

P. 135, l. 31 OR, XL, Pt. II, 216-17, 236, Pt. III, 421; MAGR for 1864-65, I, 334; Powell, *Fifth Corps*, 701; *In Memoriam, Joshua Lawrence Chamberlain*; Lewiston *Journal*, Illus. Mag. Sec., Sept. 1-6, 1900.

Chapter VI

P. 137, l. 16 Ames to Chamberlain, Oct. 18, 1864. *Cham. Paps.*, LC.

P. 138, l. 21 OR, XLII, Pt. III, 661-62, 663.

P. 138, l. 32 Joshua Lawrence Chamberlain, *The Passing of the Armies* (New York, 1915), 5. Hereafter referred to as "PA."

P. 139, l. 6 *Ibid.*, 19.

P. 139, l. 13 General Joshua L. Chamberlain, "The Army of the Potomac," in *New England Magazine*, New Series, III (Sept., 1890), 83.

P. 139, l. 17 PA, 19.

P. 139, l. 31 *Ibid.*, 40.

P. 140, l. 14 Powell, *Fifth Corps*, 748-53; Pullen, *20th Maine*, 232-34; MAGR for 1864-65, I, 334; OR, XLVI, Pt. II, 193.

P. 140, l. 19 MAGR for 1864-65, I, 334.

P. 140, l. 25 Powell speaks of Chamberlain as being in brigade command at the Hatcher's Run battles, Feb. 5-8, 1865 (*Fifth Corps*, 762, 763). But in his casualty return, he lists Sickel as in command of the brigade, while Sickel's own account of the action (OR, XLVI, Pt. I, 265-67) leaves little doubt that it was he, not Chamberlain, who commanded the brigade.

Finally, the record (NA) indicates that C. did not resume command until Feb. 27.

P. 141, l. 23 Adam Badeau, *Military History of Ulysses S. Grant* (3 vols., New York, 1881), III, 436; Grant, *Memoirs*, II, 434; *Memoirs of General William T. Sherman* (2 vols., New York, 1876), II, 324-27; Philip Van Doren Stern, *An End to Valor* (Boston, 1958), 102-9; PA, 36-38.

P. 142, l. 8 Powell, *Fifth Corps*, 774-75.

P. 142, l. 16 *Ibid.*, 777; Humphreys, *Virginia Campaign of '64 and '65*, 326; Freeman, *Lee's Lieutenants*, III, 656-57.

P. 144, l. 29 PA, 46.

P. 145, l. 4 *Ibid.*

P. 145, l. 26 *Ibid.*, 48.

P. 146, l. 11 *Ibid.*

P. 146, l. 23 *Ibid.*, 48-49.

P. 146, l. 30 *Ibid.*, 50

P. 147, l. 6 *Ibid.*

P. 147, l. 17 *Ibid.*

P. 147, l. 28 *Ibid.*, 51.

P. 148, l. 6 *Ibid.*, 51-52.

P. 148, l. 11 *Ibid.*, 52.

P. 148, l. 21 *Ibid.*

P. 149, l. 10 For the Quaker Road battle, see *ibid.*, 42-56; OR, XLVI, Pt. I, 796-802, 1286-87; Powell, *Fifth Corps*, 776-77; C. H. Porter, "Operations of the Fifth Corps on the Left, March 29 to Nightfall, March 31, 1865," in *The Shenandoah Campaigns of 1862 and 1864 and the Appomattox Campaign of 1865* (Military Historical Society of Massachusetts, Boston, 1907); Swinton, *Army of the Potomac*, 583; Stern, *An End to Valor*, 112-16; MAGR for 1864-65, I, 334-35; Pullen, *20th Maine*, 243-45; E. M. Woodward, *History of the 198th Pennsylvania Volunteers* (Trenton, 1884), 36-38.

P. 149, l. 13 PA, 56

P. 150, l. 7 *Ibid.*, 57; Woodward, *198th Pennsylvania*, 38.

P. 150, l. 18 For Chamberlain's introspection, see PA, 54-59.

P. 150, l. 28 OR, XLVI, Pt. I, 813.

P. 151, l. 18 Freeman, *Lee's Lieutenants*, III, 664-65.

P. 152, l. 1 MAGR for 1864-65, I, 335; William E. S. Whitman and Charles H. True, *Maine in the War for the Union* (Lewiston, 1865), 624.

P. 152, l. 6 Powell, *Fifth Corps*, 783.

P. 153, l. 12 *Proceedings, Findings, and Opinions of the Court of Inquiry . . . in the Case of Gouverneur K. Warren* (Washington, D. C., 1883), I, 817.

P. 153, l. 19 For the interchange among Warren, Griffin, and Chamberlain, see PA, 72-73.

P. 155, l. 9 *Ibid.*, 76. For Lee's presence, see testimony of Confederate Generals Hunton and McGowan in *Warren Court of Inquiry*, I, 625, 648.

P. 155, l. 15 PA, 76.

P. 155, l. 30 *Warren Court of Inquiry*, I, 625.

P. 156, l. 20 For the White Oak Road battle, see *ibid.*, *passim;* OR, XLVI, Pt. I, 812-17, 1287-88; Grant, *Memoirs*, II, 435; Swinton, *Army of the*

Potomac, 587-91; Humphreys, *Virginia Campaign of '64 and '65*, 330-34; Powell, *Fifth Corps*, 780-85; Porter, "Operations of the Fifth Corps on the Left," in *The Shenandoah Campaign and the Appomattox Campaign;* Freeman, R. E. *Lee*, IV, 34-35; MAGR for 1864-65, I, 335; Woodward, *198th Pennsylvania*, 39-42; Pullen, *20th Maine*, 247-48; PA, 65-83; Gen. Joshua L. Chamberlain, *Military Operations on the White Oak Road, Virginia, March 31, 1865* (Portland, 1897), 13-26. This last item, a pamphlet, is essentially the same as the pertinent material in PA but differs in a few details.

P. 156, l. 27   PA, 82-83.
P. 157, l. 5   *Ibid.*, 83.

Chapter VII

P. 158, l. 6   Stern, *An End to Valor*, 147.
P. 159, l. 2   OR, XLVI, Pt. III, 308.
P. 159, l. 18   *Personal Memoirs of P. H. Sheridan* (2 vols., New York, 1888), II, 168-69.
P. 160, l. 32   For appraisal of, and information on Fifth Corps, see Bruce Catton, *America Goes to War* (Middletown, Conn., 1958), 77-79; PA, xiii, 38-39, 112, 181; Warren to Chamberlain, Nov. 12, 1879. *Cham. Paps.* LC.
P. 161, l. 17   For this conversation, see PA, 88.
P. 161, l. 29   *Ibid.*, 89.
P. 162, l. 5   *Ibid.*, 100.
P. 163, l. 19   For orders and discussion, see OR, XLVI, Pt. I, 817-22; Powell, *Fifth Corps*, 786-93; PA, 97-99, 103.
P. 163, l. 25   PA, 103.
P. 164, l. 24.   For this exchange, see *ibid.*, 104.
P. 165, l. 7   *Ibid.*, 119.
P. 165, l. 10   *Ibid.*
P. 165, l. 24   *Ibid.*, 116
P. 166, l. 11   Sheridan, *Memoirs*, II, 160-61. During the 1880-1882 hearing on Warren's conduct, Chamberlain testified that people could easily be mistaken about Warren's attitude: ". . . those who do not know General Warren's temperament might think him to be negative when he was deeply intent. General Warren's temperament is such that he instead of showing excitement generally shows an intense concentration in what I call important movements, and those who do not know him might take it to be apathy when it was deeply concentrated thought and purpose" (*Warren Court of Inquiry*, I, 236).
P. 166, l. 23   PA, 123.
P. 167, l. 10   *Ibid.*, 124-26.
P. 169, l. 5   *Ibid.*, 130.
P. 170, l. 11   *Ibid.*, 130-31. See also D. F. Wallace to Chamberlain, March 29, 1884. *Cham. Paps.*, LC. Wallace may have been the confused soldier, though he speaks of the incident as occurring on March 29 (the Quaker Road battle) instead of April 1.

P. 171, l. 12   For exchange, see PA, 133.
P. 171, l. 25   *Ibid.*, 134.
P. 172, l. 10   *Ibid.*, 140.
P. 172, l. 21   *Ibid.*, 142.
P. 172, l. 29   *Ibid.*, 144.
P. 173, l. 7   *Ibid.*, 148-49.
P. 173, l. 27   *Ibid.*, 151; Sheridan, *Memoirs*, II, 165.
P. 174, l. 5   See *Warren Court of Inquiry* for proceedings, findings, and opinions. See also Taylor, *Warren*, 228-48.
P. 174, l. 12   PA, 153, 154.
P. 174, l. 20   Catton, *American Goes to War*, 85.
P. 175, l. 10   PA, 153.
P. 175, l. 27   New York *World*, April 4, 1865; J. Cutler Andrews, *The North Reports the Civil War* (Pittsburgh, 1955), 630-31.
P. 175, l. 30   PA, 174.
P. 175, l. 32   Chamberlain's report in OR, XLVI, Pt. I, 849-51; Griffin's report in *ibid.*, 838-40. For Five Forks in general and Chamberlain's part in particular, see also *ibid.*, *passim*, and *Warren Court of Inquiry*, *passim*, for the most complete and detailed accounts; Chamberlain's account in PA, 113-81, which is excellent and substantially the same as his pamphlet, *Five Forks* (Portland, 1902); Sheridan, *Memoirs*, II, 154-70; Powell, *Fifth Corps*, 786-828; C. H. Porter, "The Fifth Corps at the Battle of Five Forks," and W. W. Swan, "The Five Forks Campaign," in *The Shenandoah Campaigns and the Appomattox Campaign;* A. S. Perham, "Warren at Five Forks," in New York State Historical Association *Quarterly Journal* (July, 1923); Taylor, *Warren*, 207-27; Woodward, *198th Pennsylvania*, 44-46; Pullen, *Twentieth Maine*, 249-57; Freeman, *Lee's Lieutenants*, III, 661-74.
P. 176, l. 7   Stern, *An End to Valor*, 131-32, 141-42; Freeman, *Lee's Lieutenants*, III, 665-70; Rosser to A. S. Perham, Aug. 29, 1902. *Cham. Paps.*, LC.
P. 178, l. 1   OR, XLVI, Pt. I, 852.
P. 178, l. 24   PA, 227. For week's march, see *ibid.*, 192-230; OR, XLVI, Pt. I, 851-52.
P. 179, l. 2   PA, 230.
P. 179, l. 26   *Ibid.*, 232-33.
P. 180, l. 14   For the approach to the field of Appomattox, see *ibid.*, 233-35; OR, XLVI, Pt. I, 852, Pt. III, 731; Catton, *A Stillness at Appomattox*, 376-79; Burke Davis, *To Appomattox* (New York, 1959), 374-79; Gerrish, *Army Life*, 255-58; *Corn Exchange Regt.*, 588-89; Woodward, *198th Pennsylvania*, 57.
P. 181, l. 12   For incident, see PA, 235-36.
P. 182, l. 2   *Ibid.*, 237; F. C. Newhall, *With General Sheridan in Lee's Last Campaign* (Philadelphia, 1866), 211; H. E. Tremain, *The Last Hours of Sheridan's Cavalry* (New York, 1904), 252-53.
P. 182, l. 23   PA, 241.
P. 183, l. 2   *Ibid.*, 242-43; Gerrish, *Army Life*, 256-59.
P. 183, l. 10   PA, 243.
P. 183, l. 19   *Ibid.*, 244; Sheridan, *Memoirs*, II, 194-97.
P. 184, l. 14   PA, 246-47.

P. 184, l. 17   One of the best syntheses of accounts of the meeting of Grant and Lee is by Davis, *To Appomattox,* 379-90.

Chapter VIII

P. 185, l. 11   PA, 248-49.
P. 186, l. 7   *Ibid.,* 254-57. Actually it is uncertain whether Grant did anything more than approve the arrangements.
P. 186, l. 23   Tom Chamberlain to Sarah, April 11, 1865. *Cham. Coll.* MHS.
P. 186, l. 27   The terms agreed upon by the commissioners are in OR, XLVI, Pt. III, 685-86.
P. 187, l. 8   *Ibid.,* 707.
P. 187, l. 22   PA, 258-60.
P. 187, l. 26   *Ibid.,* 259-60.
P. 188, l. 1   Pullen, *Twentieth Maine,* 268.
P. 188, l. 21   PA, 260.
P. 188, l. 32   *Ibid.,* 261.
P. 189, l. 16   *Ibid.* Chamberlain wrote a number of accounts of the surrender, all essentially the same but differing slightly in details. See *ibid.,* 259-65, and his articles in Southern Historical Society *Papers,* XXXII; New York *Times,* May 4, 1901; Brunswick *Record,* Oct. 1, 1909. See also *Appomattox,* a paper read before the New York Commandery, Loyal Legion of the United States, Oct. 7, 1903; and "The Third Brigade at Appomattox," appended to Norton, *Army Letters.* For other sources on the surrender ceremony, see General John B. Gordon, *Reminiscences of the Civil War* (New York, 1903), 443-50; Gerrish, *Army Life,* 260-64; *Corn Exchange Reg't.,* 594-96; Woodward, *198th Pennsylvania,* 60-61.
P. 189, l. 32   Brunswick *Record,* Oct. 1, 1909.
P. 190, l. 6   Gordon, *Reminiscences,* 444. See also L. S. Merrick to Chamberlain, Feb. 7, 1902. *Cham. Coll.* MHS.
P. 190, l. 17   PA, 266.
P. 191, l. 6   Woodward, *198th Pennsylvania,* 61; *Corn Exchange Reg't,* 595-96; Gerrish, *Army Life,* 263-64.
P. 191, l. 31   The exchange is in PA, 266-69.
P. 192, l. 13   *Ibid.,* 56; Chamberlain file in NA; OR, XLVI, Pt. III, 730-31, 1011.
P. 193, l. 11   PA, 279-80.
P. 194, l. 25   The account of the reaction to Lincoln's assassination and the story of the funeral oration are in *ibid.,* 276-86. See also Gerrish, *Army Life,* 271-72; *Corn Exchange Reg't,* 598; Powell, *Fifth Corps,* 870.
P. 195, l. 3   PA, 289-90.
P. 195, l. 7   *Ibid.,* 301.
P. 195, l. 15   *Ibid.;* Taylor, *Warren,* 233-34.
P. 196, l. 7   PA, 308-10.
P. 196, l. 20   Gerrish, *Army Life,* 83-84.
P. 196, l. 24   PA, 310-11.
P. 197, l. 1   *Ibid.,* 313-14; Gerrish, *Army Life,* 289.
P. 197, l. 10   PA, 312.

P. 197, l. 15   *Corn Exchange Reg't*, 603.
P. 198, l. 4   PA, 315.
P. 198, l. 14   *Corn Exchange Reg't*, 604.
P. 198, l. 17   Gerrish, *Army Life*, 294.
P. 198, l. 31   PA, 316-17.
P. 199, l. 21   *Ibid.*, 324.
P. 200, l. 7   Pullen, *Twentieth Maine*, 286-87.
P. 201, l. 12   For number of actions, prisoners taken, horses shot, wounds received, etc., see MAGR for 1864-65, I, 336; Whitman and True, *Maine in the War for the Union*, 626-27; *In Memoriam, Joshua Lawrence Chamberlain*.
P. 201, l. 29   PA, 385-86.
P. 202, l. 24   *Ibid.*, 316.

Chapter IX

P. 203, l. 15   MAGR for 1864-65, I, 336. His restoration to services was sought on December 20, 1865 by Senators Morrill and Fessenden, and John H. Rice, F. A. Pike, John Lynch, S. Perham, and U. S. Grant *(Cham. Paps.* LC).
P. 204, l. 29   Chamberlain to Major General C. H. Smith of Eastport, April 12, 1866. *Ibid.*
P. 205, l. 19   Louis Clinton Hatch, *Maine, A History* (3 vols., New York, 1919), II, 533; Richard A. Hebert, *Modern Maine* (4 vols., New York, 1951), I, 230.
P. 206, l. 6   Warren to Chamberlain, Aug. 28, 1866. *Cham. Paps.*, LC.
P. 207, l. 2   Hatch, *Maine*, II, 533; Warren to Chamberlain, June 24, 1866. *Ibid.*
P. 207, l. 7   Col. Adam Badeau to Chamberlain, Dec. 26, 1866. *Cham. Paps.*, LC.
P. 207, l. 17   Godfrey to Chamberlain, Nov. 20, 1866. *Ibid.*
P. 210, l. 4   The address is to be found in *Public Documents Published by Order of the Legislature of the State of Maine* (Augusta, 1867).
P. 210, l. 8   Bangor *Daily Times*, Jan. 8, 1867.
P. 210, l. 10   Lewiston *Evening Journal*, Jan. 3, 1867.
P. 210, l. 14   Portland *Transcript*, Jan. 12, 1867.
P. 210, l. 17   Blaine to Chamberlain, Jan. 15, 1867. *Cham. Paps.*, LC.
P. 210, l. 22   Rockland *Democrat and Free Press*, Jan. 9, 1867.
P. 211, l. 7   Hebert, *Modern Maine*, I, 231; Hatch, *Maine*, II, 534.
P. 211, l. 25   Chamberlain to the Commissioners, May 9, 1867. *Cham. Paps.*, FFC,YU.
P. 212, l. 4   See correspondence of June, 1867. *Cham. Paps.*, LC; Kenneth Roberts, *Trending into Maine* (New York, 1949), 18-19.
P. 212, l. 17   Hebert, *Modern Maine*, I, 231; Hatch, *Maine*, II, 534-35.
P. 213, l. 32   The address is to be found in *Public Documents Published by Order of the Legislature of the State of Maine* (Augusta, 1868). The decline in shipping tonnage was spectacular. For example, in 1855 shipping tonnage owned in the Bangor customs district amounted to 40,297

tons; in 1890, 23,402 tons. Shipping tonnage owned in the Belfast customs district declined from about 80,000 tons in 1860 to 18,710 tons in 1890 (Munson, *Penobscot, Down East Paradise*, 145). For a splendid account of the rise and decline of sailing ships on the Penobscot, see *ibid.*, 134-46.

P. 214, l. 2   Augusta *Daily Journal*, Jan. 3, 1868.

P. 214, l. 3   Portland *Transcript*, Jan. 11, 1868.

P. 214, l. 14   Hebert, *Modern Maine*, I, 232.

P. 215, l. 17   Francis Fessenden, *Life and Public Services of William Pitt Fessenden* (2 vols., Boston, 1907), II, 207-8; Hatch, *Maine*, II, 537-38.

P. 215, l. 24   Fessenden, *Fessenden*, II, 186.

P. 215, l. 26   Claude G. Bowers, *The Tragic Era* (New York, 1929), 171. One of the best brief accounts of the impeachment is by J. G. Randall, *The Civil War and Reconstruction* (New York, 1937), 761-83.

P. 216, l. 15   Hebert, *Modern Maine*, I, 232; Hatch, *Maine*, II, 539-40.

P. 217, l. 8   See, e.g., the sentiment in the House for a reprieve as indicated in *Journal of the House of Representatives of the State of Maine, 1869* (Augusta, 1869), 147, 156.

P. 218, l. 15   The address is to be found in *Public Documents Published by Order of the Legislature of the State of Maine* (Augusta, 1869).

P. 218, l. 19   Portland *Transcript*, Jan. 16, 1869.

P. 218, l. 24   *Cham. Paps.*, LC.

P. 220, l. 11   Hatch, *Maine*, II, 562; Hebert, *Modern Maine*, I, 235.

P. 221, l. 1   H. M. Harlow to Chamberlain, Dec. 11, 1868. *Cham. Paps.*, FFC,YU.

P. 221, l. 21   The address is to be found in *Public Documents Published by Order of the Legislature of the State of Maine* (Augusta, 1870).

P. 221, l. 26   Portland *Transcript*, Jan. 15, 1870. The Bangor *Whig*, moderate on the prohibition question, was also critical (Hatch, *Maine*, II, 563).

P. 222, l. 3   Portland *Transcript*, Jan. 22, 1870.

P. 222, l. 9   The earlier states were Michigan (1847), Rhode Island (1852), and Wisconsin (1853). Although Maine abolished capital punishment in 1872, it restored it in 1878 after an insane convict attacked his keeper. Then, in 1887, Maine again abolished the death penalty.

P. 222, l. 32   See letter from British Consul Henry John Murray, March 18, 1870. *Cham. Paps.*, LC.

P. 223, l. 13   Commissioners' Report to the Legislature, 5.

P. 223, l. 15   John S. C. Abbott, *History of Maine* (Boston, 1875), 436-45; Hebert, *Modern Maine*, II, 197.

P. 224, l. 7   President Hyde's address at Chamberlain's funeral, Feb. 27, 1914. Brunswick *Record*, March 6, 1914; *Cham. Paps.*, LC.

Chapter X

P. 227, l. 16   Chamberlain to Fanny, Nov. 20, 1868. *Cham. Paps.*, FFC, YU.

P. 229, l. 12   Hatch, *Bowdoin College*, 130.

P. 229, l. 20   According to the *Faculty Records, 1871-76*, the meeting of Sept. 2, 1871 considered the first area of reform; the meeting of Sept. 4, the second area; the meeting of Feb. 5, 1872, the third area.

P. 230, l. 9   *Ibid.* for meeting of Sept. 2, 1871; George Thomas Little, "Historical Sketch," in *Bowdoin College, 1794-1894, Memorial of the One Hundredth Anniversary of the Incorporation of Bowdoin College* (Brunswick, 1894), xc-xci.

P. 230, l. 19   Bowdoin *Orient*, Oct. 2, 1871.

P. 230, l. 24   *Ibid.*

P. 231, l. 15   Little, in *Bowdoin College, 1794-1894*, xcii.

P. 234, l. 3   The complete address was carried in the Portland *Advertiser*, July 10, 1872.

P. 234, l. 22   Hatch, *Bowdoin College*, 133.

P. 235, l. 5   Quoted in *ibid.*, 134.

P. 235, l. 19   Quoted in *ibid.*, 158-59.

P. 235, l. 25   *Ibid.*, 129.

P. 235, l. 29   Little, in *Bowdoin College, 1794-1894*, xciv; Cross, *Chamberlain*, 55.

P. 236, l. 14   Chamberlain to the Trustees and Overseers, July 8, 1873. *Cham. Coll.*, MHS.

P. 237, l. 1   Minutes of meeting, Sept. 15, 1873, in *Faculty Records, 1871-76*.

P. 237, l. 8   Bowdoin *Orient*, Oct. 1, 1873.

P. 237, l. 18   Letter in Hatch, *Bowdoin College*, 136.

P. 238, l. 2   Meeting of May 21, 1874, in *Faculty Records, 1831-75*.

P. 238, l. 12   Meeting of May 26, 1874, in *ibid.;* meetings of May 18, 19, 25, and 27, in *Faculty Records, 1871-76*.

P. 238, l. 27   Form letter of May 28, 1874 is in *Faculty Records, 1831-75*.

P. 239, l. 4   Correspondence, dated May 26 and 27, 1874, is in *Cham. Paps.*, FFC,YU.

P. 239, l. 6   Meeting of May 28, 1874, in *Faculty Records, 1871-76*.

P. 239, l. 20   H. W. Benham to Chamberlain, June 3, 1874. *Cham. Paps.*, LC.

P. 239, l. 28   Newspaper clipping, dated May 31, 1874, in *Bowdoin Documentary History, 1865-1875*.

P. 240, l. 2   Quoted in Hatch, *Bowdoin College*, 144.

P. 240, l. 18   Quoted in *ibid.*, 146.

P. 240, l. 25   Quoted in Cross, *Chamberlain*, 66.

P. 241, l. 4   W. P. Morgan, *re* W. D. Washburn, future U. S. Senator, June 29, 1874. *Cham. Coll.*, MHS.

P. 242, l. 19   Chamberlain to the Trustees and Overseers, June 26, 1876. *Ibid.*

P. 243, l. 23   Joseph Titcomb to Hon. P. W. Chandler, March 4, 1874. Bowdoin College Archives, manila folder dated "1873-4."

P. 243, l. 27   Quoted in Hatch, *Bowdoin College*, 160-61.

P. 244, l. 15   President Hyde's oration at Chamberlain's funeral, Feb. 27, 1914. Brunswick *Record*, March 6, 1914; *Cham. Paps.*, LC.

P. 244, l. 29   Chamberlain to his daughter, Grace, May 29, 1876. *Cham. Coll.*, MHS.

P. 246, l. 16   Meeting of March 12, 1883, in *Faculty Records, 1874-1886*.

P. 246, l. 22   J. H. Warren, M.D., to Chamberlain, March 2, 1883. *Cham. Paps.*, FFC,YU.

P. 246, l. 30 John Pike to Chamberlain, June 18, 1883. *Cham. Coll.*, MHS.

P. 247, l. 2 Ellis Spear to Chamberlain, June 26, 1883. *Cham. Paps.*, FFC,YU.

P. 247, l. 20 Hyde's oration at Chamberlain's funeral, Feb. 27, 1914. Brunswick *Record*, March 6, 1914; Cham. Paps., LC.

Chapter XI

P. 249, l. 2 Selden Connor to Chamberlain, Feb. 28, 1876. *Cham. Paps.*, LC.

P. 249, l. 31 Joshua L. Chamberlain, *Maine: Her Place in History* (Augusta, 1877).

P. 250, l. 17 Chief Justice John Appleton to Chamberlain, March 8, 1878. *Cham. Paps.*, LC. See also Chamberlain to Peleg W. Chandler, March 7, 1878, for permission to be away from Bowdoin from June 5 to the end of the summer. *Peleg W. Chandler Papers*, Rutherford B. Hayes Library.

P. 250, l. 20 See Evarts to Chamberlain, March 11 and 19, 1878. *Cham. Paps.*, LC.

P. 250, l. 21 Passport of May 2, 1878 is in *ibid.* According to a letter of May 2, 1878 from F. W. Seward, Acting Secretary of State, Chamberlain was to receive two payments totaling $1200, one half to be paid by the State Department, presumably at once; and one half by the Commissioner General at Paris at the close of the Exposition (*Ibid.*).

P. 250, l. 31 See the interesting and amusing letter to Chamberlain from a Southerner, John C. Walker of Galveston, Dec. 15, 1878, on the latter's recollections of the trip and the Exposition. *Ibid.*

P. 251, l. 19 Hon. Joshua L. Chamberlain, "Education at the Universal Exposition," in *Reports of the United States Commissioners to the Paris Universal Exposition, 1878* (Washington, D. C., 1880), II, 181-347.

P. 251, l. 25 *Ibid.*, 342.

P. 252, l. 3 *Ibid.*, 343.

P. 252, l. 5 *Ibid.*, 344.

P. 252, l. 12 *Ibid.*, 346.

P. 252, l. 15 *Ibid.*, 227.

P. 252, l. 20 *Ibid.*, 347.

P. 253, l. 2 John D. Philbrick to Chamberlain, n.d. *Cham. Paps.*, LC.

P. 254, l. 2 For the Greenback problem and movement, see D. C. Barrett, *The Greenback and Resumption of Specie Payments, 1862-1879* (New York, 1931); F. E. Haynes, *Third Party Movements Since the Civil War, with Special Reference to Iowa* (Iowa City, 1916); Edward Stanwood, *History of the Presidency* (Boston, 1898).

P. 255, l. 10 Hebert, *Modern Maine*, I, 242-43; Hatch, *Maine*, III, 599-600, 615-19; Edward Stanwood, *James Gillespie Blaine* (Boston, 1905), 222-23.

P. 256, l. 9 *Joshua Lawrence Chamberlain, Supplement: The Twelve Days at Augusta, 1880* (Portland, 1906), 17.

P. 256, l. 19 For Conkling role, see Alfred R. Conkling, *The Life and Letters of Roscoe Conkling* (New York, 1889), 585-87.

P. 256, l. 22   Charles Edward Russell, *Blaine of Maine, His Life and Times* (New York, 1931), 111-13.

P. 256, l. 25   *Ibid.*, 116; Theron C. Crawford, *James G. Blaine* (Philadelphia, 1893), 68.

P. 257, l. 3   Russell, *Blaine of Maine*, 114-28. Blaine could also use sarcasm—and very effectively on Conkling (See David Saville Muzzey, *James G. Blaine* [New York, 1934], 61).

P. 257, l. 14   Russell, *Blaine of Maine*, 359; Gail Hamilton, *Biography of James G. Blaine* (Norwich, Conn., 1895), 452.

P. 257, l. 30   Hamilton, *Blaine*, 453; Muzzey, *Blaine*, 155-56.

P. 258, l. 25   Chamberlain to Blaine, Dec. 29, 1879. Portland *Daily Press*, Jan. 3, 1880.

P. 259, l. 11   Hatch, *Maine*, II, 604-5; Hebert, *Modern Maine*, I, 243.

P. 259, l. 19   Hamilton, *Blaine*, 454; Russell, *Blaine of Maine*, 360-61; Muzzey, *Blaine*, 156; *Twelve Days at Augusta*, 4-6; Portland *Daily Press*, Jan. 3, 1880; also accounts in New York *Tribune* (Republican), Dec. 20, 1879 and New York *World* (Democratic), Dec. 31, 1879.

P. 260, l. 17   See, e.g., Daniel White to Chamberlain, Jan. 10, 1880, and James M. Davis to Chamberlain, Jan. 13, 1880. *Cham. Paps.*, LC; Joseph B. Peaks (quoted), commanding the Piscataquis Battalion, to Chamberlain, Jan. 12, 1880. *Cham. Coll.*, MHS.

P. 260, l. 27   C. W. Goddard to Chamberlain, Jan. 10, 1880. *Cham. Paps.*, LC; Franklin Fairbanks to Chamberlain, Jan. 13, 1880. *Cham. Paps.*, FFC,YU.

P. 262, l. 6   Chamberlain to Judge Appleton, Jan. 1, 1881. *Cham. Coll.*, MHS.

P. 263, l. 11   Memorandum of a conversation with Bradbury, Jan. 10, 1880, in *Twelve Days at Augusta*, 21-22; Hatch, *Maine*, II, 610-11.

P. 263, l. 23   Chamberlain to Judge Appleton, Jan. 12, 1880. *Cham. Coll.*, MHS.

P. 264, l. 3   For incident, see Hatch *Maine*, II, 611. Hatch based his account on the biography of Nelson Dingley by Dingley's son, p. 169.

P. 265, l. 2   *Twelve Days at Augusta*, 24-25; Hatch, *Maine*, II, 611.

P. 265, l. 21   "To the People of Maine," Jan. 15, 1880. *Cham. Paps.*, LC.

P. 266, l. 2   For revocation of Chamberlain's orders, see Smith's letter from the Adjutant General's Office, Jan 16, 1880. *Ibid.*

P. 267, l. 2   For Davis' letter of Jan. 17, 1880 to Chamberlain and the General's reply, see *Cham. Coll.*, MHS. Actually after Chamberlain retired from the city, the situation grew worse and Governor Davis summoned several militia companies to keep the peace where Chamberlain by himself had succeeded before (Hatch, *Maine*, II, 613-15; Hebert, *Modern Maine*, I, 245).

P. 267, l. 11   *Twelve Days at Augusta*, 18.

P. 267, l. 13   A. P. Gould to Chamberlain, Jan. 15, 1880. *Cham. Paps.*, FFC,YU.

P. 267, l. 28   G. H. Manley to Chamberlain, Jan. 10, 1880, and F. A. Wilson to Chamberlain, Jan. 13, 1880. *Cham. Coll.*, MHS; Geo. W. Quimby to Chamberlain, Jan. 15, 1880. *Cham. Paps.*, FFC,YU.

P. 268, l. 4   Wilbur D. Spencer, *Maine Immortals* (Augusta, 1932), 51; Richard Hallet, "The Happy Warrior," in *Down East Magazine* (Nov.-Dec., 1956), 33. Stanwood (*Blaine*, 222) is one of the few admiring biographers of Blaine who concede that Chamberlain had something to do with keeping the peace.

P. 268, l. 7   Charles D. Gilmore (then a proprietor of the Washington News Association) to Chamberlain, Jan. 11, 1880. *Miscellaneous Papers*, Rutherford B. Hayes Library.

P. 268, l. 19   J. Warren Brown to Chamberlain, June 18, 1879. *Cham. Paps.*, FFC,YU.

P. 268, l. 27   Chamberlain to General J. W. Spaulding, Oct. 4, 1880. *Cham. Coll.*, MHS. See also letters of Oct. 8 to C. O. Farrington, A. H. Walker, General B. A. Murray, and Ephraim Flint. *Ibid.*

P. 269, l. 6   As has been aptly said, his political friends censured him for his objective attitude, "and many joined themselves to other leaders who were willing to take care of themselves and their friends better." ("Chamberlain, Joshua Lawrence," in *Men of Progress, Maine, 1897* [Boston, 1897]).

P. 269, l. 26   Charles E. Nash to Chamberlain, Jan. 3, 1881. *Cham. Coll.*, MHS.

P. 270, l. 15   Hebert, *Modern Maine*, I, 245-46; *National Cyclopedia of American Biography*, I, 290 (Frye), XX, 220 (Hale); *Dictionary of American Biography* and Hatch, *Maine*, II, 619-22 for both Frye and Hale.

P. 271, l. 8   Dexter A. Hawkins to President Arthur, March 1, 1884; Hawkins to Chamberlain, March 1, 1884; Chamberlain to President Arthur, March 4, 1884. *Cham. Paps.*, FFC,YU; N. P. Banks to Stephen M. Allen, May 8, 1876, *re* London post. *Cham. Paps.*, LC; Chamberlain to A. H. Rice, Governor of Mass., April 28, 1877, *re* French mission. *Hayes Papers*, Rutherford B. Hayes Library. It has been alleged that when Chamberlain returned to Maine after the Civil War, he was offered the choice of several diplomatic posts (*Joshua Lawrence Chamberlain, A Sketch*, 16). In my researches I have found nothing to substantiate this assertion. It has also been observed that Horace Greeley encouraged him to go on the national ticket with him as a candidate and that Chamberlain declined (*ibid.*, 19; Spencer, *Maine Immortals*, 54). A careful search of both the Chamberlain and the Greeley papers as well as of numerous secondary sources has uncovered no evidence to support this contention. The statement may have been made on the basis of hearsay.

P. 272, l. 12   Chamberlain to President Hayes, March 8, 1877. *Hayes Papers*, Rutherford B. Hayes Library.

P. 272, l. 25   Boston *Post*, Aug. 7, 1884.

Chapter XII

P. 274, l. 6   George M. Barbour, *Florida for Tourists, Invalids and Settlers* (New York, 1882), 16.

P. 275, l. 9   Chamberlain to 'Sadie' Chamberlain Farrington, Jan. 29, 1882. Letter in possession of Miss Alice Farrington, Brewer, Maine.

P. 275, l. 15 Davis Tillson to Chamberlain, May 16, 1881. *Cham. Coll.*, MHS.

P. 275, l. 20 H. W. Chamberlain to Fanny, Jan. 27, 1884. *Ibid.*

P. 276, l. 10 Charles Ledyard Norton, *A Handbook of Florida* (New York, 1891), 233.

P. 276, l. 15 Notice of Sale of Hyde Park Orangery by A. L. Eichelberger, Ocala, Fla. *Cham. Coll.*, MHS.

P. 276, l. 27 Report to Stockholders, March 17, 1886; understanding with Willard, Jan. 20, 1886. *Cham. Paps.*, FFC,YU.

P. 277, l. 20 Many of the details of Chamberlain's Florida ventures may be found in *ibid.*

P. 278, l. 1 H. W. Chamberlain to Chamberlain, May 7, 1888 and March 22, 1889. *Ibid.*

P. 279, l. 3 Evidence of Chamberlain's numerous business activities may be found in *ibid.*

P. 279, l. 9 See the Bates case in correspondence folder for 1896. *Ibid.*

P. 280, l. 4 Chamberlain to the Reverend Searles, Nov. 13, 1893. *Cham. Coll.*, MHS.

P. 280, l. 24 Undated notes in Chamberlain's handwriting, probably written in 1892 or 1893. *Cham. Paps.*, FFC,YU.

P. 281, l. 6 Description of Domhegan in Cross, *Chamberlain*, 85.

P. 281, l. 12 Notice in *Cham. Paps.*, FFC,YU.

P. 282, l. 9 *Joshua Lawrence Chamberlain, A Sketch*, 23.

P. 284, l. 3 The address is in *Maine at Gettysburg*, 546-59.

P. 284, l. 27 *Dedication of the Twentieth Maine Monuments at Gettysburg October 3, 1889. Speeches by Howard L. Prince and Joshua L. Chamberlain* (Waldoboro, Maine, 1891).

P. 285, l. 19 Springfield *Republican*, June 4, 1897.

P. 286, l. 16 Joshua L. Chamberlain, *Property: Its Office and Sanction*. A Discourse before the Benevolent Society of Portland, Maine, January 21, 1900 (Portland, 1900).

P. 288, l. 17 Thomas H. Hubbard to the Secretary of War, Feb. 15, 1893. NA.

P. 288, l. 22 The correspondence concerning the Medal of Honor is in the NA, File No. C411(CB)1866 relating to the service of Joshua Lawrence Chamberlain.

P. 288, l. 31 Tom died Aug. 12, 1896, leaving Chamberlain and his sister 'Sadie' the survivors of their family: Horace had died Dec. 7, 1861; John —whose widow, Delia, Tom married—Aug. 11, 1867; Joshua, their father, Aug. 10, 1880; and Sarah, their mother, Nov. 5, 1888.

Chapter XIII

P. 291, l. 8 There were five articles in all, but see especially the Bangor *News* for March 5, 21, and 26, 1898.

P. 291, l. 13 Powers to Chamberlain, April 5, 1898. *Cham. Paps.*, LC.

P. 291, l. 16 Chamberlain to the Secretary of War, April 22, 1898. NA.

P. 291, l. 27   Chamberlain to the Honorable Wm. P. Frye, April 22, 1898. *Ibid.*

P. 292, l. 4   The Secretary of War to Chamberlain, April 30, 1898. *Ibid.*

P. 292, l. 7   See their letters of Aug. 20 and 21, 1898. *Cham. Paps.*, LC.

P. 292, l. 10   George D. Cutler to the Honorable John D. Long, Secretary of the Navy, May 6, 1898. NA.

P. 292, l. 15   William P. Whitehouse to the President of the United States, Nov. 17, 1899. *Cham. Coll.*, MHS.

P. 292, l. 20   A copy list of this petition is in the *Cham. Paps.*, FFC,YU.

P. 292, l. 26   James P. Baxter to the President, Nov. 22, 1899. *Cham. Coll.*, MHS.

P. 292, l. 31   F. M. Drew to Chamberlain, Dec. 1, 1899. *Ibid.*

P. 293, l. 1   See Frye's letter, Nov. 19, 1899. *Cham. Paps.*, FFC,YU.

P. 293, l. 25   Chamberlain to Amos L. Allen, Dec. 1, 1899. *Cham. Coll.*, MHS.

P. 294, l. 6   Abner O. Shaw (surgeon of the 20th Maine) to Chamberlain, Dec. 5, 1899. *Ibid;* Amos L. Allen to Chamberlain, Feb. 12, 1900. *Miscellaneous Papers*, Rutherford B. Hayes Library.

P. 294, l. 11   The Chief of the Division of Appointments, Treasury Department, wrote Chamberlain on March 27, 1900 of his appointment by commission of March 20 (*Cham. Paps.*, FFC,YU). The Federal Records Center, of the National Archives and Records Service, St. Louis, Mo., wrote the author on May 28, 1958 that according to the records received from the U.S. Civil Service Commission, Chamberlain was appointed on April 12. The apparent discrepancy may not really exist since, according to Amos Allen, from the time of the President's appointment "It would take about two weeks to be confirmed and commissioned" (Allen to Chamberlain, Feb. 12, 1900. *Miscellaneous Papers*, Rutherford B. Hayes Library).

P. 295, l. 27   Chamberlain to Gen. John T. Richards, Dec. 26, 1899. *Cham. Coll.*, MHS.

P. 296, l. 5   Chamberlain to the Secretary of the Treasury, Oct. 22, 1900. *Ibid.*

P. 297, l. 8   For Chamberlain's Egyptian experiences, see his letter to Moses, Dec. 18, 1900, published in the Portland *Press*, Jan. 10, 1901 and the Brunswick *Telegraph*, Jan. 12, 1901; his reminiscences in the Lewiston *Journal*, Illus. Mag. Sec., Aug. 17-21, 1907; Nimr to Chamberlain, April 19, 1901. *Cham. Coll.*, MHS. The Bible-Koran story was given the author by Chamberlain's niece, Miss Alice Farrington of Brewer, Maine.

P. 297, l. 20   James McKeen to Chamberlain, Oct. 31, 1901[5]. *Cham. Coll.*, MHS.

P. 298, l. 3   Frye offered a bill to this effect: S6150, on May 14, 1906, and another in the first session of the 59th Congress (S2162).

P. 298, l. 30   Letters from Edith and Mary Dalton and from Elizabeth Kendall Upham are to be found in the *Cham. Coll.*, MHS and the *Cham. Paps.*, FFC,YU. Letters from Sarah S. Sampson are in the *Cham. Coll.*, MHS.

P. 299, l. 16   Letters from Myra E. Porter are in *ibid.*

P. 300, l. 4   Letters from Mary P. Clark are in *ibid.*

P. 300, l. 22   Chamberlain to Fanny, May 28, 1852. *Ibid.*

P. 301, l. 3   Published in *Ceremonies and Commemoration of the One Hundredth Anniversary of the Birth of Abraham Lincoln, Philadelphia, February 12, 1909* (no place, 1909) and in *The Magazine of History,* Extra Number 32 (New York, 1914).

P. 302, l. 22   *Cosmopolitan Magazine,* LIV (Dec., 1912–May, 1913).

P. 302, l. 25   *Hearst's Magazine,* XXIII, No. 6 (June, 1913).

P. 303, l. 4   Published in Portland, 1897.

P. 303, l. 8   Published by G. P. Putnam's Sons, New York, 1915.

P. 304, l.26   There are many good accounts of the ceremony. See, e.g., the Boston *Journal,* June 26, 1908.

P. 305, l. 14   Portland *Eastern Argus,* June 2, 1913.

P. 305, l. 22   Chamberlain's reply is in the folder marked, "General Chamberlain, 1852," Bowdoin College Library.

P. 306, l. 30   Account based on article in the Portland *Press,* July 2, 1912.

P. 306, l. 3   A recollection of Chamberlain's granddaughter, Miss Eleanor Allen.

P. 307, l. 17   An interesting, detailed description of the house and its contents may be found in Little, *Genealogical and Family History of Maine,* I, 138-140.

P. 307, l. 31   See Chamberlain to the President, Dec. 11, 1891; Adelbert Ames to Chamberlain, Feb. 18, 1895, Ames remarking, "I understand Merriam's offense is that is is not a West Pointer. I *am one* and I protest such injustice to him and to West Point." *Cham. Paps.,* LC. See also Merriam to Chamberlain, Feb. 20, 1903. *Ibid.;* Merriam to Chamberlain, Aug. 27, 1898. *Cham. Paps.,* FFC,YU.

P. 308, l. 5   Chamberlain to the Hon. E. P. Mayo, Jan. 16, 1907. *Cham. Coll.,* MHS.

P. 308, l. 13   See, e.g., Chamberlain's letter to the Hon. Isador Rayner, Senator from Maryland, July, 1912. *Ibid.*

P. 308, l. 28   An inventory of his estate after his death revealed that he held real estate in Brunswick, Portland, South Portland, and Brewer appraised at $10,840; a personal estate of goods and chattels (violin, furniture, schooner *Pinafore,* etc.) appraised at $1675; and rights and credits (bonds, shares, notes, coupons, cash in bank, etc.) valued at $21,093.11. Total: $33,608.11 (Detailed inventory in *Cham. Paps.,* FFC,YU).

P. 309, l. 3   Chamberlain to H. W. Chamberlain, Oct. 18, 1913. *Cham. Coll.,* MHS.

P. 309, l. 21   This paragraph is based on recollections of Miss Rosamund Allen of St. Petersburg, Florida and Miss Eleanor Allen of London, England.

P. 310, l. 4   Chamberlain to 'Sadie' Chamberlain Farrington, Jan. 20 and Feb. 4, 1914. In possession of Miss Alice Farrington.

P. 312, l. 14   Newspaper accounts of Chamberlain's life and of plans for the funeral ceremonies or of those actually held may be found in the Portland *Evening Express and Advertiser,* Feb. 24-28, 1914; Portland *Eastern Argus,* Feb. 25 and 28, 1914; Portland *Daily Press,* Feb. 25-27, 1914; Brunswick *Telegraph,* Feb. 26 and 27, 1914. An excellent account is also given in *In Memoriam, Joshua Lawrence Chamberlain*. President Hyde's address may be found excerpted or in full in the Portland and Brunswick papers. A complete version is in the *Cham. Paps.*, L.C.

P. 312, l. 16 Chamberlain is buried in Pine Grove Cemetery, Brunswick, Maine. His grave lies in the section nearest the Bowdoin College campus. It is a section shared by a number of Bowdoin's most famed and beloved faculty—among others, men like Professors Cleaveland, Packard, and Smyth, and President Hyde. Beside the boundary fence stands a grove of pine trees beneath which grow lilies-of-the-valley and myrtle. Near Chamberlain are the graves of his wife Fanny (d. 1905), his son Wyllys (d. 1928), and his daughter Grace (d. 1937). Chamberlain's own grave is next to the cemetery drive and half shadowed by two maples across the drive. For a man who was a major general in the Union army, governor of Maine, and president of Bowdoin College, his grave stone bears only the brief and simple inscription:

Joshua L. Chamberlain
1828–1914

Bibliography

Abbott, John S. C., *History of Maine,* Boston, 1875.
Andrews, J. Cutler, *The North Reports the Civil War,* Pittsburgh, 1955.
Annual Reports of the Adjutant General of the State of Maine (for the years 1862 through 1865), Augusta (Maine), 1863-66.
Appleton's Cyclopedia of American Biography.
Augusta (Maine) *Daily Journal.*

Badeau, Adam, *Military History of Ulysses S. Grant,* 3 vols., New York, 1868-1881.
Bangor *Daily News.*
——— *Daily Times.*
——— *Historical Magazine.*
——— *Whig.*
Barbour, George M., *Florida for Tourists, Invalids and Settlers,* New York, 1882.
Barrett, D. C., *The Greenback and Resumption of Specie Payments, 1862-1879,* New York, 1931.
Battles and Leaders of the Civil War, edited by Robert Underwood Johnson and Clarence Clough Buel, 4 vols., New York, 1884-87.
Boston *Journal.*
——— *Post.*
Bowdoin College. *Documentary History,* Scrapbook.
——— *Orient.*
——— *Records of the Executive Government, Faculty Records.*
Bowdoin College, 1794-1894, Memorial of the One Hundredth Anniversary of the Incorporation of Bowdoin College, Brunswick, 1894.
Bowers, Claude G., *The Tragic Era,* New York, 1929.
Brunswick. *The First Parish Church in Brunswick, Maine,* no author, place, or date.
——— *Record.*
——— *Telegraph.*

Campfire Sketches and Battlefield Echoes of the Rebellion, edited by W. C. King and W. P. Derby, Springfield (Mass.), 1887.
Catton, Bruce, *America Goes to War,* Middletown (Conn.), 1958.

341

Catton, Bruce, *A Stillness at Appomattox*, New York, 1957.
———, *Glory Road*, New York, 1952.
———, *Mr. Lincoln's Army*, New York, 1951.
Chamberlain Collection, Maine Historical Society, Portland, Maine.
——— File, National Archives, Washington, D. C.
——— *Letters*, in possession of Miss Alice Farrington, Brewer, Maine and Miss Rosamond Allen, St. Petersburg, Florida.
——— *Letters* in *Miscellaneous Papers*, Rutherford B. Hayes Library, Fremont, Ohio.
——— *Papers*, Frost Family Collection, Yale University, New Haven, Conn.
——— *Papers*, Library of Congress, Washington, D. C.
——— Joshua L., "Abraham Lincoln Seen from the Field," *Ceremonies in Commemoration of the One Hundredth Anniversary of the Birth of Abraham Lincoln, Philadelphia, February 12, 1909*. Also published in The Magazine of History, Extra Number — No. 32 (1914).
——— Address (untitled), *Dedication of the Twentieth Maine Monuments at Gettysburg, October 3, 1889*, Waldoboro, 1891.
——— "Appomattox," New York *Times*, May 4, 1901.
——— *Appomattox*. A Paper read before the New York Commandery, Loyal Legion of the United States, Oct. 7, 1903.
——— "The Army of the Potomac," *New England Magazine*, New Series, III (1890).
——— "Education at the Universal Exposition," *Reports of the United States Commissioners to the Paris Universal Exposition, 1878*, 5 vols., Washington, D. C., 1880 (vol. II).
——— *Five Forks*, Portland (Maine), 1902.
——— Gubernatorial Addresses, *Public Documents Published by Order of the Legislature of the State of Maine*, Augusta (Maine), 1867-1870.
——— Inaugural Address at Bowdoin College, Portland *Advertiser*, July 10, 1872.
——— *Maine: Her Place in History*, Augusta (Maine), 1877.
——— *Military Operations on the White Oak Road, Virginia, March 31, 1865*, Portland (Maine), 1897.
——— "My Story of Fredericksburg," *Cosmopolitan Magazine*, LIV (December, 1912-May, 1913).
——— *The Passing of the Armies*, New York, 1915.
——— *Property: Its Office and Sanction*. A Discourse before the Benevolent Society of Portland, Maine, January 21, 1900. Portland, 1900.
——— "The Third Brigade at Appomattox," *Army Letters* by Oliver Willcox Norton, Chicago, 1903.
——— "Through Blood and Fire at Gettysburg," *Hearst's Magazine*, XXIII, No. 6 (June, 1913).
——— (Editor-in-Chief), *Universities and Their Sons* (6 vols., Boston, 1898-1923).
Chandler (Peleg W.) Papers, Rutherford B. Hayes Library, Fremont, Ohio.
Cleaveland, Nehemiah, and Packard, Alpheus Spring, *History of Bowdoin College*, Boston, 1882.
Commager, Henry Steele, *The Blue and the Gray*, 2 vols., New York, 1950.

Conkling, Alfred R., *The Life and Letters of Roscoe Conkling*, New York, 1889.

Cross, Robert M., *Joshua Lawrence Chamberlain*, Bowdoin College, unpublished Senior essay, 1945.

Davis, Burke, *Gray Fox: Robert E. Lee and the Civil War*, New York, 1956.

——, *To Appomattox: Nine April Days, 1865*, New York, 1959.

Dictionary of American Biography

Downey, Fairfax, *The Guns at Gettysburg*, New York, 1958.

Fessenden, Francis, *Life and Public Services of William Pitt Fessenden*, 2 vols., Boston, 1907.

Freeman, Douglas Southall, *Lee's Lieutenants*, 3 vols., New York, 1942-44.

——, *R. E. Lee*, 4 vols., New York, 1935.

Freemantle, Arthur L. J., *Three Months in the Southern States*, New York, 1864.

Gerrish, Theodore, *Army Life, A Private's Reminiscences of the Civil War*, Portland, 1882.

Gordon, General John B., *Reminiscences of the Civil War*, New York, 1903.

Grant, U. S., *Personal Memoirs*, 2 vols., New York, 1886.

Hallet, Richard, "The Happy Warrior," *Down East Magazine*, Nov.-Dec., 1956.

Hamilton, Gail, *Biography of James G. Blaine*, Norwich (Conn.), 1895.

Haskell, Frank A., *The Battle of Gettysburg*, Harvard Classics, New York, 1910.

Hatch, Louis C., *The History of Bowdoin College*, Portland (Maine), 1927.

——, *Maine, A History*, 3 vols., New York, 1919.

Hayes Papers, Rutherford B. Hayes Library, Fremont, Ohio.

Haynes, F. E., *Third Party Movements Since the Civil War, with Special Reference to Iowa*, Iowa City, 1916.

Hebert, Richard A., *Modern Maine: Its Historic Background, People, and Resources*, 4 vols., New York, 1951.

History of the 118th Pennsylvania Volunteers, Corn Exchange Regiment. By the Survivors' Association, Philadelphia, 1905.

Hood, John B., *Advance and Retreat*, New Orleans, 1880.

Humphreys, Andrew A., *The Virginia Campaign of '64 and '65*, New York, 1883.

In Memoriam: Joshua Lawrence Chamberlain, Late Major-General, U. S. V. Circular No. 5, Series of 1914, Whole Number 328, Military Order of the Loyal Legion of the United States, Commandery of the State of Maine, Portland, 1914.

Joshua Lawrence Chamberlain, A Sketch. Prepared for the Report of the Chamberlain Association of America, no author, place, or date.

Joshua Lawrence Chamberlain, Supplement: The Twelve Days at Augusta, 1880, Portland (Maine), 1906.

Journal of the House of Representatives of the State of Maine.
Judson, A. A., *History of the 83rd Regiment Pennsylvania Volunteers,* Erie, no date.

Lewiston *Evening Journal.*
Little, George Thomas, *Genealogical and Family History of the State of Maine,* 4 vols., New York, 1909.
Longstreet, James, *From Manassas to Appomattox,* Philadelphia, 1896.

Maine at Gettysburg. Report of the Commissioners, Portland (Maine), 1898.
Meade, George, *The Life and Letters of George Gordon Meade,* 2 vols., New York, 1913.
Medical and Surgical History of the War of the Rebellion, 2 vols., each in 3 parts, Washington, D. C., 1870-88.
Men of Progress, Maine, 1897. Boston, 1897.
Munson, Gorham, *Penobscot, Down East Paradise,* Philadelphia, 1959.
Muzzey, David Saville, *James G. Blaine, A Political Idol of Other Days,* New York, 1934.

Nash, Eugene Arus, *A History of the Forty-Fourth Regiment, New York Volunteer Infantry,* Chicago, 1911.
National Cyclopedia of American Biography.
Newhall, F. C., *With General Sheridan in Lee's Last Campaign,* Philadelphia, 1866.
New York *Times.*
———— *Tribune.*
———— *World.*
Norton, Charles Ledyard, *A Handbook of Florida,* New York, 1891.
————, Oliver Willcox, *Army Letters, 1861-1865,* Chicago, 1903.
————, *The Attack and Defense of Little Round Top,* New York, 1913.

Oates, William C., *The War Between the Union and the Confederacy and Its Lost Opportunities,* New York, 1905.

Palfrey, Francis Winthrop, *The Antietam and Fredericksburg,* New York, 1893.
Pennsylvania at Gettysburg, 2 vols., Harrisburg, 1904.
Perham, A. S., "Warren at Five Forks," New York State Historical Association *Quarterly Journal,* July, 1923.
Porter, C. H., "Operations of the Fifth Corps on the Left, March 29 to Nightfall, March 31, 1865," and "The Fifth Corps at the Battle of Five Forks," *The Shenandoah Campaigns of 1862 and 1864 and the Appomattox Campaign of 1865,* Military Historical Society of Massachusetts, Boston, 1907.
Portland (Maine) *Advertiser.*
———— *Daily Press.*
———— *Eastern Argus.*
———— *Evening Express and Advertiser.*
———— *Transcript.*

Powell, William H., *The Fifth Army Corps*, New York, 1896.
Pullen, John L., *The Twentieth Maine, a Volunteer Regiment in the Civil War*, Philadelphia, 1957.

Randall, J. G., *The Civil War and Reconstruction*, New York, 1937.
Rockland *Democrat and Free Press*.
Russell, Charles Edward, *Blaine of Maine, His Life and Times*, New York, 1931.

Sheridan, P. H., *Personal Memoirs*, 2 vols., New York, 1888.
Sherman, William T., *Memoirs*, 2 vols., New York, 1876.
Spencer, Wilbur, *Maine Immortals*, Augusta (Maine), 1932.
Stackpole, Edward J., *They Met at Gettysburg*, Harrisburg, 1956.
———, *Drama on the Rappahannock*, Harrisburg, 1957.
Stanwood, Edward, *History of the Presidency*, Boston, 1898.
———, *James Gillespie Blaine*, Boston, 1905.
Stern, Philip Van Doren, *An End to Valor*, Boston, 1958.
Swan, W. W., "The Five Forks Campaign," *The Shenandoah Campaigns of 1862 and 1864 and the Appomattox Campaign of 1865*, Military Historical Society of Massachusetts, Boston, 1907.
Swanberg, W. A., *Sickles the Incredible*, New York, 1956.
Swinton, William, *Campaigns of the Army of the Potomac*, New York, 1866.
Sypher, J. R., *History of the Pennsylvania Reserve Corps*, Lancaster, 1865.

Taylor, Emerson Gifford, *Gouverneur Kemble Warren*, Boston, 1932.
Tremain, Henry Edwin, *The Last Hours of Sheridan's Cavalry*, New York, 1904.
Tucker, Glenn, *High Tide at Gettysburg*, New York, 1958.

Walker, Francis A., *History of the Second Army Corps*, New York, 1891.
War of the Rebellion: A Compilation of the Official Records of the Union and Confederate Armies, 70 vols., in 128 parts, Washington, D. C., 1881-1902.
Warren. *Proceedings, Findings, and Opinions of the Court of Inquiry ... in the Case of Gouverneur K. Warren*, 3 parts, Washington, D. C., 1883.
Whitman, William E. S., and True, Charles H., *Maine in the War for the Union*, Lewiston, 1865.
Who's Who in America, 1912-1913.
Williams, Kenneth P., *Lincoln Finds A General*, 4 vols., New York, 1949-56.
Williams, T. Harry, *Lincoln and His Generals*, New York, 1952.
Wilson, Forrest, *Crusader in Crinoline*, Philadelphia, 1941.
Wise, Jennings Cropper, *The Long Arm of Lee*, 2 vols., Lynchburg, 1915.
Woodward, E. M., *History of the 198th Pennsylvania Volunteers*, Trenton, 1884.

Index

347

Suggested reading list:

Army Life: A Private's Reminiscences of the Civil War (20th Maine Volunteer Infantry) by Reverend Theodore Gerrish

Through Blood and Fire at Gettysburg: My Experiences with the 20th Maine Regiment on Little Round Top by General Joshua Lawrence Chamberlain

"Bayonet! Forward": My Civil War Reminiscences by General Joshua Lawrence Chamberlain

Soul of the Lion: A Biography of General Joshua Lawrence Chamberlain by Willard Wallace

The Passing of the Armies: The Last Campaign of the Armies by General Joshua Lawrence Chamberlain

The Attack and Defense of Little Round Top, Gettysburg, July 2, 1863 by Oliver W. Norton

Sickles the Incredible: A Biography of General Daniel Edgar Sickles by W. A. Swanberg

The Life and Letters of General George Gordon Meade by George Meade

A Diary of Battle: The Personal Journals of Colonel Charles S. Wainwright 1861-1865 edited by Allan Nevins

"Over a Wide, Hot ... Crimson Plain", The Struggle For The Bliss Farm by Elwood Christ

High Tide at Gettysburg: The Campaign in Pennsylvania by Glenn Tucker

Crisis at the Crossroads: The First Day at Gettysburg by Warren Hassler

The Killer Angels: A Novel About the Four Days of Gettysburg by Michael Shaara

The Great Invasion of 1863 or General Lee in Pennsylvania by Jacob Hoke

At Gettysburg or What a Girl Saw and Heard of the Battle: A True Narrative by Tillie (Pierce) Alleman

Gettysburg Sources: 3 Volumes, compiled by James L. McLean, Jr. and Judy W. McLean

The History of the Fighting Fourteenth: 14th Brooklyn State Militia compiled by C. Tevis and D. R. Marquis

Major-General John Frederick Hartranft: Citizen, Soldier and Pennsylvania Statesman by A. M. Gambone

The Civil War Letters of Dr. Harvey Black: A Surgeon with Stonewall Jackson edited by Glenn L. McMullen

Historical Record of the First Maryland Infantry by Charles Camper and J. W. Kirkley

The Baltimore and Ohio (Railroad) in the Civil War by Festus Summers

The History of the Tenth Massachusetts Battery of Light Artillery in the War of the Rebellion by John Billings

Whatever You Resolve To Be: Essays on Stonewall Jackson by A. Wilson Greene

Lee: A Biography by Clifford Dowdey

Pickett and His Men by LaSalle Corbell Pickett

A Texan in Search of a Fight: Being the Diary and Letters of a Private Soldier in Hood's Texas Brigade by John C. West

A Lieutenant of Cavalry in Lee's Army by George Beale

Letters of a Confederate Officer to His Family During the Last Year of the War of Secession by Richard Corbin

Death of a Nation: The Story of Lee and His Men at Gettysburg by Clifford Dowdey

Four Years in the Saddle by Colonel Harry Gilmor

Return to Bull Run: The Campaign and Battle of Second Manassas by John Hennessy

Confederate Monuments at Gettysburg: The Gettysburg Battle Monuments by David Martin

To the Gates of Richmond: The Peninsula Campaign by Stephen Sears

Mine Eyes Have Seen The Glory: The Civil War in Art by Harold Holzer and Mark E. Neely Jr.

All of the above titles are available from the Publisher:
Stan Clark Military Books
915 Fairview Avenue
Gettysburg, Pennsylvania 17325
(717) 337-1728